Irish Pilgrimage

Michael P. Carroll

Irish Pilgrimage

*Holy Wells
and Popular
Catholic
Devotion*

THE JOHNS HOPKINS

UNIVERSITY PRESS

BALTIMORE AND

LONDON

This book has been brought to publication
with the generous assistance of
the J. B. Smallman Publication Fund
administered by the Faculty of Social Science
at the University of Western Ontario.

Published 1999
Printed in the United States of America
on acid-free paper
2 4 6 8 9 7 5 3 1
THE JOHNS HOPKINS UNIVERSITY PRESS
2715 North Charles Street
Baltimore, Maryland 21218-4363
www.press.jhu.edu

Library of Congress Cataloging-in-Publication Data
Carroll, Michael P., 1944–
    Irish pilgrimage : holy wells and popular Catholic devotion /
Michael P. Carroll.
        p.   cm.
    Includes bibliographical references and index.
    ISBN 0-8018-6190-X (alk. paper)
    1. Catholics—Ireland. 2. Ireland—Religious life and customs.
I. Title.
BX1504.C37 1999
263'.042415—DC21   99-24137
                                                                         CIP

A catalog record for this book is available from the British Library.

Pilgrimages to "holy wells" were once a very cherished
and a very popular devotion amongst the Catholics
of Ireland. . . . In latter years pilgrimages have been discouraged,
in consequence of the degeneracy of the times, and the dangers
of abuses; and the pastors have exhorted their flocks
to pray and prepare for the sacraments where they can do so
with security, and without disedification—namely, in their parish
churches. Much, however, of the poetry of religion,
of the chivalry of lively faith—much that was grand
and romantic in the heartfelt devotion of
a truly Catholic people, is intertwined
with the memory of the
holy wells of Ireland.

—Rev. Anthony Cogan,
The Diocese of Meath,
Ancient and Modern (1867)

Contents

vii

Acknowledgments

This book owes its greatest debt to my parents, William Carroll and Olga Ciarlanti, whose sacrifices and constant encouragement enabled me to pursue an academic career. Funding for much of the research reported here was very generously provided by the Social Sciences and Humanities Research Council of Canada. I also want to thank the Royal Irish Academy for permission to quote from the typescript copies of the Ordnance Survey Letters in their possession. Finally, I need to thank Sharon Gmelch, anthropologist and friend, and Sam Clark, sociologist and friend, for reading and commenting on the manuscript.

Prologue

In 1500 there were likely only a million or so people living in Ireland. By 1791, that number had grown to nearly four and a half million, and by 1841 it was just over eight million. This pattern of surging population growth ended in the 1840s. In retrospect, the first signs of the great tragedy that would reshape Irish culture forever likely went unnoticed by most of the population. In 1845, here and there throughout Ireland, the leaves and stalks of a few potato plants shriveled and turned black. When dug up, the tubers themselves at first appeared sound, but shortly they too blackened and turned rotten and soggy. Irish commentators of the time noted that the potato crop had in recent years failed both in the eastern United States and in England and in areas on the western edge of Continental Europe. Fortunately, they noted, the Blight—variously called, at least in this early period, "potato cholera," "potato rot," or simply "the disease"— seemed restricted to a few areas.

By October 1845, however, it was apparent that the potato crop was being assaulted in almost all areas of the island. Irish farmers scrambled to separate good potatoes from bad and to store the good ones in pits, all to no avail. The earth itself was infected and about one-third of the crop failed. The losses in 1846 and 1848 were even higher. For a nation in which more than a third of the population subsisted mainly on the potato, and in which it was not uncommon in this section of the population for adults to consume over fifty potatoes a day, it was a disaster. To this dramatic decline in the availability of such a central dietary element was added the inability of many tenant farmers to pay their rents and a willingness, if not an eagerness, on the part of many landlords to exploit the situation in order to merge small holdings. Mass evictions followed, and entire areas were cleared of people whose families had worked the land as far back as anyone could remember.

Popular accounts of the Great Famine like to deal in round numbers, and so it is conventional to say that between 1845 and 1851 one million people died—mainly from fever, dysentery, or outright starvation—and that eventually another two million were forced to emigrate. More detailed considerations of the available evidence suggest that the number of dead was a bit higher and the number of emigrants a bit lower. Whatever the precise numbers, it was a tragedy of horrific proportions.

The Famine was a watershed in Irish history and it continues to loom large in the thinking of many contemporary Irish (and many contemporary Irish-Americans, Irish-Canadians, Irish-Australians, etc.). In particular, the Famine has become a master symbol of England's oppression of Ireland, and academics who seek to minimize the role of the British government of the time in making the Famine a worse experience than it needed to have been do so at their peril. Even a casual remark can provoke a torrent. Walking out of the Royal Irish Academy one cold Dublin day with a local historian who, like me, had spent the morning and afternoon going through old texts, I mentioned that a conference on the Famine was to be held later that week at Dublin Castle. For the next thirty minutes I was nailed to the street corner by his conversation, as he railed against the insensitivity of overfed and overclothed academics who pontificated on experiences of which they had no inkling. Still, though professional academics and the general public may disagree on the precise causes of the misery occasioned by the Famine, what remains constant and agreed upon by all is that the sheer amount of human misery and human suffering was enormous.

My personal and private link to that misery and suffering is a woman named Margaret Fogarty Larkin. Margaret was born in County Tipperary in 1811 and at age twenty-five she married a farmer named John Larkin. For all I really know, John may have been a cottier or even a landless laborer, who was later construed as a farmer in order to make him more important in the eyes of his family. In the first nine years of their marriage, Margaret and John had four children. Sometime in late 1845 or early 1846 John became part of the first wave of Famine dead. Margaret was forced to emigrate to the United

Prologue

States with her four children, the oldest of which was only nine. She arrived at New York in late 1846 and set out immediately for Ohio, since she knew that she had relatives there, somewhere.

I have tried to reconstruct, with little success, what it must have felt like to set off to what was literally a New World. All I have are scraps of information about her first few years in her new home. A letter sent to my paternal grandmother in 1925, for instance, tells the story of Margaret Larkin's very first day in Cincinnati. It seems she was traveling up the Ohio River and arrived in Cincinnati on a Sunday. Leaving her children on the ferry, she set off with a woman she had met on the trip to find a Catholic church where she could attend Mass. At the church that she eventually found she met a cousin of hers. He inquired after her husband, and, learning that John was dead, insisted that Margaret and her children stay with him and his young bride as long as necessary.

The story could end here and still be a good story, but it doesn't. It seems that when Margaret and her children first arrived at the man's house, everybody—including the children—was served a hot toddy laced with alcohol. Not having any experience of alcohol, Margaret's six-year-old daughter—also named Margaret—drank the contents of her cup down fast and shortly fell off her chair "dead drunk" (as she herself would later say when relating these events). *That*, my grandmother was told, was how her grandmother, the second Margaret Larkin, had spent her very first day in Cincinnati.

The formula evident in this story is a familiar one, and can be found beneath any number of folktales and Hollywood movies: the experience of great tragedy, a heroic journey characterized by much uncertainty and many obstacles, and a happy ending laced with comic relief. It is a formula that makes retelling the story easier, and, who knows, for that very reason maybe the story was shaped to fit the formula as it was told and retold over the decades. Such postmodern cynicism notwithstanding, it's a good story and one that holds a number of lessons. At one level, it's a story about looking to the future no matter how dark the present may seem. Indeed, it was told to my grandmother at a time when her own world was falling apart. Her father had just died, she had just separated from her husband (it was the first separation in the history of the family), and she was facing the future as a single mother having to raise three children.

What the story shows, said the author of the letter (a cousin), was that "God never sends us heavier crosses than we can bear." Maybe.

For me, the story holds a different lesson, and it is one that has guided my thinking as I wrote this book. As we shall see, the form of popular Catholicism I describe was already in decline when the elder Margaret Larkin was born. Consequently, it is entirely possible that she knew little of the holy wells, rounding rituals, pilgrimages, patterns, and the like that I talk about here. Margaret Larkin, however, was an active agent. Within the constraints that undeniably set limits to what she could achieve, she built for herself and her children a new life in a new land even as the world she knew was collapsing around her. She may have cringed at the thought, and she may have felt overwhelmed by the enormous challenge of what she had to do, but she did it. The lesson here is simply this: in discussing Irish history, the Irish must not be construed as passive agents, that is, as individuals who cling unthinkingly to tradition as they are buffeted about by forces beyond their control. Like Margaret Larkin, they quite often reacted to changed circumstances in bold new ways. Such a conclusion may seem obvious, even banal, but it is nevertheless a conclusion that is sorely needed in the study of Irish popular Catholicism.

Simply put, I argue that almost all previous accounts of popular Catholicism in Ireland during that perplexing period that stretches from the Reformation to the Famine have failed to capture the historical reality of the Catholic experience during this period because they have failed to grant to Irish Catholics the sort of creative agency that Margaret Larkin so obviously had.

Introduction

Ireland has the dubious distinction of being a case that is forever subverting patterns that are otherwise well established in the study of Catholic societies. In most Catholic societies, for instance, rates of weekly attendance at Sunday Mass are notoriously low. Not so in Ireland. During the latter half of the nineteenth century, attendance at Sunday Mass was well over 90 percent in most areas, and even now Irish Catholics are more likely to go to Sunday Mass than are Catholics almost anywhere else in the world. Then there is the matter of the Reformation. In most European societies, local populations matched the religious preferences of their rulers; where princes and kings embraced Protestantism their subjects eventually followed suit. In Ireland, by contrast, the vast majority of the population remained Catholic despite the fact that the governing authorities were thoroughly Protestant. Similarly, the Reformation in most areas of Europe was in the first instance a distinctively urban phenomenon, and the urban mercantile class, in particular, proved especially receptive to Protestantism. Even in a Catholic society like Italy, where the Reformation would eventually fail, Protestantism for a time won over substantial minorities in those cities—like Genoa, Venice, and Florence—that were heavily involved in trade. But cities and merchants played a much different role in Ireland. Irish cities—in particular, port cities like Wexford, Waterford, Cork, and Limerick—proved receptive most of all to Counter-Reformation ideologies, and became the nodes from which the Counter-Reformation was carried to the rest of the island. Moreover, the Irish mercantile class in these cities played a leading role in this process. Finally, but most importantly, Ireland is distinctive among Catholic societies by virtue of the rituals and beliefs that were central to the everyday experience of "being

Catholic." In most Catholic societies, popular Catholicism revolved around cults associated with saintly relics and miraculous images. But cults of this sort have always been less important in Ireland. For Irish Catholics, both the laity and the local clergy alike, the cults most central to the experience of "being Catholic" were far more likely to be organized around springs or shapeless piles of stone than around images or relics.

While scholars have never lacked for ways to explain (or really, to explain away) the peculiarities of the Irish case, these explanations inevitably have an ad hoc quality that undermines their force. Ireland is still (with apologies to Herbert Spencer) that troubling little fact that so often kills grand theories relating to the history or psychology of European Catholicism.

Yet despite the undeniable importance of the Irish case to the study of Catholicism, scholarly thinking about popular Catholicism in Ireland is still very much shaped by a "pagan survivals" model that rose to prominence in the early nineteenth century. Within the logic of this model, Irish popular Catholicism is a syncretic mix of (1) truly Catholic elements (the Mass, the sacraments, a belief in Christ's divinity, etc.) and (2) a variety of beliefs and practices inherited from a distant Celtic past. In many accounts this model is only implicit, but it is not difficult to find authors—even authors who are otherwise quite knowledgeable about Ireland and Irish history—who state it explicitly, for example:

> There are two main types of magical practice that exist within Irish Catholicism: (1) traditional practices, rituals, and superstitions which are pagan, i.e., non-Christian, in origin, and (2) sacred objects and practices approved by the Church and used to obtain temporal favors. (Inglis 1987, 18)

> And we find that Cogan [a nineteenth-century priest/historian] ... supported the notion of local pilgrimage to holy wells in spite of official opposition to such ancient piety on the part of his own hierarchy. [These] gatherings at wells and other ancient cult centres combined genuine primitive Christian penitential spirituality with equally strong elements of pre-Christian carnival and licence. (Smyth 1992, 21)

Introduction

Until [the Famine] the religion of Ireland's poor Catholics contained admixtures of folk practices and pagan influences. Many nominal adherents did not receive the sacraments and embarrassingly large numbers rarely if ever attended Mass. (Guinnane 1997, 70)

One unfortunate effect of the widespread and uncritical acceptance of this pagan origins model is that those beliefs and practices that were central to the experience of Irish popular Catholicism have been defined as "folklore"—and so as something that can be safely ignored by scholars interested in "religion." Even now most studies of Catholicism in Ireland continue to be studies concerned with the difficulties encountered by Church elites as they tried to promote the rituals and beliefs favored by the official Church. By contrast, anyone who does have an interest in the rituals and beliefs central to popular Catholicism in pre-Famine Ireland is forced to rely mainly on obscure folkloric publications that are generally descriptive and generally little concerned with relating these rituals to the Catholicism of the official Church or to key events like the Reformation.

What is perhaps most puzzling about the continuing influence of the pagan origins hypothesis on the study of Irish popular Catholicism is that this hypothesis is so much at variance with two intellectual revolutions that have otherwise revamped our view of both "tradition" and "popular religion" in European societies.

Tradition Isn't What It Used to Be, or, Pity the Poor Clachan

For nearly two thousand years Ireland has been regarded by the rest of Europe as a society existing on the fringes of European civilization. For scholars in the nineteenth and twentieth centuries, this long-standing conceptualization of Ireland inevitably led to the belief that traditions that had long ago died out in the rest of Europe might still be found in Ireland. "The outstanding interest of Ireland for the student of European origins," intoned E. Estyn Evans (1957, xiv) in his still-popular book on Irish folk ways, "lies in the fact that in its historic literature, language, and social organization, as well as in its folklore, and folk customs, it illustrates the marginal survival of archaic elements of the Indo-European world."

But even fringes have fringes, and in Irish historiography the counties along Ireland's Atlantic seaboard were seen as the areas where an enterprising investigator might best discover archaic traditions that have died out in the rest of Europe. Evans himself, for example, drew disproportionately from the Atlantic counties in collecting material for the book cited above. Similarly, until quite recently it was conventional to take Conrad Arensberg's *The Irish Countryman* (1937) and Arensberg and Kimball's *Family and Community in Ireland* (1940), both of which were based on fieldwork done in County Clare, as providing an account of "traditional" peasant life in Ireland. But tradition—in Ireland and in the rest of Europe—just isn't what it used to be.

Starting in the late 1970s and early 1980s, a number of scholars came increasingly to argue that many traditions were not traditional at all but rather cultural inventions that had emerged in the relatively recent past. While much of this work was in anthropology (see Handler and Linnekin 1984; Hanson 1989), the approach was popularized most of all by historians working with European materials. The essays in Eric Hobsbawm and Terence Ranger's *The Invention of Tradition* (1983) were particularly influential. In that book, for instance, Hugh Trevor-Roper (1983) shows that the kilt and the use of tartans to distinguish among different Scottish clans were not, as so many people think, part of an archaic Highland tradition; rather, both were cultural inventions that emerged only in the eighteenth century. In the same book, Prys Morgan examines the invention of a Druidic and Celtic past in eighteenth-century Wales; David Cannadine shows that many of the "traditional" rituals surrounding the British monarchy only came into existence during the nineteenth and twentieth centuries; and so on.

As research on "the invention of tradition" has continued, it has become apparent that the scholarly community itself has been as much predisposed to invent tradition as the general public. Richard Suggett (1996), for example, demonstrates this in connection with the Welsh *mabsant*, a type of secular fair that flourished at the parish level in Wales during the eighteenth century. The usual scholarly interpretation of the mabsant is that it was originally a medieval religious celebration in honor of a parish's patron saint. Following the success of the Reformation in Wales, so the argument goes, the mabsant supposedly lost its religious significance and became a purely secular gathering concerned with eating, drinking, games-playing, and general rowdiness. Suggett, however, challenges this view, pointing out that there is little or no evidence for parish-based festivals of this sort prior to the Reformation. He goes on to suggest that such festivals only became commonplace in the wake of legislation passed in the mid-1600s that made the parish an important administrative unit in regard to things like care for the poor. In short, although the mabsant was very much a creation of the post-Reformation period, scholars insisted on projecting its origins back into an imagined medieval past.

This questioning of tradition by European historians eventually spilled over into Irish historiography. The result has been a radical rethinking of some very familiar Irish institutions. A good example here involves the Irish *clachan*. A clachan is a nucleated settlement, that is, a cluster of households gathered together in one location and usually associated with a rundale system of farming. Clachans, along with holy wells and virtually everything that might be classed as a "site," were mapped by the men who conducted the Ordnance Survey in Ireland in the 1820s and 1830s. In plotting out the distribution of the clachans encountered by these nineteenth-century investigators on a map of Ireland (see McCourt 1971), a clear pattern emerges: clachans were concentrated in a dense, crescent-shaped cluster that hugs Ireland's Atlantic coast along the north, west, and southwest. They were generally absent in an oval-shaped area that pushes up from the southeast into central Ireland. This patterning seemed to have an obvious explanation: clachans were a traditional form of settlement in Ireland but had been undermined by processes of modernization. This is why, so the usual reasoning went, clachans were found mainly in those areas least touched by modernization (the areas along Ireland's Atlantic periphery) and were generally absent in areas that had been most affected by modernization (the east and southeast). As late as the 1970s, some scholars (McCourt 1971, 153) were still suggesting that the clachans found in the nineteenth century were the remnants of a settlement tradition that had originated as far back as the Neolithic. But this view of the Irish clachan, particularly as it applies to those clachans found in Ireland's western periphery, has now changed quite dramatically.

Using a variety of data, but relying mainly on the Poll Tax Returns from 1660, William J. Smyth (1988; 1992) plotted the distribution of Ireland's population in the mid-seventeenth century. Looking at the result, he points out that "the far west [that is, the Atlantic periphery] emerges as distinctively in the mid-seventeenth as it did in the mid-nineteenth century but for different reasons" (1988, 60). Simply put, the data indicate that "[Atlantic] areas with the greatest densities [just before the Famine] are often the least densely settled parts of mid-seventeenth century Ireland" (Smyth 1988, 60). The proximate cause of this reversal is not problematic. From 1500 to 1840, Ireland's population increased from one million to just over eight million. This dramatic increase in population put increased pressure on the land, with the result that previously marginal areas came to be settled and farmed. What all this means is that the clachans found by the Ordnance Survey investigators in the western counties in the early nineteenth century were relatively new settlements, having only been established within the preceding two centuries. Furthermore, there is no need to appeal to "tradition" to explain why clachan settlement flourished in these areas. On the contrary, there are good reasons for believing that it was mainly because clachan settlement and the associated rundale system of farming is an efficient way to farm marginal land (Whelan 1991).

In short, although clachans certainly existed in some areas of Ireland in earlier centuries, the hypothesis that clachan settlement was "traditional" or "premodern" was not so much wrong as misleading, in that it prevented nineteenth-century investigators from seeing other possibilities that were in fact better supported by the historical record. In particular, it prevented them from seeing the clachans clustered along the Atlantic periphery as relatively recent adaptations to a specific set of historical and environmental circumstances.

The stem family is another "traditional" institution in Ireland that, like the clachan, has been rethought in recent years. For decades, the stem family described by Arensberg and Kimball (1940) was taken as the form of family organization that was typical in the Irish countryside. By contrast, Birdwell-Pheasant (1992; see also Guinnane 1997, 134–65) presents data showing that the stem family was less a family type than a cluster of attributes that have each changed over time in response to changing economic and social conditions.

Generally, historians and anthropologists studying Ireland are

Introduction

now more skeptical of all claims that presuppose a stable and homogeneous Irish past and are now as likely to be concerned with discontinuities as with continuities (see Silverman and Gulliver 1992 for a review of this new literature). And yet, as pervasive as this newfound skepticism toward "traditional" institutions in Ireland is, it has not as yet led Irish historians to look carefully at the presumed pagan origins of the rituals and beliefs that were associated with Irish popular Catholicism. Doing just that is one of the goals of this book.

The Second Revolution: Allowing for Popular Creativity

Starting in the early 1970s a number of scholars began to challenge the conceptual dichotomies that had structured perceptions of popular religion since the Enlightenment. Specifically, they called into question the sharp distinctions that had been drawn by earlier scholars between magic and religion, between official religion and popular religion, between reasoned faith and superstition, and between the religious elites who actively promoted true religion and the peasant masses who passively clung to inherited tradition. Such distinctions, they argued, are misleading, and misleading most of all because they obscure the dynamic and creative processes that so often gave rise to the beliefs and practices that constituted popular religion.

In what would turn out to be a seminal work in this new tradition, Jean Delumeau (1977, originally 1971) argued that the Catholic Counter-Reformation took a lot longer to penetrate into the countryside in Italy and France than had previously been thought. But in considering the religion that persisted in the French and Italian countryside in the centuries after Trent, Delumeau specifically rejected the view that it had been a religion permeated by elements inherited from a distant pagan past. Such a view, he argued (1977, 166), was seductive but facile, and usually fell apart if particular examples of so-called pagan survivals were examined carefully. The religion of the countryside was in reality a "folklorised Christianity," by which he meant that rural Catholics had taken elements promulgated by the official Church and shaped these elements using modes of thought that derived from the nature of life in a peasant society.

Building upon Delumeau's work, Natalie Zemon Davis (1974) criticized all models of popular religion that depicted the great mass of ordinary people as essentially passive, and suggested instead that historians pay more attention to the ways in which "traditional" forms of religion have been reworked by the laity in response to changing social conditions. She illustrated what might be accomplished here by considering the emergence of confraternities for young males in fifteenth-century Florence. Although sharing a number of elements in common with traditional confraternities, these "young male" confraternities, Davis demonstrates, also embodied certain new features that made them ideally suited to the needs of prosperous nonpatrician families that were otherwise cut off from sources of political power.

In the Italian scholarly tradition, this emerging emphasis upon recognizing "creativity from below" came to be merged with a perspective on Catholicism associated with Antonio Gramsci (d. 1937). The essence of Gramsci's approach is summarized in the following passage, which is one of the most commonly encountered citations in Italian-language studies of religion:

> Every religion, even Catholicism (in fact especially Catholicism, precisely because of its efforts to maintain a superficial unity and not allow itself to be fragmented into national churches or along class lines) is really a multiplicity of religions that are distinct and often contradictory: there is a Catholicism of the peasant, a Catholicism of the petty bourgeoisie and urban workers, a Catholicism of women and a Catholicism of the intellectuals. (Gramsci 1966, 120)

Gramsci suggested, in other words, that in a society like Italy there were several variants of Catholicism. The scholar's task is to study the nature of these different variants and the ways in which they interact, not to decide which is "more authentic" or "more Catholic." Within the Gramscian perspective, we can associate "official Catholicism," like all Catholicisms, with a specific social group. That group consists mainly of the bishops of the institutional Church. In other words, the bishops of the Church and the intellectuals and administrators who surround them are simply one social group among many, and their "Catholicism" only one variant among many.

Although Gramsci's "many Catholicisms" model influenced any number of subsequent investigators in Italy, the most important of these is undoubtedly Gabriele De Rosa. In a number of works De

Introduction

Rosa has traced out in some detail the ways in which different Italian bishops "adapted" the Tridentine Catholicism of the official Church to the specific social and economic conditions characteristic of their dioceses. De Rosa's work on the type of Catholicism that developed at the local level in Mezzogiorno communities is especially well known.[1]

Since the early work by Delumeau, Davis, Gramsci, De Rosa, and others, there has been a veritable explosion of studies documenting the ways in which both the laity and the clergy in different societies have constructed for themselves a type of religious experience that was adapted to the particular cultural context in which they found themselves. In a particularly impressive series of studies dealing with Spanish Catholicism, for example, William Christian Jr. (1981, 1992, 1996) has linked the emergence of new Catholic devotions in Spain to changing social conditions across a variety of historical periods. In his study more specifically of Andalusian Catholicism, Timothy Mitchell (1990) shows that the cultic activities favored by Andalusian Catholics have modified the account of Christ's Passion found in the Gospels so as to give more emphasis to his suffering and pain while simultaneously de-emphasizing his eventual Resurrection; this "Passion according to Andalusia," Mitchell argues, is perfectly suited to a fatalistic culture in which there are no happy endings and in which the experience of emotion is the only reward to which ordinary people can reasonably aspire. Sandra Zimdars-Swartz (1991) examines several well-known Marian apparitions and shows how in each case the apparition account was modified over time as it came to be shaped and reshaped simultaneously by the seers who experienced the apparition and by the various audiences (both lay and clerical) who received their reports.

Looking carefully at the records of ecclesiastical trials held in Terra d'Oltranto (the "heel" of the Italian boot) during the seventeenth and eighteenth centuries, David Gentilcore (1992) shows how the members of this essentially agricultural society often borrowed from the official Catholic tradition in order to create new forms of Catholic devotion and how these forms, in turn, were then appropriated by the Catholic clergy. In her study of a Greek Orthodox shrine on the Aegean Island of Tinos, for example, Jill Dubisch (1995) argues that the penitential activities associated with the shrine—activities that often strike outside observers as extreme—provide modern Greek women with a way of "being good at being a woman" in a society in which the poetics of womanhood are bound up with notions of constant suffering. Finally, in his analysis of the cult of St. Jude in the United States, Robert Orsi (1996) has shown how during the 1930s and 1940s the daughters and granddaughters of immigrants from various European locations embraced the cult of this initially obscure saint and shaped it in such a way that they were able to give voice to issues and concerns that were deeply troubling to them but which they would not otherwise have been able to express.[2]

Interestingly, the occasional exception such as Dubisch notwithstanding, most studies of popular religion in European (and more generally, Western) societies which have highlighted the role played by popular creativity have been studies specifically concerned with popular Catholicism. Possibly this reflects simply the biases of the investigators, but it may also reflect some very basic sociocultural differences between the Protestant and Catholic traditions. Although this is a topic that cries out for further investigation, a few scholars have already suggested what the nature of those differences might be. Ellen Badone (1990, 21), for example, suggests that the more highly developed processes of rationalization in Protestant contexts narrow the gap between official and popular styles of religious expression, thus making it unlikely that popular religiosity will diverge much from officially sanctioned religiosity.

By contrast, the irrepressible Andrew Greeley (1995)—when not overwhelming us with data that shatter myths about Catholics (it turns out, you see, that Catholics like sex more, not less, than Protestants; that Catholics are more, not less, tolerant of homosexuality; etc.)—has argued that the thought of ordinary Catholics (but not ordinary Protestants) has for centuries been shaped by what he calls the "analogical imagination." It is a way of thinking that proceeds from the particular to the particular using analogy, rather than from the general to the specific, and one that enables Catholics to easily assimilate new images and ideas to older patterns. The net result (if I am reading Greeley correctly) is that Catholics are more likely than Protestants to embrace a wide variety of beliefs and images that— the obvious differences evident in these beliefs and images notwithstanding—are all recognizably "Catholic."

In any event, whatever the cause turns out to be, given that the

Introduction

perspective pioneered by Delumeau, Davis, Gramsci, De Rosa, and others has proven especially useful in the study of popular Catholicism, it is hardly surprising that some investigators have brought this perspective to bear on the study of popular Catholicism in post-Famine Ireland. As we shall see (chap. 4), it is now commonplace to suggest that many of the devotional changes that occurred in Ireland during the latter half of the nineteenth century were shaped by the particular interests of the tenant farmer class. Similarly, Lawrence Taylor (1995) has looked carefully at the stories that modern Irish Catholics in County Donegal tell about drunken priests, pilgrimages to Medjugorje, local holy wells, and the like, and shows that these stories have been shaped and revised over time in order to more perfectly represent local experiences and concerns.

And yet, even though the call to take "popular creativity" into account when studying popular religion (popular Catholicism in particular) is now several decades old, and even though scholars studying Catholicism in post-Famine Ireland have heeded that call, there has been little if any change in the way scholars have approached the study of popular Catholicism in pre-Famine Ireland. In this area the pagan origins hypothesis still reigns supreme and the great mass of pre-Famine Catholics are still being construed as individuals who clung passively to traditions inherited from a distant Celtic past and who just as passively received (and occasionally absorbed) new beliefs and practices sent down from above. I want to demonstrate that this view of pre-Famine Catholics is wrong and that the variant of Catholicism to which they were attached was not simply a recent phenomenon but also something that was brought into existence by processes in which ordinary Catholics played a decisive role.

A Framework for the Study of Popular Catholicism in Ireland

As salutary as the emphasis upon popular creativity has been for the study of popular Catholicism, it is important to recognize that such creativity is not unbounded. The conceptual framework that guided my work on Italian Catholicism (Carroll 1992; 1996) suggests that the logic of official Catholicism sets certain very broad constraints on what can be considered legitimately Catholic, and so the popular Catholicism that develops at the local level must develop within these broad constraints. Two constraints are particularly important.

First, to be considered legitimately Catholic, a popular belief or ritual must be at least loosely associated with the supernatural beings who are important in the pantheon of the official Church (namely, Christ, Mary, or the saints). Second, public rituals must be given legitimacy by the clergy, at least the local clergy.

Precisely because these constraints are broad, local populations are free to develop variants of popular Catholicism that can (and do) differ significantly from official Catholicism. In Italy, for instance, it is relatively easy to demonstrate that saints and madonnas have independent power and are far more important than the "Christ" favored by the official Church. It is also easy to demonstrate that different madonnas, although they might indeed be vaguely associated with the "Mary" of the official Church, are nevertheless considered separate and distinct personalities. The fact that all variants of popular Catholicism develop within the broad constraints allows all the groups associated with these variants to maintain what Gramsci called a sense of "superficial unity."

The value of the framework just outlined is entirely pragmatic: in studying Italian Catholicism I found that it provided a useful way of organizing much of what was already known about popular Catholicism in Italy and was useful in directing attention to patterns that had previously gone undetected. As will become clear, I have found the same perspective useful in the study of Irish Catholicism as well.

The Organization of This Book

The starting point of any analysis of Irish popular Catholicism must be a description of the thing itself. For that reason, chapter 1 presents an account of those elements—mainly having to with holy wells, the gatherings called "patterns," and rounding rituals—that made this variant of Catholicism so distinctive. My concern in this section is to describe each of these elements in detail and to lay out the implicit cultural logic that binds them together.

As mentioned, it is an accepted part of most scholarly thinking about pre-Famine Catholicism that holy well cults, patterns, and rounding rituals were part of an archaic Celtic inheritance. The first part of chapter 2 examines the evidence that nineteenth-century commentators brought forward to support this hypothesis. What emerges is that such evidence was minimal and, in any event, could

Introduction

easily have been interpreted differently if the will to do so had been present. This chapter then considers some of the intellectual fashions that prevailed in the late eighteenth and early nineteenth centuries and that facilitated the rise of the "Celtic origins" hypothesis despite the paucity of evidence. The final section of the chapter looks at information from a variety of sources—including recent archaeological discoveries, the Irish penitentials, Irish vernacular literature, medieval accounts of Ireland, and so forth—which suggests that not only were holy well cults and rounding rituals not a part of *Celtic* tradition in Ireland, they were not an important part of the *Christian* tradition in Ireland through to the sixteenth century.

Chapter 3 considers the one pilgrimage site in Ireland that has been described on a more or less continuous basis since the twelfth century: St. Patrick's Purgatory in County Donegal. In sifting through the various accounts of this site, it is possible to detect changing devotional patterns in Ireland that would otherwise be difficult to perceive. Specifically, it is possible to observe a fairly dramatic shift in the nature of Irish popular Catholicism that was well under way by the early seventeenth century.

Chapter 4 deals with those areas of Leinster and Munster that scholars like Kevin Whelan and Emmet Larkin have identified as Ireland's Catholic heartland. It seems clear that this area has long been characterized by a dynamic and creative culture associated with both the Anglo-Irish and the Gaelic-Irish, and was the area of Ireland in which Counter-Reformation practices (including regular attendance at Mass) took root as early as the seventeenth century. Most previous studies of the culture that prevailed in this region have assumed implicitly that the commitment of heartland Catholics to the Catholicism of the official Church would have diminished their attachment to the practices and beliefs associated with popular Catholicism. Much of this chapter is devoted to a consideration of evidence that undermines this assumption and to a consequent rethinking of the relationship that likely existed between the Counter-Reformation ideologies imported from Continental Europe and the popular Catholicism that came to prevail in Ireland.

Chapter 5 continues the argument developed in chapter 4. It starts by describing the social processes operative in the sixteenth and early seventeenth centuries which led Anglo-Irish and Gaelic-Irish elites in Leinster and Munster to develop and practice a new variant of Catholicism. This new variant was formed by merging Counter-Reformation emphases imported from the Continent with older cultural emphases that had long prevailed in Ireland. It was this process, I suggest, that brought into existence that variant of Irish popular Catholicism that later generations of scholars would see as a "Celtic inheritance." The second half of the chapter describes the sociocultural processes operative in the late eighteenth and early nineteenth centuries that caused this variant of Catholicism to go into decline.

The sixth and last chapter is really more of an addendum. Whereas the theoretical argument developed in earlier chapters can explain many of the empirical patterns associated with pre-Famine Catholicism, it cannot explain them all. It is to account for these remaining patterns that this chapter constructs a frankly speculative account of the psychology of pre-Famine Catholicism.

Chapter One

Popular Catholicism before the Famine

In the two and a half centuries before the Famine, what did "being Catholic" mean for most Irish Catholics? What, in other words, did they "do" and "think" that validated their identity as Catholics? Of course participating in the rituals, notably the Mass, that were central to official Catholicism was a great part of this expression. The evidence that weekly attendance at Mass was relatively low by post-Famine standards should not blind us to the likelihood that a majority of Irish Catholics probably attended Mass several times during the year. Even during the period of the Penal Laws, Mass-houses were common and were allowed to function even though their locations were usually known to the authorities.[1] Nevertheless, for most Catholics it was participation in rituals at local holy wells, far more than simple attendance at Mass, that validated their Catholic identity. Consequently, an understanding of holy well cults is central to an understanding of popular Catholicism in pre-Famine Ireland.

The Nature and Distribution of Holy Wells in Ireland

Foreign tourists who visit Ireland, and who find themselves with a free afternoon in the Dublin area, commonly decide to visit Glendalough. Located just to the south of Dublin in County Wicklow, Glendalough can be reached easily either by rented car or by tour bus. Although it was once one of the four greatest pilgrimage sites in Ireland, tourists go to Glendalough today mainly to see its spectacular round tower and its monastic ruins, or—more simply—to walk through one of Ireland's most beautiful valleys (see figure 1). What today's tourists won't see as they walk around Glendalough are its holy wells. That such wells once existed, however, is beyond doubt. In June 1714, the local high sheriff and his (Protestant) posse dispersed the annual gathering at Glendalough in honor of St. Kevin, and in his official report of the incident the sheriff says, "Wee pulled down their Tentes, threw down and demolished their superstitious crosses [and] destroyed the wells" (cited in Burke 1969, 310). In the spring of 1996, when I asked one of the staff at Glendalough's visitor center where the wells mentioned in this report had been located, he pointed to a stand of brush on the other side of the river and said that one of the wells was still there. It was overgrown, he said, and it would likely take ten minutes or so of searching to find it. In fact, after thirty minutes of wandering through the brush in the area indicated, I still had not found the well and gave up.

It would be easy to conclude from this experience at Glendalough that Ireland's holy wells are quite literally being swallowed up by a land in which they are no longer relevant. But that would be misleading. Glendalough notwithstanding, a far more common experience as I traveled through Ireland was to ask about holy wells in a local pub, variety store, gas station, or such and be directed to some out-of-the-way but nevertheless accessible location in which a well-maintained holy well (or at least a well that had once been holy) still existed. In short, while Ireland's holy wells may no longer be the focus of cultic activities, at least not to anywhere near the extent that they were before the Famine, and while such wells may not be on display in the places where tourists are most likely to gather, something about these wells has induced local populations to preserve and maintain them. Anyone who wants to find them, can.

In his popular book on holy wells, Patrick Logan (1980) describes 207 such wells scattered throughout Ireland. Everyone, including Logan, agrees that this is only a small fraction of the total that once existed. So how many holy wells have there been in Ireland? One estimate, repeated in any number of commentaries (see, e.g., Evans 1957, 298; Logan 1980, 14; Harbison 1991, 229), is that there have been "over 3,000" holy wells in Ireland. Unfortunately, none of the many authors who repeat this "over 3,000" figure give a source for this estimate or indicate how it was derived. In fact, the earliest use of the "over 3,000" figure that I have been able to locate occurs in W. G. Wood-Martin's *Traces of the Elder Faiths of Ireland* (1902, 47). Since Wood-Martin also says that the systematic enumeration of holy wells has only been attempted for Counties Clare and Sligo (1902, 90), it seems evident that the now commonly encountered "over 3,000"

Popular Catholicism before the Famine

Table 1.1
Published Surveys Listing the
Holy Wells Found in Different Areas of Ireland

Study	Area Surveyed	Number of Holy Wells Reported
Wood-Martin (1902, 88)	County Sligo	59
Wood-Martin (1902, 90–91)	County Clare	92
Carrigan (1905)	Diocese of Ossory*	123
Stubbs (1908/11)	County Louth	24
O'Toole (1933)	County Carlow	28
Ó Muirgheasa (1936)	County Donegal	106
Ó Coindealbhain (1946)	"in and around the city of Cork"	7
Hartnett (1947)	barony of East Muskerry, County Cork	18
Ó Danachair (1955)	County Limerick	134**
Ó Danachair (1958a; 1960b)	northern County Kerry, including the Dingle Peninsula	70**
Ó Danachair (1958b; 1960b)	County Dublin	89**
Jackson (1977/86)	County Kildare	72
Mooney (1990)	County Meath	83

* The Diocese of Ossory includes most of County Kilkenny
  and the southwestern portion of Queens County.
**Excludes wells that Ó Danachair classes as "doubtful."

figure was originally just an impressionistic estimate. It is an estimate, however, that became a bit of scholarly folklore and as such
has been passed on uncritically for almost a century.

On the other hand, there are now more than a dozen published
studies that list the holy wells found in some particular area of Ireland, and collectively these studies identify more than nine hundred
holy wells (see table 1.1). Since these studies cover less than half the
counties in Ireland and are for the most part based on materials gathered in the nineteenth and twentieth centuries (and so could easily
have missed wells that had ceased to be the focus of cultic activity
prior to the nineteenth century), it seems clear that the "over 3,000
holy wells in Ireland" estimate, however it originally came into existence, is well within the bounds of plausibility.

Although I am using the term *well* in this discussion in deference
to popular usage in Ireland, most holy wells are really springs. A holy
well, in other words, usually consists of a water source that flows out
of the ground rather than being a deep hole in the ground that leads

down to water (which is, I think, what most North Americans think of when they hear the word *well*). Some holy wells are quite uncomplicated, being nothing more than the small pool of water that collects around the outlet to a spring. In many other cases a stone structure has been erected over a spring. Some of these stone structures are quite small; others more closely approximate what in other contexts would be called oratories and are large enough to hold two or three people comfortably. In the case of these "oratory" wells, the spring water usually flows just under the stone floor (in which case a hole in the floor provides access to the water) or exits from an outlet in the wall and flows freely across the stone floor itself.

Most holy wells in Ireland were (and are) located in the countryside. It would be wrong to conclude from this, however, that holy well cults were popular only with rural populations. On the contrary, such cults held as much appeal (and maybe more appeal) for urban Catholics as for rural Catholics. Writing early in the seventeenth century, for example, the Protestant commentator Barnaby Rich (1610, 51) talked about "the superstitious conceit that is holden of the Irish about certaine Wels" and says that "Dublin is quartered out" with such wells, with St. Patrick's Well located just to the east of the city, St. James's Well to the west, St. Sunday's Well to the south,[2] and St. Dolock's Well (see figure 2) to the north. Each of these wells attracted large numbers of Catholics on the festival day associated with its saint, and Rich is very clear in saying that most of the Catholics who flocked to these wells on these particular days were from within the city of Dublin itself:

> On the East part, they have Sai. Patricks Well, the water whereof, although it be generally reputed to bee very hot, yet the very prime of the perfection, is upon the 17. of March, which is Sai. Patricks day, and upon this day, the water is more holy then it is all the yeare after, or else the Inhabitants of Dublin are more foolish upon that day, then they be al the yeare after. For upon that day thither they wil run by heapes, men, women, and children, and there, first performing certain superstitious ceremonies, they drinke of the water. (Rich 1610, 52)

Rich's account, incidentally, is one of the earliest documentary sources we have attesting that large numbers of Irish Catholics were gathering at holy wells dedicated to Catholic saints and performing religious rituals. His account predates, if only by a few years, the synodal legislation that mentions such cults. In other words, when holy well cults first appear in the documentary record as an important tradition among Irish Catholics, such cults are associated with urban centers. Note too that Rich's reference to the "men, women, and children" who poured out of Dublin almost certainly means that entire families came to participate in the rituals associated with these cults.

Nor was Dublin the only Irish city that had a holy well within easy reach. At Galway there were three holy wells clustered together at the water's edge just beyond the walls of the old city. We know from a remark made in passing by John Lynch (1848[1662], 1:57), during the course of a discussion of the atrocities committed by English authorities in Ireland, that one of these wells attracted large numbers of people: "Not long ago, a great multitude of persons, men, women, and children, assembled to bathe in a well near Galway, expecting to benefit their health by the salubrity which the waters have from nature or the prayers of St. Augustine, whose name it bears. The Governor of Galway . . . headed the soldiers of the garrison against that inoffensive crowd, and ordered them to discharge, without the slightest warning, a shower of bullets among the poor innocents." A holy well dedicated to St. Augustine, and possibly the one referred to in this passage, still exists at Galway (see figure 3). There were also two holy wells near Kilkenny (dedicated to St. Rioc and St. Kenny), each located just a few hundred yards beyond the city walls (O'Carroll 1994, 23–24, 26). St. Kenny's Well can still be visited just off (appropriately enough) Kennyswell Street in the modern city of Kilkenny (see figure 4). Ó Coindealbhain (1946) describes seven holy wells in or near the city of Cork. John Rutty (1767, 273) suggests that one of these wells, dedicated to St. Bartholomew, was the site of an especially well attended pattern.

Holy Wells and Spa Wells

Consciously, Irish Catholics went to holy wells for two reasons: to secure relief from a physical ailment and/or to discharge a penance. With regard to the former, holy wells often specialized in the ailment they cured. Wells that specialized in curing eye problems or headaches were especially common, but there were wells that cured rheumatism, nervous disorders, worms, and so on. Still, the fact that a well's water cured some physical ailment did not in itself make it holy.

There were many wells in Ireland whose water was thought to have curative properties but which were not considered holy and so not made the focus of religious rituals. Such wells were called spa wells, and the distinction between holy wells and spa wells was well established in the popular imagination. Writing in the mid-seventeenth century, for example, Gerard Boate (1652, 55) noted:

> A few yeares since some fountains have been discovered in Ireland, some of them not far from Dublin, and others in other parts, whose veines running through certain Minerals, and washing off the virtue of the same, yeeld a Medicinall water, apt to open the obstructions of a mans body, and to cure other accidents thereof; which kind of Fountains are commonly called Spaes. . . . Besides these Spaes there are also a great number of other Fountains throughout all the land, called Holy-wels by the inhabitants, whose water not differing from that of other Wels, in smell, tast, or in any other sensible quality, nevertheless is believed to be effectual for the curing of several diseases. But experience doth shew, that those virtues are not found in the Springs themselves, but only in the vain imagination of the superstitious people; the which also having dedicated every one of those to some particular Saint, do expect the supposed vertue rather from the power of them, than from any naturall efficaciousness inherent in the water itself.

Nearly two centuries later, the same distinction that Boate draws in this passage—between "spa wells" and "holy wells"—reappears in the Ordnance Survey Letters (hereafter OSL) written by John O'Donovan and others in the 1830s and 1840s.[3]

What most distinguished a holy well from a spa well was that the holy wells were associated with supernatural power. This power, in turn, was usually (but not always) seen to derive from one of the supernatural beings—usually Christ, Mary, or a saint—considered legitimate by the official Church. As often happens in Catholic societies, however, the rank ordering of these beings in the popular tradition was not congruent with their rank ordering in the official tradition.

Saintly Preeminence

A few holy wells were dedicated to the God of the Tridentine Church, usually under some variant of the title *Rí an Domhnaigh* (the King of Sunday, i.e., Christ) or by virtue of being called Trinity Well, Well of the Cross, and so forth. Others were dedicated to Mary, either by way of the Gaelic *Tobermuire* (variants: Tobermurry, Tobar Muire, etc.), which means "Mary's well," or the English "Lady's well." A minority of wells, even though considered "holy" in local tradition, were not explicitly associated with a supernatural being at all. In these cases, the wells might be associated with individuals who were not saints (e.g., Egan's Well, Grumley's Well, Ward's Well, Priest's Well), with "generic" labels indicating their status as holy wells (e.g., Rag Well, Blessed Well, Holy Well), with a particular cure (Eye Well, Ear Well, Well of the Head), with some detail associated with the legends surrounding the well (Salmon Well, Poor Man's Well, etc.). Nevertheless, the majority of holy wells, in all areas of Ireland, were dedicated to a saint. The data in table 1.2 gives the relative frequency of each type of dedication as established by six different studies, each of which surveyed the holy wells in a different part of Ireland.

The vast majority of the saints associated with Irish holy wells were male. The simple fact that male saints were predominant in Ireland does not in itself make Ireland distinctive among Catholic societies. Male saints outnumber female saints by a ratio of at least four to one in almost all national traditions in Catholic Europe (see Delooz 1969). What *is* distinctive about Ireland, however, is the association between male saints and pilgrimage sites. For example, the analogue to holy wells in Italy would presumably be sanctuaries, which by definition are churches that are the object of pilgrimage. What is most striking about Italian sanctuaries is that most (87 percent) are dedicated to a madonna rather than to a saint or to Christ (see Carroll 1992, 23–25). In Italy, that is to say, the supernatural beings whose power drew pilgrims to specific locations were usually female; in Ireland, they were usually male. Similarly, in their survey

Table 1.2
The Dedications Associated with Holy Wells,
for Selected Areas of Ireland*

Location	Number (%) of Holy Wells Dedicated to				
	Christ/God	Mary	Saint	Other	Total
County Kildare	4	4	43	21	72
	(5%)	(5%)	(60%)	(30%)	(100%)
County Carlow	—	—	20	8	28
			(71%)	(29%)	(100%)
County Dublin	4	11	59	14	88
	(5%)	(12%)	(67%)	(16%)	(100%)
County Limerick	15	20	76	23	134
	(11%)	(15%)	(57%)	(17%)	(100%)
northern County Kerry,	11	5	31	24	71
incl. Dingle peninsula	(15%)	(7%)	(44%)	(34%)	(100%)
Diocese of Ossory	6	15	74	28	123
	(5%)	(12%)	(60%)	(23%)	(100%)

*Based on the information provided in the published surveys listed in table 1.1.

of over six thousand shrines in Western Europe Mary Lee and Sidney Nolan (1989, 120) found that Ireland had the highest proportion of shrines dedicated to a saint, and the lowest proportion of shrines dedicated to Mary. Generally the Irish Catholic predilection for associating pilgrimage sites with male figures sets Ireland apart from almost all other Catholic societies.

Looking at holy well dedications in Ireland as a whole, there is little doubt that the two most popular saints are St. Patrick and St. Brigid. Even so, the more significant pattern is that the holy wells found in any one area are usually dedicated to a wide variety of saints, with no one saint being predominant. For instance, the Ordnance Survey Letters for County Galway (written in 1839) identify sixty-three holy wells, and forty-six of these are dedicated to saints. One well in this latter category is called simply "the well of the saints," but the others are dedicated to specific individuals. The saints associated with these wells are Albae, Allachtan, Anne (two wells), Augustine (two wells), Beanan, Brendan (five wells), Brigid (two wells), Briocain (two wells), Cavan, Ciarán, Colman MacDuach (four wells), Dima, Donriuc (two wells), Enda, Greallan (two wells),

Iarlath, Imor (two wells), James, Odrani, Patrick (six wells), Peter, Rondearg, Seanain, Sornach, and Suibhne (two wells). There is some duplication here (in the sense that occasionally a given saint is associated with more than one well), but the more general tendency is clearly for different holy wells to be dedicated to different saints. This same emphasis upon saintly "variety" is found in all areas of Ireland.

Finally, the vast majority of the saints associated with holy wells in Ireland, whether male and female, were distinctively Irish. The dizzying array of distinctively Irish saints encountered in connection with holy wells in Ireland will come as no surprise to anyone familiar with Irish hagiography. However, it just might come as a surprise to other readers, if only because at least two well-known studies of Catholic sainthood have suggested that Ireland has traditionally produced very few saints in comparison with other Catholic societies. For that reason a brief digression seems in order.

Ireland and the Geography of Catholic Sainthood

Pierre Delooz (1969, 169) devotes two entire chapters to "geography" in his massive statistical study of Catholic sainthood. Among the 1,969 European saints in his sample, Italy accounts for the lion's share (with 32 percent of the total), followed by France (29 percent), England (12 percent), and Germany/Austria (6 percent). By contrast, Delooz's sample includes only fourteen Irish saints and another seven saints that he associates with "Ireland and Scotland" jointly; taken together, these two categories account for a mere 1 percent of all Delooz's European saints. The predominance of Italian and French saints in his sample is not due to the fact that Italy and France have exercised more influence over the formal canonization process than other societies. On the contrary, Italy and France still account for the vast majority of Catholic saints even if we limit our attention to those 1,042 European saints whose cults were established on the basis of local tradition long before they received official approval from Rome (Delooz's "Deuxième classe").

Unfortunately, it seems clear that Delooz's results were shaped less by the geography of Catholic sainthood than by the geographic biases of his sources. In particular, he relies heavily on hagiographical works—French hagiographical works in particular—whose authors were either unfamiliar or unconcerned with Irish hagiography. To get a sense of just how much Irish saints are under-represented in Delooz's sample, consider the saints listed in *The Martyrology of Donegal*. This is a work compiled around 1630 by the Franciscan scholar Michael O'Clery on the basis of a variety of Irish martyrologies then in existence. Although called the "martyrology" of Donegal, because O'Clery worked on it while residing in a Franciscan convent in Donegal, it was meant to be a relatively complete listing of all Irish saints and their associated feast days.

In the end, O'Clery was able to identify 2,230 saints. This means that the total number of Irish saints in *The Martyrology of Donegal* alone exceeds the sum total of all the European saints in Delooz's sample. To be fair, there is likely some duplication in O'Clery's listing. For instance, he lists 102 saints named "Colman." Seventy-three of these had different family names and so were clearly conceptualized as different individuals. The remaining twenty-nine Colmans, however, are considered to be different individuals mainly because their feast days are different; in this case, we might easily be dealing in several instances with different local traditions concerning the same saint. But even if we were to reduce O'Clery's overall list by 50 percent, the number of Irish saints remaining (in excess of a thousand) should still make us wonder about the very small number of Irish saints who show up in the sources used by Delooz.

Donald Weinstein and Rudolph Bell (1982) have also published a statistical study of Catholic sainthood (I suspect that this is the study that will be most familiar to readers of this book) and they devote an entire chapter to geography. In this case there are so few Irish saints in their total sample (of 864 saints) that Ireland is lumped together with England, Scotland, and Wales into a general "British Isles" category, and "Ireland" does not even appear as a separate entry in the index. Their study, like Delooz's, might thus be taken as indicating that Ireland has produced few saints relative to other areas of Catholic Europe. But once again the result is artifactual: Weinstein and Bell constructed their sample using Delooz's much larger sample as a base (see Weinstein and Bell 1982, 278–79) and so their study simply incorporates the bias against Irish hagiographical materials that was a part of Delooz's original work.

The under-representation of Irish saints in the well-known studies by Delooz and by Weinstein and Bell is worth noting if only because the inclusion of a larger number of Irish saints would have forced a modification of some of the conclusions that these authors reached about Catholic sainthood. For example, at several points in his discussion (see in particular 207–8, 219–20) Delooz cites the fact that Latin countries like Italy, France, Spain, and Portugal account for something like 70 percent of the European saints in his sample as evidence that Catholicism was strongly implanted in "l'Europe latine" and that as a result "l'Europe latine" must be regarded as the heart of the Catholic Church. But it is precisely conclusions of this sort—those that establish a distinction between Latin Catholicism and Catholicism elsewhere—which are subverted by the data from Ireland. After all, while Ireland may not have been as productive of saints as Italy, it seems entirely possible—even given only the number of saints listed in *The Martyrology of Donegal*—that on a per capita basis Ireland has produced more saints than Spain and Portugal, and maybe even France.

In a similar vein, Weinstein and Bell (1982, 166–93) argue that the great divide among Catholic saints has been between "Mediterranean saints" (mainly Italian and Spanish) and "northern European saints." Their conclusion here is based less on simple numbers (as was the case with Delooz) than on the characteristics associated with saints in these two areas. Mediterranean saints, they argue, were far more likely to be characterized by visual displays of supernatural power, by asceticism, and by evangelical activity. Northern European saints, by contrast, were more likely to be associated with visionary experiences. Yet here again including a substantial number of Irish saints in the analysis would undermine the distinction being advanced. The legends surrounding early Irish saints (see, e.g., Anderson and Anderson 1991; Bieler 1979; Plummer 1968; Stokes 1887) make it clear that these saints were well-known miracle workers, were deeply committed to evangelical activity, and were engaged in any number of extremely ascetic practices, but were not particularly prone to visionary experiences. In short, their geographical location notwithstanding, Irish saints conform far more closely to Weinstein and Bell's so-called Mediterranean type than to their northern European type. In other words, the Irish case works to undermine that overly neat distinction between Mediterranean Catholicism and northern European Catholicism that is often encountered in existing scholarly works.

A complete statistical analysis of the cult of the saints in Europe is beyond the scope of this book. My point is only that the under-representation of Irish saints in existing studies of Catholic saint-hood means that the geography of Catholic sainthood in Europe is a subject that has not yet been effectively investigated, claims to the contrary notwithstanding.

Rounding Rituals and Penitence

Because holy wells were associated with supernatural (mainly saintly) power, they, unlike spa wells, could be used to serve a penitential purpose. Sometimes this meant that devotees went to a well to dis-charge a penance established by a priest during Confession. In other cases it meant that devotees thought they were earning what the of-ficial Church would call an indulgence, an action that, performed correctly, leads to the remission of some portion of the punishment occasioned by their sins.

Surprisingly, the water found at holy wells, as important as it was to the cure of physical ailments, played little or no role in the peni-tential rituals at these sites. What *was* central to these rituals was the practice of "making rounds." In its simplest form, making rounds meant walking around a well in a clockwise direction for a specified number of times (usually three, seven, nine, or fifteen) while saying certain prayers. Traditionally, these prayers included some set num-ber of Our Fathers, Hail Marys, Creeds, and Glorias. It was also com-mon to gather up some pebbles and to "count off" rounds by depos-iting a pebble in a pile somewhere on or near the well as each round (and the associated set of prayers) was completed.

Rounding rituals were generally not restricted to the well itself. On the contrary, the well at any particular location was usually only one of a series of stations that each had to be rounded. The well itself aside, the most common sort of station was an amorphous pile of stones (sometimes standing alone, sometimes surrounded by a low circle of stones). In the OSL for County Mayo (1838, 1:411), for ex-ample, O'Connor provides a succinct account of a holy well and its associated station in Killbride parish: "Bride's well . . . is surrounded with a wall of stone work that supports a great heap of stones loosely placed over it as a tegument. There is at the Well a Station Monument, a heap of stones thrown loosely together, with a stone about three feet high . . . placed in an inclining position in the center of it." Often there were several piles of stone that had to be rounded. O'Donovan (OSL, 1838, County Mayo, 2:8), for example, says that "in the Glebe of Aghadovey there is a holy well called Tobar Bearoige . . . or well of St. Bearog [also called] Well of the Eyes, because it is resorted to by pilgrims for the cure of diseases of the eye; and a short distance to the south of it a green spot with piles of stone or penitential leachtas or monuments, at which pilgrims kneel, pray and perform their turas, or circumgyratory rounds." Large stone slabs (often with indentations or basins) and/or "coffins" made of flat stones could also serve as stations. Any pile of stones or stone structure that served as a station would typically be called a "saint's bed."

The various stations at a given location had to be visited in a predetermined order. For example, during the nineteenth century an inscription at Scattery Island (County Clare) instructed pilgrims to round the eleven stations there in the following order:

> In the name of God Amen/ Bare head, bare feet, all pious Christians are to kneel/ At every station say or read, 5 paters aves & a creed/ 5 times round each blessed place/ singing hymns & partner [sic] beads/ Round the Altar is a first/ and 2 noted stations on the strand annex/ Round the Island at water's edge; 4th the Nun's tomb on the strand du [sic] west/ Whoever kneel & read a prayer will not meet a watery grave/ Bring up a stone to monument hill perform there and thats the 5th./ 6th, N-East a place called Loath & at our lady's church women stop/ 8th, the large church, 9th is the Srs, 10th is the bed called St. Synan's grave. The well is 11th, finish & pray for ye souls of ye Erectors of this Blessed Place. (cited in Westropp 1911, 332)

Notice that in this case the saint's bed was called "St. Synan's grave." Generally, the term *bed* meant only that local legends described the saint involved as having "rested" (in any sense of the word) on that spot in the distant past.

As in many Catholic areas, physical pain was seen to heighten the value of penitential rituals. The result was that devotees often walked barefoot or on their knees while making rounds. Given the stony ground around most stations, such practices often caused minor lacerations and a consequent "bloodiness"—a feature of Irish devotional practice that disdainful Protestant observers were always quick to note. Nevertheless, my reading of the reports suggests that the lacerations involved were relatively minor and that the actual amount of physical pain involved was likely far less than, say, the pain often found associated with devotional practices in Italy or Spain.

The centrality of "making rounds" (and its associated penitential emphasis) to the Irish Catholic experience must be emphasized, if only because this is what most differentiates the Irish Catholic experience from a more broadly defined "Celtic" experience. After all, people in other parts of the British Isles sought out the curative waters of their own local wells, both before and after the Reformation. John Brand (1849, 2:366–67), for instance, brings together several dozen reports from the period 1600–1800 which make it clear that there were lots of holy wells in England, Scotland, and Wales which attracted large numbers of people (both Catholic and Protestant). Furthermore, just as in Ireland, many of the wells in these other areas were dedicated to saints, and—again, as in Ireland—devotees often left rags tied to nearby trees (see below). In all cases, however, the wells in England, Scotland, and Wales were sought out primarily for the curative nature of their water, and the most common ritual performed at these wells, if it can be called a ritual, was simply drinking the water or immersing one's self in it. What is missing in these other areas, in other words, is that strong emphasis on rounding, and in particular the view that rounding rituals earned the remission of punishment for sin, which was so central to the experience at holy wells in Ireland.

This is not to say that rounding rituals per se were completely unknown in these other areas. In his account of the visits he made to three dozen islands in the Scottish Hebrides in the 1690s, Martin Martin (1970 [1716], 99, 277–78) did find Roman Catholics making rounds at a local church or at a holy well on two of these islands. Reports of "making rounds" also exist for a few wells in both Wales and England (see, e.g., Brand 1849, 2:375; Knowlson 1910, 192–94). Nevertheless, we must keep in mind that as an *occasional* practice, the simple act of "walking around" a sacred site is commonly encountered in several Catholic societies. At many sanctuaries in southern Italy, for instance, pilgrims routinely walked around the church building three times before entering and engaging in other ritual acts (Rossi 1969, 92; Cipriani et al. 1979, 74–75; Gentilcore 1992, 119). The important point (given our concerns here) is that in England, Scotland, and Wales "making rounds" was not central to the rituals performed at holy wells, in the way that rounding *was* central to holy well devotions in Ireland, and that in these other areas (as well as in other Catholic areas, like Italy) whatever rounding rituals existed were not associated with penitence, as was the case in Ireland.

Leaving Sin and Sickness Behind

It was common at many holy wells in Ireland for devotees to leave something behind after they had visited the well. Quite often they tied a bit of cloth—usually torn from their own clothing—to a tree or bush near the well (see figure 5). Other objects included pins, nails, buttons, bits of clipped hair, broken crockery, braided thread taken from the fringe of a shawl. Starting in the late nineteenth century, it also became common (at the holy wells that were still the object of cultic attention) to leave religious objects with a more "romanized" cast, like holy cards, rosaries, and so forth. Although the objects left at holy wells are often called "votive offerings," this term is misleading since it suggests that these objects can be equated with the ex-votos brought to sanctuaries in other areas of Catholic Europe.

In Latin Catholic societies, ex-votos are objects brought to a sanctuary as the result of a vow. In a typical case, for instance, a devotee will call upon a madonna or saint for supernatural assistance during the course of an accident or an illness (their own or someone else's) and promise (vow) to bring an offering to the shrine of that madonna or saint if the favor is granted. In Italy the two most common forms of ex-votos are body-part ex-votos (pressed-metal representations of the body part that was healed) and painted ex-votos (small paintings, usually specially commissioned from an artisan, that depict the danger from which the devotee was delivered).[4] Painted ex-votos were also common in France, although by the late nineteenth century these came increasingly to be replaced by carved marble plaques (Cousin 1977). In Hispanic areas of North and South America, ex-votos were commonly very small representations of different body parts or animals, usually made from silver or a metal that had the appearance of silver (Egan 1991). What is common to all these different forms of ex-votos, however, is the fact that they were brought to a shrine *after* the receipt of a supernatural favor. This is not what was happening in Ireland.

Irish Catholics came to holy wells because they were in search of a favor, either the cure of some physical ailment or release from sin and its associated punishment, not because they had received it. The act of leaving behind some object was a metaphor that allowed them to visualize in a concrete manner what they wanted to achieve: to separate themselves from the ailment that afflicted them (either a physical ailment or the punishment and guilt occasioned by their sins) and leave it behind. In discussing the practice of leaving rags at holy wells, William Hackett (1861–62, 258) stated the general principle succinctly: "This [practice] is generally regarded in the light of a votive offering, but it is of a character altogether different. . . . The intent with which this is done [is] that all the spiritual and corporeal ailments of the votaries are deposited in the rag. The words used on such occasions by the Irish votary clearly express this object [namely] 'invoking the Lord, my ailments are deposited in this place.'" What allowed devotees to "separate" themselves from their physical ailments at holy wells was mainly the water itself, which was either drunk or applied to the afflicted area (the eyes, forehead, etc.). In the case of their spiritual ailments (the guilt and punishment associated with sin), however, it was the rounding rituals that effected the separation.

That devotees felt they were "detaching" themselves from their physical or spiritual ailments probably explains the particular nature of the objects they left behind at holy wells. Since they had been in "close association" with the ailments they were leaving behind, it was only fitting that they represent this materially by leaving behind concrete objects with which they had been in close association (e.g., strips torn from their clothing, strands of their hair, threads from their shawls, etc.). Similarly, the emphasis upon "detachment" or "unfastening" could be represented by leaving behind objects that would normally be removed during a process of "unfastening"—like nails, pins, and buttons. The concrete objects left behind at a holy well, in other words, served as metaphorical representations of that process of "detachment" from physical and spiritual ailments that was a primary purpose of visiting the well.

At the same time, in at least one way the objects left at holy wells in Ireland were similar to the ex-votos brought to Catholic sanctuaries elsewhere in Europe: in both cases, the display of these objects was a visible manifestation of the potency associated with the supernatural force (usually personified as a saint) that was associated with the site. In other words, the hundreds of cloth strips that might adorn a tree near an Irish holy well and the hundreds of painted ex-votos that might cover the walls of an Italian sanctuary conveyed the same message: the supernatural power associated with this place was especially potent and under the right conditions could be tapped for the benefit of human beings.

Patterns and Patrons

In many cases a holy well was visited on a particular day or during a particular period. On these occasions, a fairly large number of people might gather at the well for what was called a "pattern" or "patron" (two variants of the same word), because the celebration was at least loosely in honor of the well's patron saint. The largest patterns attracted several thousand people. A newspaper account published in 1710, for example, suggests that ten thousand Catholics had attended the annual pattern at St. John's Well in County Meath (Brady 1965, 14). Similarly, an observer who attended the pattern at Ardmore in 1841, using a relatively careful estimation procedure, suggested that somewhere between twelve thousand and fifteen thousand people had taken part in the religious rituals there (Hall and Hall 1841–43, 1:284–85).

During the course of a pattern, devotees did rounds at the well itself and any associated stations. But patterns were also the occasion for secular activities. Tents were usually erected to dispense food and drink, and to serve as a staging area for a variety of activities such as gaming, singing, dancing, horse racing, and such. Mason's account (1814, 1:494) of the annual pattern at St. Bridget's Well in the parish of Kilmanaheem (County Clare) provides a good example of how the secular and the sacred were mixed:

The last Sunday in July is a patron day, when a number of people assemble at Lahinchy: they amuse themselves with horse racing on the strand, dancing, etc. . . . On Saturday evening preceding this Sunday, numbers of people, male and female, assemble at St. Bridget's well, and remain there the entire of the night. They first perform their rounds, and then spend a good part of the time in invoking this saint Bridget over the well, repeating their prayers and adorations aloud, and holding conversations with the saint, etc. When this ceremony is over, they amuse themselves until morning by dancing and singing, etc. They then on Sunday morning repair to Lahensey [*sic*], distant from this well at least three miles.

Note that although a pattern involved both sacred and secular activities, the distinction between these two types of activity was not blurred. In the pattern described above, as was the case with most if not all patterns in Ireland, there was a clear sequencing to the activities: the roundings and other religious rituals were performed first, and only then did devotees begin their dancing, singing, and playing.

Although most patterns were held in rural areas, it would be wrong to think of them as rural activities. Patterns routinely drew devotees from urban areas, which is why many of the most well attended patterns were those held on the fringes of major urban centers. I have already cited Rich's (1610) account of the "heapes" of people who poured out of Dublin to visit St. Patrick's Well on March 19. Nearly two centuries later, Edward Wakefield (1812, 2:505) made much the same point about Dublin Catholics by suggesting that the annual pattern held at St. John's Well in County Meath was especially well attended because it was near Dublin.

The patterns held at holy wells were distinctively local, or at best regional, affairs. But there were other sacred places that consistently attracted Catholics from all over Ireland. Prior to the emergence of the sanctuary at Knock in the late nineteenth century, the two most important of these national sites were St. Patrick's Purgatory and Croagh Patrick. What might at first sight seem odd, given the importance of holy wells at the local level, is that neither of these sites was associated with a holy well. St. Patrick's Purgatory will be discussed at length in chapter 3. It will be useful, however, to discuss Croagh Patrick here.

County Mayo's Holy Mountain

So much of what we know about religious practice in Ireland, whether in the Middle Ages or the early modern period, comes to us in the form of passing remarks made in discussions concerned mainly with other things. Like most of the annalistic sources, for example, the *Annals of Loch Cé* is for the most part concerned with listing the never-ending series of deaths, battles, assassinations, sieges, invasions, sackings, and so on that occurred in Ireland over the course of the centuries. A single sentence found buried in the entry for the year 1113, however, tells us that "a thunderbolt fell on Crua-chan Aigle [Croagh Patrick], on the night of the festival of Patrick, which destroyed thirty of the fasting people" (Hennessy 1871, 103). As brief as it is, this statement is evidence that by the early twelfth century Croagh Patrick was an established pilgrimage site and that fasting at that site was an established devotional practice for the pilgrims who came there.

The medieval pilgrims who went to Croagh Patrick to fast almost certainly felt that they were imitating St. Patrick himself. After all, one of the earliest legends about Patrick, preserved in the *Book of Armagh* (see Bieler 1979, 153), says that he climbed Cruachan Aigle (Croagh Patrick) and fasted there for forty days and forty nights in order to "follow the example of Moses, Elias and Christ." Moreover, the account closes with a divine injunction to follow Patrick's example: "To all the holy men of Ireland, past, present and future, God said: 'Climb o holy men, to the top of the mountain which towers above, and is higher than all the mountains to the west of the sun in order to bless the people of Ireland,' so that Patrick might see the fruit of his labours" (Bieler 1979, 153).

On the other hand, it is now generally recognized that much of what is found in the stories about St. Patrick are very much "invented traditions" that were designed to serve some particular function. De Paor (1971), for example, suggests that many of the stories about Patrick in the *Book of Armagh* were shaped by a concern (which emerged long after the death of the historic Patrick) to establish the primacy of the Church at Armagh. It seems likely, then, that the story of Patrick's climbing Cruachan Aigle is an example of what Malinowski called a "charter myth," that is, a myth that emerges in order to give legitimacy (or greater legitimacy) to an already existing practice. In short, the pilgrimage to Croagh Patrick is likely much older than the myth that legitimates it and likely was originally not associated with Patrick at all.

Whenever Croagh Patrick emerged as a pilgrimage site, there is nothing about the practice of making a pilgrimage to some out-of-the-way spot and fasting there that is distinctively Irish. On the contrary, such practices were found throughout the Christian world. Indeed, the explicit statement in the *Book of Armagh* story suggesting that Patrick was following the example of Moses, Elias, and Christ seems an attempt to associate the devotional activity at Croagh Patrick with the Christian tradition that prevailed in Europe generally. In particular, what is missing from all medieval accounts that mention Croagh Patrick is any suggestion that the pilgrims going there performed rounding rituals. By contrast, accounts of the pilgrimage experience at Croagh Patrick written in the early nineteenth century—and there are several (see Hughes 1991)—suggest that by this time rounding rituals were as central to the pilgrimage experience there as they were to the experience at local holy wells.

During the early nineteenth century there were three stations at Croagh Patrick that had to be rounded (see figure 6). The first was Leacht Benain, the Monument of St. Benignus, which was located just at the base of the cone that forms the upper portion of Croagh Patrick (see figure 7). Here the pilgrim said seven Our Fathers, seven Hail Marys, and one Credo and walked seven times around the Leacht. The second station was the summit itself. Here the pilgrim first said some prayers in the chapel and then walked fifteen times around the circular perimeter of the summit. The pilgrim next went to Lectus Patricii, or St. Patrick's Bed, a structure that looks like a grave just to the south of the chapel, said seven Our Fathers, seven Hail Marys, and one Credo, and then walked round the bed seven times. The third and final station was Roilig Mhuire, or Mary's Cemetery. This station is located down from the summit, on the southwest side, and consists of three stone cairns. Pilgrims went seven times around all three cairns collectively, and then rounded each cairn individually seven times. Prior to each set of rounds, they repeated the now standard formula, consisting of seven Our Fathers, seven Hail Marys, one Credo, and a walk around the cairn seven times. The modern ritual at Croagh Patrick is much the same.

Commentators, at least those not writing from a devotional perspective, inevitably commented on the "shapelessness" of the stone cairns associated with the Croagh Patrick stations. O'Donovan (OSL, County Mayo, 434), for instance, describes Leacht Benain simply as "a heap of stones at the east base of the mountain," and William Makepeace Thackeray (1843, 236)—who visited the area in 1842 and obtained his information from a friend who climbed the mountain— called the altar at the summit "a shapeless heap of stone." Today, this shapelessness is probably most evident at Roilig Mhuire, where the stations consist of relatively large mounds of loose and irregularly sized stones.

There was a strong penitential emphasis associated with Croagh Patrick. Pilgrims often walked up the stony mountain barefoot and moved around the three stations on their knees. Thurston (1905, 461), for example, says that at the summit one round on bare knees was often substituted for fifteen rounds on bare feet. Even now, such practices are not unknown. As I was going down Croagh Patrick in 1997, I encountered a group of teenaged schoolchildren going up, and at least one of the boys was barefoot and very doggedly trying to avoid the sharpest stones in the path. Here again, as with holy wells, this sort of penitential activity routinely resulted in lacerations, and the resulting bloodiness was something that unfriendly Protestant commentators were always quick to stress. Thackeray (1985 [1843], 237) reports that people often came away from the mountain "suffering severe pain, wounded and bleeding in the knees and feet, and some of the women shrieking with the pain of their wounds." Having completed the penitential rounding, pilgrims to Croagh Patrick visualized their separation from their sins and the associated punishment in the same way they did at holy wells: they left something behind. O'Donovan reports, for instance, that pilgrims tore strips of cloth from their clothing and left them stuck in between the stones of the chapel.

What is easy to overlook in considering the different accounts of the pilgrimage to Croagh Patrick is what is missing. Simply: there is no strong tradition of its pilgrims' receiving miraculous cures, even though such cures are routinely associated with holy wells. Indeed, there is no strong tradition of miraculous cures associated with any of Ireland's "national" pilgrimage sites. Even hostile Protestant commentators, for instance, conceded that Catholics did not associate the pilgrimage to St. Patrick's Purgatory with miracle working (see, for instance, Hewson 1727 [1701], 136).

A consideration of the activities associated with holy well cults and pilgrimage sites like Croagh Patrick suggests that popular Catholicism in Ireland rests mainly upon two separate elements: the first links rounding rituals with penitence and the second associates water with miraculous cures. Although these two elements could be combined, as they were combined in the case of holy well cults, they are analytically and empirically separable. Moreover, the fact that penitential rounding rituals is the only one of these elements in evidence at both "national" pilgrimage sites like Croagh Patrick and local holy wells suggests that it was this element (of the two) that was more central to the experience of popular Catholicism in Ireland.

Catholic to the Core

The variant of Catholicism described in the preceding sections is clearly different from the orthodox variant formulated by the good bishops who had gathered at the Council of Trent in 1545–63. Unlike the Tridentine variant, Irish popular Catholicism was a Catholicism in which the figure of Christ played only a small role, and which was blissfully unconcerned with esoteric doctrines about Transubstantiation, the Virgin Birth, or the Immaculate Conception; in fact its central ritual involved walking several times around a holy well and shapeless piles of stones. So why call it "Catholicism" at all? The answer to that question takes us back to the modified Gramscian perspective described in the introduction. I suggested there that "popular Catholicism" is best viewed as the type of Catholicism that emerges spontaneously at the local level within certain broad constraints laid down by official Catholicism. The most important of those constraints are that popular rituals must be (1) at least loosely associated with the supernatural beings considered important by the official Church and (2) legitimated by the clergy of the official Church. The strong association between holy wells (and other pilgrimage sites) and Catholic saints means that the first condition is certainly met in the Irish case. But what about the second condition? Did the Catholic clergy legitimate the popular devotions at holy wells and elsewhere? The evidence clearly suggests that they did.

Even in relatively recent periods, for example, it seems clear that local priests affirmed and encouraged popular attitudes about the miraculous powers of the water at holy wells (Taylor 1990, 173–74). Local priests also attended popular patterns and took an active part in the proceedings by staging some suitably Tridentine ritual that functioned as a complement to the rounding rituals associated with stations. In some cases, this might mean something as simple as a priest's reading from the Bible. Writing in 1802, one observer (cited in Westropp 1912, 111) described a pattern held at Downpatrick (County Mayo) by saying, "Hither the common people resort to do penance about a number of stone crosses going round and round again, and dropping beads . . . on Good Friday where the priest attends to read the Passion of our Saviour." More usually, however, at least until the late 1700s, the priests who came to patterns incorporated the two rituals central to Tridentine Catholicism—confession and the Mass—into the pattern experience.[5]

Irish priests also shared the popular view that rounding rituals had penitential value and so legitimated popular Catholic practice by assigning "making rounds" as penance. A pilgrimage to Lough Derg, for instance, was typically assigned as a penance for sins that were especially grave; for lesser sins a visit to a local holy well was sufficient. In other words, when Irish Catholics went to a pilgrimage site and made their rounds at the various stations there, they had often (maybe even usually) been instructed to do that by Catholic priests.

This legitimation of popular practice by the local clergy was not given reluctantly, and indeed there is no reason to think it would be. Although most secular priests were allowed to operate in a relatively undisturbed manner even under the period of the Penal Laws, their legal and economic position was precarious and this worked to minimize the gap between priests and people. Until the late 1700s, for instance, priests did not wear distinctive garb, and they often worked at "regular" jobs and lived with relatives (see Brady and Corish 1971, 49–57; McCullough 1992, 55–62). It is hardly surprising, then, that priests would share the values and beliefs of other local Catholics.

But it was not just the fact that the devotions at holy wells were associated with Catholic saints, and the fact these devotions were given legitimacy by the local clergy, that made these devotions seem "Catholic" for the people involved. There was something else: in the minds of ordinary Catholics these popular devotions had a clear and obvious affinity with traditions of penitential pilgrimage that stretched back to the earliest days of the Irish Church. As a result, some understanding of that ancient tradition is necessary if we want to recapture what going to a holy well "meant" to Irish Catholics.

Pilgrimage and Penance

Pilgrimage is an activity mentioned often in the legends about early Irish saints. A succinct statement of what counted as an ideal pilgrimage in the early Irish Church appears in the *Book of Lismore* (see Stokes 1890, 168–70), which says that the perfect pilgrimage is one in which a person "leaves his fatherland completely in body and in soul." This meant that the ideal pilgrim was someone who left Ireland entirely, thereby cutting himself off from his kin, and wandered in other lands for a number of years. If he converted some pagans along the way, so much the better. The *Book of Lismore* also makes it clear that this "leaving behind" of one's native land had also to be accompanied by a "leaving behind" of past sins and vices: "For when one leaves his fatherland in body only, and his mind doth not sever from sins and vices, and yearneth not to practise virtues or good deed, of the pilgrimage, then that is made in that wise [way], there groweth neither fruit nor profit to the soul, but labor and motion of the body idly" (Stokes 1890, 169). This leaving behind of sin and vice allowed the pilgrim to use the pilgrimage experience as a way of atoning for past sin and vice.

Several early legends suggest that St. Columba had played a role in causing a battle that resulted in a large loss of life. As penance, he embraced precisely that form of perfect pilgrimage described in the *Book of Lismore:* he left Ireland, established a monastery on the island of Iona, and with Iona as a base spent the rest of his life missionizing pagan populations throughout the British Isles. The legends about

Popular Catholicism before the Famine

Columba also provide several instances of the saint himself imposing pilgrimage on others as a penance for grave sin. In one case, Columba imposes twelve years of wandering among the Britons as a penance for an Irishman who had killed his own brother and had had sexual intercourse with his own mother (Anderson and Anderson 1991, 51).

By the early modern era, the practice of spending years wandering in foreign lands was no longer widely practiced in Ireland. What had remained intact, however, was a strong emphasis on pilgrimage as a penitential activity, and this emphasis was shared by both the laity and the clergy in Ireland. Sometime in the early 1540s, for instance, Heneas MacNichaill, a layman of Armagh, appealed to Dean Edmund MacCawell (who was administering the See of Armagh at the time) for absolution. MacNichaill's sin was that he had strangled his own son. The penance that MacCawell imposed required that MacNichaill visit fifteen different pilgrimage sites scattered throughout Ireland. After MacNichaill had completed his pilgrimage, he appeared before George Dowdall, Archbishop of Armagh. Dowdall inspected the certificates attesting to the fact that the penitent had visited all fifteen sites and only then granted absolution.[6]

A pilgrimage did not have to be assigned in order for it to have penitential value. In 1507, the prior of St. Patrick's Purgatory certified that Nylan Oledan was "a devout priest and pilgrim" who had visited the purgatory as part of his intention to visit "all the approved places of pilgrimage of the whole of Ireland, for the salvation of his soul and of the souls of his benefactors" (see Bieler 1958). Oledan, in other words, appears to have been a priest of good character who was making a pilgrimage at least as extensive as MacNichaill's in order to earn —for himself and those who contributed to his expenses—something akin to an indulgence that could be used to remit the punishment due to sin.

Strictly speaking, the practice of rounding the stations at local holy wells would hardly count as the sort of penitential pilgrimage envisioned in the *Book of Lismore* and practiced by early saints like Columba. A visit to a holy well was usually of short duration, and —far from cutting one off from kin—was undertaken, especially if done on the occasion of a pattern, in the company of family and friends. Moreover, the secular activities associated with patterns clearly undermined the ascetic emphasis that was a feature of early

43

Irish pilgrimage. Nevertheless, however wrong it might seem when set against the strict Columban ideal, the fact remains that Irish Catholics in the post-Reformation period, priests and people alike, did think of their rounding rituals as pilgrimage (which is why they used the term *turas*, which means pilgrimage, to describe these rituals), and they did believe that these rounding rituals served a penitential function. This means that when ordinary Catholics performed these rituals, and when their priests assigned the rituals as penance, they all experienced a sense of affinity with a distinctively Irish tradition of penitential pilgrimage that was over a thousand years old and impeccably Catholic. To have said that these popular rituals were not "really" instances of penitential pilgrimage and so not "really" Catholic would have seemed as nonsensical to Irish Catholics as the suggestion that Communion was not "really" a reenactment of Christ's distribution of bread and wine at the Last Supper because it did not take place in Jerusalem.

The Church Hierarchy

So far I have been discussing the attitudes of the laity and the local clergy toward the popular devotions associated with holy wells and other sites. What about the Church hierarchy? How did they feel about these same devotions? The available evidence suggests that the Irish hierarchy was generally supportive of these devotions so long as they did not in any obvious way violate any of the doctrines that were laid down at the Council of Trent. In 1614, for example, the Synod of Drogheda passed the following legislation for the ecclesiastical province of Armagh:

> Superiors should also oppose those superstitious practices which occur sometimes at wells, trees, etc. If it be certain that these waters have naturally, or through the intercession of a particular saint, the power of healing, or any virtue, the people are not to be prevented from assembling there, provided the danger of abuse be removed. (cited in Renehan 1861, 433)

This legislation clearly suggests that in many cases the water from wells dedicated to Catholic saints may indeed have supernatural potency and that assembling at such wells is a legitimate religious activity. The assembled prelates had only two concerns: first, that the water's supernatural potency be attributed to the intercession of the saint involved (thus reaffirming Trent's insistence that saints had no independent power but could only intercede with God) and second, that "superstitious practices" not be a part of the ceremonies. Although the Drogheda synod does not specify the nature of these superstitious practices, a clue to what might have been involved here appears in the legislation passed at a synod in the Province of Tuam in 1660:

> Dancing, flute-playing, singing in harmony, intermingling [of the sexes?] and other such abuses are all forbidden during the visitation of wells and other holy places, especially during the periods when indulgences can be earned. Also forbidden are those practices that involve a striving to have children and such, since such practices smack more of superstition than devotion. Take care too that people do not use the appearance of devotion during these visitations to avoid hearing Mass on Sundays and holy days.

The reference to practices that involve a striving to have children is presumably a reference to magical procedures designed to make women fertile. If so, then the legislation was probably directed as much at the clergy as at the laity, since—as hostile Protestant commentators like Rich (1610, 47) were quick to point out—Catholic priests of this period were well known for giving blessings that were designed to "fructify" wives.

The Tuam legislation is valuable for other reasons as well. First, its prohibition of dancing, flute playing, and so forth during the visitation of holy wells and other sites is clear evidence that these secular activities were already an integral part of the pattern experience by the seventeenth century. This undermines the suggestion, implicit in many commentaries, that these elements only crept into patterns during the eighteenth and early nineteenth centuries, as these events began to lose their "original" religious function. Second, in expressing concern that the proper decorum be maintained especially during the period when indulgences can be earned, the Tuam legislation is also evidence that Irish prelates were quite willing to legitimate yet another popular belief, namely, that the rituals performed at holy wells could and did earn the remission of punishment due to sin.

It must be emphasized that the toleration of holy well cults by the

Irish hierarchy did not derive from an unwillingness to challenge popular custom. In other contexts Irish prelates were more than willing to wage a determined campaign against practices that violated either the spirit or the letter of Tridentine Catholicism. They certainly took a hard line against the traditional Irish funeral. The legislation passed at the Provincial Synod of Armagh in 1618, for instance, which was later adopted throughout the island, condemned the traditional Irish funeral because the "festive rejoicings" that took place at such funerals ensured that "all fear of death is banished from the mind [of those attending], although the image of death itself, in the body of the deceased, is present before them" (Moran 1864, 1:274). In short, traditional Irish funerals needed to be stamped out because their festive nature negated the concern with securing salvation after death that was so central to Tridentine Catholicism.

Other practices and behaviors that the hierarchy tried to stamp out can be identified by looking at the records of pastoral visits. In 1668, for instance, Rome sent James Taafe, a Franciscan, to Ireland to caution the Irish clergy in the Dublin area against certain irregularities. One of the first things Taafe did was to organize "visitations" of local parishes, and as part of this he issued a list of twenty-nine specific questions that were to be investigated (reproduced in Millett 1965, 123–28). Some were concerned with parish organization or with disputes between the secular clergy and the regular clergy. Most, however, concerned the material condition of altars, chalices, albs, and so forth, and with the character of local priests. In regard to the latter, visitors were instructed to determine what books local priests read, how often they administered the sacraments or preached, how well versed they were in doctrine, whether they were "liars, quarrelers, whoremongers, tipplers, players of dice and cards." Despite the detailed nature of the questionnaire, there is not the slightest hint that Taafe was concerned with the degree to which priests or laity were participating in the popular devotions associated with holy wells, patterns, or pilgrimages. This is true, remember, despite the evidence from Rich's (1610) account, published earlier in the century, that holy well cults were extremely popular with Dublin Catholics and, in particular, that Dublin Catholics turned out in large numbers to attend the patterns at nearby holy wells.

It would later be determined that Taafe had overstepped his authority in organizing the visitation. Still, once recalled to Rome, he was cleared of all wrongdoing, something that suggests some degree of official approval for what he had tried to do. In any event, the visitations organized and conducted by Irish bishops themselves throughout most of the eighteenth century, although usually less rigorous than the one envisioned by Taafe, were generally concerned with the same issues and also ignored holy well cults (see Cogan 1870, 3:25–44; Flood 1913).

Starting in the latter half of the eighteenth century, Irish bishops did begin to issue edicts designed to curtail the participation of the clergy in patterns or to eliminate patterns altogether, and these edicts are often cited (see Brady and Corish 1971, 79–81; Connolly 1982, 14–42) as evidence of a shift in official attitudes, that is, as a move from a policy of encouraging or at least tolerating these popular devotions to a policy of actively seeking their elimination. Yet, as Donnelly (1988, 28) points out, the primary concern of these edicts was always with the licentious and unruly behavior associated with the secular activities that accompanied the patterns and not with the religious activities at these wells. Thus, when the Archbishop of Dublin published a decree in 1787 forbidding attendance at the pattern held at St. John's Well, he made reference to the people who "scandalise their holy religion and disturb public peace by many criminal excesses" and to "the dangerous opportunities of intoxication [and] riot" associated with the pattern (Brady 1965, 256), but he made no reference to rounding or to any of the popular beliefs associated with the water at this well.

In some cases, bishops condemned the unruliness at patterns because it detracted from the religious nature of the event and so interfered with the penitential value of the pattern experience. In 1761, for instance, Thomas Burke, bishop of Ossory, issued an edict in which he called attention to the "mobbing, rioting, cursing, swearing, thieving, excessive drinking and other great Debaucheries [that] are constantly practiced at St. John's Well near Kilkenny" and which worked to ensure that "many Reflections are cast upon the Roman Catholic Religion and its Pilgrimages" (Carrigan 1905, 1:170). Burke went on to suggest that this rowdiness was entirely the result of the fact that this pattern attracted swarms of beggars from all over Ireland. His solution: to prohibit the Catholics attending the pattern from giving alms and to warn them that "if they transgress this most just command of their Spiritual Superior [i.e., him], instead of reaping any benefit by going to the said Well, they'll return greater sinners from it than they went to it" (Carrigan 1905, 1:170). The implication of this passage, of course, is that Catholics *would* reap the benefits of going to this well so long as they refrained from giving alms to beggars.

In the end, of course, what an Irish bishop himself felt about the value of holy well cults and patterns was less important than the position he took in regard to the participation of the local clergy in his diocese in such activities. It was, remember, the participation of the local clergy that made these activities legitimately "Catholic" and so ensured their popularity. In regard to clerical participation, Irish bishops—even in the late eighteenth century—adopted a view that was relatively tolerant and certainly pragmatic. In 1771, for instance, the bishop of Ferns (a diocese that includes County Wexford and the southern part of County Wicklow) issued a set of regulations for the clergy in his diocese (see Flood 1914). Most of these regulations are quite firm in their prohibitions of certain behaviors. Priests are absolutely forbidden to say a mass for the dead without the permission of the pastor of the local parish church; to "act the Fairy Doctor" by blessing water to be sprinkled over sick persons or cattle or fields; to dine with "impious Catholicks that scoff at Religion"; and so on. When the regulations come to the matter of patterns, however, the tone becomes less harsh and the regulation is phrased more as a recommendation, to be implemented if possible, than as an absolute prohibition:

> [Rule] 18. I earnestly recommend to ye to put back and discourage as much as ye can Patrons or Pilgrimages, or Meetings of pretended Devotion, or rather of real Dissipation and Dissoluteness; wh. Bring nothing but reflection and ridicule on our Holy Religion, from those that are without, according to St. Paul's phrase I Cor. v. 12 &c. At least ye must not say Mass at the Places of Patrons or Pilgrimages, but in ye Chapels or near them. (Flood 1914, 118)

As always, the primary concern is with the rowdiness associated with patterns and with the concern that such rowdiness brings the Catholic religion into disrepute. Priests are simply asked to "do as much as ye can" in discouraging these rowdy activities. There is certainly no condemnation of the rounding rituals associated with patterns or of any of the beliefs associated with holy wells. And finally, notice that this regulation does not really forbid priests from saying Mass in connection with the celebration of a pattern; it simply says that if such masses are said they must be said in or around chapels.

In summary, then, over the progression from the seventeenth to the eighteenth century there was little or no change in the way Irish bishops evaluated the different activities associated with patterns: in both centuries Irish bishops disapproved strongly of the secular activities and magical rituals associated with patterns but were neutral in regard to rounding rituals. To the extent that there was a change at all, it had to do with a political calculation: on balance, bishops in the late eighteenth and early nineteenth centuries were far less likely than their seventeenth-century predecessors to believe that the unwanted elements associated with the pattern experience could be eliminated while maintaining the pattern's religious focus. Even then, many bishops remained sympathetic to holy well cults and patterns and did not strongly discourage local priests from taking part in these activities.

Missing Figures

There is one final thing that made popular Catholicism in Ireland so distinctive, but to understand what it was it is necessary to elaborate upon something that until now has only been mentioned in passing: the nature of the physical objects that were invested with supernatural power in Ireland. Although Irish Catholics were as likely as Catholics elsewhere to invest physical objects with supernatural force, they showed a clear predilection for objects that were relatively shapeless and nonfigurative. In Ireland, popular rituals generally coalesced around shapeless piles of stones, pools of water, irregularly shaped boulders, and such, while in Catholic areas like Italy and Spain popular cults and devotions coalesced most often around images (a painting, fresco, statue) that depicted a figure that was usually a madonna or saint (and less often Christ) but almost always recognizably human.

It would be easy to dismiss this lack of a figurative emphasis in

Irish Catholicism on force of circumstance, that is, on the fact that the civil authorities who ruled Ireland after the Reformation were Protestant and Protestants were generally hostile to image cults. While Protestant iconoclasm cannot be ruled out in trying to explain the "shapelessness" that pervades Irish Catholicism, another possibility is simply that ordinary Irish Catholics were psychologically predisposed against associating such power with figurative representations. Consistent with this latter possibility is the fact that image cults were not especially popular in Ireland even before the Reformation.

Irish churches, of course, did contain sacred images in the pre-Reformation era, and a few of these images were every bit as miraculous as images found in Italy or Spain. A government report written in 1460, for instance, says in passing that a man whose tongue had been cut out and whose eyes had been gouged out (by an enemy) was restored to sight and speech after appealing to the miraculous image of Mary at the abbey church in Navan, County Meath (Cogan 1862–70, 1:225–26). We know of additional miraculous images if only because they came to be destroyed during the Reformation. In 1538–39 Protestant authorities suppressed fifty or so Irish shrines (mainly in Counties Meath and Dublin, but including cities like Limerick as well), and in the process they seized the cult images associated with these shrines. Catholic accounts of this iconoclastic campaign make it clear that at least some of these images were associated with miracle working. The *Annals of Loch Cé*, for example, says: "The very miraculous image of Mary which was in the town of Ath-Truim [Trim; see figure 8], in which all the people of Erinn believed for a long time previously, which healed the blind and deaf, and lame, and every other ailment, was burnt by Saxons [English] . . . and not this alone, but there was not in Erinn a holy cross, or figure of Mary, or an illustrious image, over which their power reached, that was not burned" (Hennessy 1871, 2:316–17).

Still, notwithstanding the annalist's claim here that the image at Trim was one "in which all the people of Erinn believed for a long time previously," there is nothing in the historical record to suggest that the outburst of iconoclasm in 1538–39 generated any significant degree of popular resistance. Moreover, this silence of the historical record in regard to the matter of popular resistance is likely not due to the scarcity of the documentation that has survived from this period. As Bradshaw (1974, 105) points out in his own discussion of the 1538–39 campaign, there is ample evidence of popular resistance to other reforms that had been introduced just the year before and ample evidence too of popular resistance on the part of Irish Catholics to reforms introduced later under Edward. I suggest that the most straightforward way to account for the relative ease with which image cults were suppressed in Ireland is on the hypothesis that such cults never had a particularly strong appeal for Irish Catholics.

A few image cults continued to exist in Ireland well into the seventeenth century. Writing in 1612, the archbishop of Cashel and others complained that Protestant authorities had seized and burned "an image of our Lady renowned for its miracles, which was the pride of the Christians [in this] part of the country" (see Moran 1874, 120). Similarly, an Irish Franciscan traveling through Ulster around 1648 described a church dedicated to "St. Broncha, a most noble virgin, at whose statue God has performed many miracles in our day" (Reeves 1854, 48). Nevertheless, the point being made here is not that there were no miraculous images in Ireland (there clearly were) but that such images never came close to playing the role in Ireland that they played in other Catholic societies. Simply put, images in Ireland were never a source of supernatural favors (nor were they seen to bleed, cry, become surrounded by strange lights, etc.) on anything like the scale that was typical of Italy or Spain.[7] Moreover, my own sense is that the popularity of the few image cults that did exist in Ireland can usually be traced to the influence of some segment of the regular clergy who were trying to introduce into Ireland a devotional form that had proven popular on the Continent.

The matter of miraculous images aside, images in general seem not to have been central to the Catholic experience in Ireland. This is why the images that were found in Irish churches were more likely to be there as the result of official policy than by popular preference. For instance, the Synod of Cashel held at Limerick in 1453 specified that every church should have at least a crucifix, a statue of the Virgin Mary, and a statue of the church's patron saint. When statutes of this sort were passed at synods in Italy, the clear intent was always to limit the number of images in a church; the intent of the Synod of Cashel seems to have been to establish a minimum number of images in churches. (On the Synod of Cashel and its legislation see Begley 1906; Burrows 1989.) Even in the early nineteenth century, when Catholic churches were no longer subject to the restrictions of the Penal period and were being built in ever-increasing numbers, both foreign and Irish commentators observed that these churches were notably devoid of images (Connolly 1982, 94–96). This lack of concern with images lasted well into the twentieth century. Lawrence Taylor (1989, 186; 1995, 70), for example, points out that most of the images of Mary now encountered in Ireland were put in place only subsequent to 1954, the first Marian Year.

The lack of a figurative emphasis that seems a feature of Irish popular Catholicism is also evident in something else: the relative rarity of apparitions in Ireland. In Catholic areas like Italy, Spain, and France, it was and is relatively common to find ordinary Catholics reporting that a madonna (or, less frequently, a saint or Christ) has come down to Earth and appeared to them. Reports of this sort are rare in Ireland. The special importance that now attaches to the sanctuary at Knock (County Mayo), which was the site of a series of apparitions in 1879,[8] should not blind us to the fact that Catholics in pre-Famine Ireland were simply not prone to the experience of apparitions. In their survey of 135 pilgrimage sites in Ireland, the Nolans (1989) found only three that were established on the basis of an apparition, and one of these was Knock. The paucity of apparitions in pre-Famine Ireland does not seem to be the result of any suppression by ecclesiastical authorities, Protestant or Catholic; rather, it would seem that Irish Catholics simply did not experience apparitions. Certainly apparition stories are rare, and when they do occur the force of the story is usually weakened by an explicit acknowledgment that the supernatural being involved appeared during the course of a dream (for an example of this sort of story, see Hackett 1861–62, 268). In countries like Italy, by contrast, seers usually claimed that the madonna or saint who appeared to them appeared as they were going about their daily business and not while they were asleep.[9]

There is little doubt as to the terminus ad quem that should be associated with the variant of Catholicism that I have been describing in this chapter. As will be documented in detail later on (chap. 5), this variant of Catholicism began to decline in popularity during the late

1700s, and that decline continued steadily through to the 1830s. Although holy well cults and rounding rituals never completely died out (and still haven't died out), the truly "popular" variant of Catholicism in the post-Famine period was the strongly Romanized variant that has been described by Emmet Larkin (1972) and others, and in which Sunday Mass was the central ritual and the local parish church the focal point of all devotional activity. But what about the terminus a quo? When, in other words, did popular Catholic devotions incorporating holy wells, rounding rituals, penitence, patterns, and so forth first become popular in Ireland and first become central to the Catholic experience there? As discussed in the introduction, for nearly two centuries now the commonly accepted answer to this question, among both scholars and the educated public generally, has been that these devotions date back to the earliest days of the Irish Church and reflect the absorption of Celtic traditions that predated the introduction of Christianity in Ireland. It is time to consider this "Celtic origins" hypothesis in detail and to indicate where it goes wrong.

Chapter Two

The Rise of the "Celtic Origins" Hypothesis

Today, William Wilde (1815–76) is likely known to most of the non-Irish audience mainly as the father of Oscar Wilde. In his time, however, Wilde père was well known in his own right. Wilde's reputation rested upon his accomplishments as a medical doctor, notably his role in founding St. Mark's Ophthalmic Hospital in Dublin and his willingness to treat the poor for free. Partly, too, the elder Wilde (as would come to be the case with his son) came to be known on account of his association with a court case in which his sexual improprieties were a central issue. But for many people Wilde was known most of all because he wrote on a variety of antiquarian subjects in a manner that appealed to a popular audience.

One of Wilde's more extensive works was *The Beauties of the Boyne, and Its Tributary, the Blackwater* (1850), in which he described the structures of antiquarian interest that a genteel rambler (like himself) might encounter in County Meath. Moving through the Meath that emerges from Wilde's account, the reader encounters megaliths, round towers, the ruins of ancient castles and churches—and, of course, holy wells.

For William Wilde there was never any doubt about the historic origins of these wells: they were part of a great Celtic inheritance that had once covered much of Western Europe but whose visible remains were now preserved most of all in Ireland. Moreover, he argued, many of the modern practices associated with these wells (and in this regard he made explicit reference to rounding rituals) were a direct continuation of various Celtic practices that early on had been absorbed into Irish Christianity. The following passage is typical: "Most of our holy wells were objects of veneration, perhaps of worship, long prior to the spread of Christianity in Ireland, when the Pagan altar, the sacred grove, and Druid priest, were their general accompaniments; and therefore, it cannot be wondered that so many unchristian rites and ceremonies should still attend the practices observed there by the uneducated" (46–47). The suggestion that Irish holy wells and their associated rounding rituals were a Celtic inheritance was by no means novel. On the contrary, it was an idea that had been steadily gaining ground in the early nineteenth century and had already been incorporated into several books addressed to the general public (see Hardy 1840; Hall and Hall 1841–43). By mid-century, when Wilde was writing, it was the dominant view among both scholars and the educated public alike.

For someone like William Wilde, the Celtic origin of modern holy well devotions was too self-evident to require documentation. Many of his contemporaries, however, were more than willing to lay out the evidence in support of this view. In hindsight, what is most striking about the evidence they presented is how meager it was.

Evidence from the Legends about Early Irish Saints

Roman armies never arrived in Ireland and so there were no Roman generals or natural philosophers on hand to describe the indigenous population, in the way that such commentators had described indigenous populations in Gaul or Germania. The closest that nineteenth-century scholars could come to "eyewitness" accounts of life in pre-Christian Ireland were the stories about what early Irish saints had encountered in their efforts to convert the Irish to Christianity. Nineteenth-century commentators knew full well that such stories had been compiled some time after the events they described. Even so, they routinely assumed that these stories, at least when stripped of their overtly miraculous elements, were only slightly distorted accounts of what had actually happened in history; and two of these stories did seem to suggest that Irish Celts had gathered at holy wells to engage in religious activities.

One of these two stories concerned St. Columba. As already mentioned, the historic Columba had founded a monastery on the island of Iona during the sixth century, and with Iona as a base had traveled throughout the British Isles as a missionary. In Adomnán's *Life of Columba* (c. 690) we are told that during a mission to the Picts (in northern Scotland) Columba came to a well whose water caused blindness and leprosy and which for that reason was feared and venerated as a god by the local population. Columba blessed the well in Christ's name and then washed himself in its waters without ill effect (much to the dismay, Adomnán says, of the Pictish magicians who had gathered at the site). From that day forward, the story continues, the water of that well cured, rather than caused, infirmity.

The second story used to support the view that well cults were popular with pagan Celts appears in a collection of legends about St. Patrick compiled by bishop Tírechán around 700 and which came to be preserved in the *Book of Armagh*. In the course of his travels in Ireland, we are told, Patrick came to the well of Findmag, called Slán, and learned "that the druids honored the well and offered gifts to it as to a god" (Bieler 1979, 153). The reason for this, the druids told Patrick, was that a wise man had made a stone sarcophagus for himself under the well's capstone so that the water might forever wash his bones and thereby protect him from fire. In the presence of a great crowd of druids and other pagans of that region Patrick lifted the stone and showed them that there was no body underneath.[1]

I must stress that these two stories, involving Columba and Patrick, were not just the stories cited "most often" in support of the view that Irish holy wells were of Celtic origin; they were the only stories from the literature on early Christian saints that were ever cited in this regard and they were cited over and over again (see, e.g., Petrie 1841; Joyce 1875, 449–50; Wood-Martin 1902, 47; MacCulloch 1911, 181–82, 193). Given the pivotal role that these two stories played for proponents of the Celtic origins hypothesis, it is easy to overlook the fact that each story could have been interpreted differently.

Scholars could, for example, have stressed that only the story about the well called Slán was set in Ireland. They could also have stressed that this well was the burial place of a Druidic priest and so might have argued that *this* (and not an emphasis on the sacredness of spring water) was the reason that the site was the focus of cultic activity. Certainly modern commentators, in considering this same story, have suggested that a druid's being buried at this site is central to an understanding of what the story would have meant to contemporary audiences (Carey 1996).

The two wells mentioned in these stories could also have been set against the sum total of all the wells mentioned in the legends about early Irish saints. After all, over and over again these early legends say that Patrick (or Columba or Senan or whoever) went to such and such a well, blessed it, and then proceeded to use the well's water to baptize dozens (or hundreds or thousands) of pagans. St. Columba alone is recorded as having blessed three hundred wells (Stokes 1890, 177). Often, if a well is not initially available, these stories tell us, one was created in a miraculous way. Usually, this means that a saint simply strikes the ground with his staff and water pours out. Irish saints, however, could and did create wells simply by saying prayers, making the sign of the cross, having drops of their blood fall on the ground, pouring water out of a bell, and so on.[2] The point is that none of the hundreds of wells mentioned in the legends about early Irish saints—save the two exceptions mentioned above—are ever associated with pagan rituals. Indeed, since the vast majority of wells mentioned in the stories about early Irish saints are associated with baptismal activities, these stories could easily have been read as suggesting that an emphasis on holy wells had been a Christian innovation in Ireland that had no widespread analogue in pagan practice.

The Evidence from Medieval Legislation

It was also common to support the "Celtic origins" hypothesis by pointing to bits and pieces of medieval legislation that seemed to prohibit pagan rituals at wells. Mentioned most often in this regard was the legislation promulgated by Edgar, king of England from 959 to 975, and that promulgated by Canute, the Danish king of England from 1016 to 1035. Edgar's legislation stipulated that "every priest do forbid the worship of fountains, and necromancy, and auguries, and enchantments, and sooth-saying, and false worship, and legerdemain, which carry men into various impostures, and to groves and Ellens, and also many trees of divers sort, and stones" (Petrie 1841, 402). Canute's was similar: "Heathenism is that men worship idols— the sun or moon, fire or rivers, water-wells or forest-trees" (Hogan 1874, 273). In both cases, the legislation seems obviously concerned with suppressing a pantheistic religion that invested a variety of natural elements, notably including springs, with supernatural power. As a result, many Irish scholars (see, e.g., Petrie 1841; Hogan 1874, 273) suggested that these pieces of legislation provided clear evidence that well cults had existed in Celtic Ireland and so, by extension, clear evidence that the well cults associated with Catholics in modern Ireland were a Celtic inheritance. Here again, though, the evidence could easily have been viewed differently.

As L. Perry Curtis (1968) points out, educated publics in both England and Ireland during the nineteenth century saw "Irish Celts" and "English Saxons" to be separate and distinct racial groups, who differed from one another both in their innate temperaments and in the nature of the institutions they had inherited from their ancient ancestors. Given this view of things, Irish commentators could have focused on the fact that both Edgar and Canute were English (not Irish) kings ruling over mainly Saxon (not Celtic) populations and so could have interpreted the pagan rituals targeted by their legislation as having been part of a continuing tradition of Saxon paganism. Indeed, this is precisely how modern commentators have tended to interpret these same pieces of legislation (see, e.g., Laing and Laing 1979, 99). But, again, such an interpretation did not suit the purpose of most Irish scholars, anxious as they were to promote the Celtic origins approach to Irish holy wells, and so it was an interpretation that was ignored.

Celtic Rounding Rituals

Irish scholars who wanted to derive the holy well cults that were so much a part of popular Catholicism in Ireland from Celtic sources knew that they needed to explain more than just an emphasis on well sites. As we saw in the last chapter, one element that made Irish holy well cults so distinctive were the rounding rituals performed there. If holy well cults had been inherited from a distant Celtic past, then rounding rituals had to be Celtic in origin as well. To support this claim they did occasionally (but only occasionally) draw on distinctively Irish materials. J. A. MacCulloch (1922, 841), for instance, supports a supposed Celtic origin for rounding by noting that "in the Cúchulainn cycle, when [Queen] Mebd is setting out for the war, her charioteer makes her chariot describe a right-hand turn." Similarly, W. G. Wood-Martin (1902, 53) cites "an old Irish ms." that recounts how a battle standard that was "carried three times to the right around the army of the Cinel Conaill" would always ensure victory. For the most part, however, the view that rounding rituals were of

The Rise of the "Celtic Origins" Hypothesis

Celtic origin was supported using non-Irish examples. In retrospect, what is most striking about these non-Irish examples is that they were largely non-Celtic as well.

In Wood-Martin's discussion (1902, 52–57) of rounding rituals in antiquity, for instance, most of his examples are taken from Roman sources. Romans, he says, moved rightward around sacred images when adoring their gods; Roman prisoners moved rightward around their captors; Romans moved rightward around a funeral pyre to ensure the safe passage of the person's ghost to the otherworld, and so forth. Why these Roman examples of rounding (none of which, incidentally, involved holy wells) supported the view that the rounding rituals in Ireland were Celtic in origin was never explained. The general idea, quite simply, seems to have been that if rounding rituals had been practiced in any context by any group in the classical world, then, by a process of evidentiary osmosis, this supports the view that Irish Celts engaged in similar rituals.

Unwittingly, it turns out, scholars who sought a pre-Christian origin for rounding rituals accumulated evidence that could have been used to support the view that rounding rituals had developed spontaneously in Christian Ireland. After all, it quickly became apparent that rounding rituals of one sort or another had existed in a wide variety of the world's societies. In his well-known work on Semitic religion, W. Robertson Smith (1972 [1889], 338–39) cites an account by Nilus (a Christian ascetic who lived in the Sinai during the fifth century A.D.) which describes a sacrificial rite performed by Bedouins: they set a bound camel upon an altar, collectively walk three times in procession around the altar, and then kill and devour the animal. Similarly, Goblet D'Alviella (1922), after running through the standard list of examples from Greece, Rome, and contemporary Celtic areas, gives examples of rounding in cultures as diverse as ancient Egypt, contemporary Islamic societies, and North American Indian societies like the Navaho and the Pawnee. Since no one ever claimed that the rounding rituals performed by the Bedouin, the ancient Egyptians, the Navaho and Pawnee were of Celtic origin, it was clear that rounding rituals could develop independently of the Celtic tradition. It thus should have been clear that Catholic rounding rituals in Ireland could have developed spontaneously, without regard to Ireland's Celtic past.

Irish Pilgrimage

Circular Reasoning

Apart from the textual evidence culled from ancient and medieval sources—whether relating to Irish saints, medieval legislation, Roman religious practice—there was one other thing that was routinely mentioned by proponents of the Celtic origins hypothesis. In a particularly blatant example of circular reasoning commentators routinely cited modern instances of rounding in "Celtic areas" as evidence that rounding had been practiced by the ancient Celts. Thus Edward Dwelly (1911, 328) argues for the Celtic origins of rounding rituals by citing the references to rounding in Martin's (1716) account of his visit to the Scottish Hebrides. Similarly Wood-Martin (1902, 52) and D'Alviella (1922) support a Celtic origin for rounding rituals by pointing out that the ritual rounding of some object was still being used in parts of Ireland or Scotland to ensure good health or good luck. Nor is this sort of circular reasoning a thing of the past. On the contrary, here is how one recent author continues to argue for the importance of rounding rituals in Celtic religion:

> It is important to emphasize that, although circumambulation [rounding] is not known as an exclusively Celtic ritual, its cultic significance and prolific practice has been argued credibly by prominent students of Celtic custom. *The most persuasive testimony comes from surviving folk customs in Ireland, in Gaelic Scotland, the Isle of Man,* as Goblet d'Alviella, J. A. MacCulloch and Edward Dwelly have demonstrated in now classical contributions. (Haderlein 1992, 16–17; emphasis added)

Of course the only way that rounding rituals in modern Ireland, modern Scotland, and so on can be taken as "persuasive testimony" that such rituals were important in Celtic tradition is on the a priori assumption that such rituals are survivals of Celtic practice. The argument succeeds, in other words, only by presupposing what it wants to prove.

In the end, then, nineteenth-century commentators supported the hypothesis that Irish holy well cults were of Celtic origin with bits and pieces of evidence that in all cases could have been interpreted in other ways. But if the evidence for the Celtic origins hypothesis was so flimsy, why was that hypothesis so popular?

The Rise of the "Celtic Origins" Hypothesis

The Romantic Movement and the Invention of Ireland's Celtic Past

We live in a time when Celtic music of one sort or another is popular with large audiences, when any number of feminist authors have written glowingly about Celtic society and the relatively high status it accorded women, and when Celtic news groups on the Internet regularly attract hundreds of discussants each day. Moreover, for most modern consumers of Celticism, the societies with the strongest Celtic tradition are almost certainly Ireland, Scotland, and Wales. Given all this, it is something of a surprise to learn that the popular image of what constituted "Celtic society" is largely an invention of the eighteenth century, and that prior to this time the ancient inhabitants of Ireland, Scotland, and Wales were not generally linked with the Celts of the classical world.

The terms *keltoi* and *celtae* first appear in the writings of Greek and Roman historians, who used these terms to refer to a variety of different peoples living on the fringes of the civilized (read: Mediterranean) world. Quite often "Celts" was used interchangeably with "Gauls." Most likely all these terms were little more than racist epithets meaning, as Malcolm Chapman (1992, 33–34) suggests, "uncivilized barbarians to the north." In any event, none of the classical writers ever used the term *Celts* to refer to the ancient inhabitants of the British Isles (Dietler 1994, 585–86). It was only in the early 1700s that a few scholars with an interest in linguistics began to suggest links between Welsh, Cornish, Breton, Scots Gaelic, and Irish, and to trace all these languages back to the Celts mentioned in classical sources.[3] Even so, these early linguistic investigations had little impact on the popular imagination. What did have an impact on the popular conceptualization of the ancient Celts was the Romantic movement of the late eighteenth century.

The Romantic movement was in the first instance a literary and philosophical tradition whose practitioners self-consciously set out to negate the emphases that were characteristic of mainstream Enlightenment thought. The Enlightenment thinkers stressed reason and the slow building up of objective arguments; authors in the Romantic tradition stressed emotion, impulsive action, and imaginative leaps. Enlightenment thinkers sought to uncover the processes that promoted the advance of civilization (which always meant the advance of European civilization); authors in the Romantic tradition—Rousseau and his followers in particular—were more likely to see civilization as corrupting and to seek a return to the more natural condition that had prevailed in primitive human societies. Enlightenment thinkers believed that human reason would eventually solve all mysteries; authors in the Romantic tradition saw mystery and the mysterious as things to be embraced for their own sake. Finally, and most importantly (as far as the rise of Celticism was concerned) Enlightenment thinkers rooted European civilization—and their own theories—squarely in the Greco-Roman tradition; authors in the Romantic tradition sought out exotic nonclassical societies, especially societies associated with the emphasis on emotion, nature, and so forth that was so central to the Romantic program. Some of the societies favored by Romantic authors (and their audiences) were overtly fictional, but others were societies that had supposedly existed in the distant past; one of these was the society of the ancient Celts. Although a number of literary works published in the late eighteenth century depicted Celts and Celtic society in a manner that appealed to the Romantic imagination, the most influential were unquestionably those written by the Scottish author James Macpherson (1736–96).[4]

In the early 1760s Macpherson published a series of poems that had supposedly been composed by a third-century Scottish bard named Ossian. Macpherson's claim was that Ossian's poems had been passed down orally over the centuries until he himself had reconstructed these poems using ballads collected in the Scottish Highlands. The Ossianic poems were an immediate literary success. Several editions were brought out in English in quick succession, and the poems were quickly translated into a variety of European languages, including Italian, German, Spanish, Dutch, Danish, Swedish, Russian, and Polish (see Stafford 1988, 163–83; Snyder 1923, 76–77). The poems were especially popular in Germany, France, and Italy, where they were received "with an excitement bordering on hysteria" (de-Gategno 1989, 118).

In large part the immense popularity of the Ossianic poems derived from the fact that the "Celtic society" which emerged from these poems was a society perfectly suited to the Romantic imagination. Macpherson himself provided a succinct characterization of this society in a scholarly history of the Celts published shortly after the success of the Ossianic poems:

> The Ancient British Nations, like their Celtic brethren on the Continent, were fierce, passionate, and impetuous; sudden in resolution, sanguine in expression, impatient under disappointment. They were in love with slaughter . . . and born as it were in the midst of battle and depredation. . . . [Yet] with all this violence and fierceness of disposition, they were in private life plain and upright in their dealings, and far removed from the duplicity of modern times. They were always open, sincere, and undisguised; simple, good-natured, and void of malignity; and though cruel, and sometimes barbarous, to their enemies, they were kind and compassionate to the supplicant and unfortunate. (Macpherson 1771, 188–89)

The Celtic society that emerges in Macpherson's work is thus an egalitarian society that existed in harmony with its natural surroundings and a society whose members are refreshingly honest, driven by strong emotion, and compassionate. It is, in short, a society that embodied all the elements central to the Romantic philosophy.

Macpherson's work did not go unchallenged. Very early on a number of scholars suspected that his Ossianic poems were a forgery, and a report published in 1805 by the Highland Society of Scotland supported this view. It was clear then and now that Macpherson had produced Ossian's poems by merging material from a number of different Highland ballads with much material of his own creation. Nor was suspected forgery the only grounds for criticizing Macpherson, especially in Ireland.

Macpherson had wounded Irish pride by reversing the historical relationship previously assumed to have existed between Ireland and Scotland. For centuries it had been taken for granted that Scotland had been settled by Irish colonists. Macpherson reversed this relationship and argued that Ireland had been settled by Scottish Celts. Among other things, such a view allowed Macpherson to view Irish epics, which were undeniably similar to the poems supposedly composed by Ossian, as derivative. But as Clare O'Halloran (1989, 72) points out, what was most central to the Irish rejection of Macpherson was that Macpherson's view of the Celts as primitive—and in particular as ferocious, bloodthirsty, and driven by emotion—seemed too close to the disparaging view of the uncivilized Irish that had for so long been promulgated by English historians. Irish scholars— themselves influenced by Romanticism—had constructed a different image of the ancient Irish. In their vision, Celtic society had been a superior society (read: better than contemporary English society), founded originally by the Phoenicians but with links to Egypt and India, and one in which sacred knowledge had been preserved for centuries by a Druidic priesthood (see Hutchinson 1987, 48–73).

Nevertheless, as much as Irish scholars might reject the specifics of Macpherson's argument in favor of their own Phoenician-flavored vision, and despite the evidence of fakery on Macpherson's part, there is no denying that Macpherson's work had an impact on Irish scholarship. Some scholars, like Sylvester O'Halloran, took up Celtic studies for the express purpose of "regaining" for Ireland the pagan heroes that Macpherson had appropriated for Scotland (Hutchinson 1987, 72). More generally, the great popularity of the Ossianic poems captured the imagination of educated elites in Ireland as much as elsewhere and so created a demand for a better sense of what Celtic society in ancient Ireland had been like. This heightened interest in scholarly accounts of things Celtic was one of the factors that contributed to the formation of scholarly bodies like the Royal Irish Academy, founded in 1785 (Cooney 1996, 150).

A core element in this first Celtic revival was the belief that remnants of ancient Celtic tradition had persisted in modern folk practice. After all, the whole premise of the Ossianic enterprise was that Ossian's work had been handed down orally over the centuries and was still evident—albeit in corrupted form—in contemporary Scottish ballads. If ballads could be used to reconstruct the society of the ancient Celts, so could other folk beliefs and practices. In discussing the religious ceremonies of the ancient Celts, for example, Macpherson (1771, 163–66) himself saw three ceremonies to have been especially important: (1) Celtic peoples lit the "fire of the rock" on the first of May, (2) they avoided bathing in certain springs, and (3) they never mentioned "the water of rivers without prefixing to it the epithet of excellent." And how did he know all this? In each case, he tells us, he knows these things because these practices can still be detected in folk practice in the Scottish Highlands. True, he concedes, modern Highlanders no longer realize that the practice of lighting fires on the first of May was originally a solar ritual used for divination and enchantment, nor do they know that they avoid bathing in certain springs because their ancestors wanted to avoid offending the deity that resided there. Modern Highlanders, in short, had forgotten the original meaning of these ancient ceremonies; even so, he argued, they continued to engage in behaviors that preserved the form of these ceremonies.

Macpherson did not discuss rounding rituals, and he certainly did not suggest that rounding rituals had been central to Celtic religion. And why should he? Macpherson was clearly reconstructing Celtic religion by working backward from contemporary folk practice. Given that rounding rituals were not extensive in Scotland, there was nothing in the Scottish data that would lead him to envision long-dead Celts walking in circles around holy wells and stone cairns. But Irish scholars working to reconstruct Celtic religion were in a different situation. Contemporary Ireland was a society in which rounding rituals were central to popular religious practice. It is hardly surprising, then, that the vision of Celtic religion that emerged in Ireland suggested that both well cults and rounding rituals had been an integral part of that religion.

The Needs of a Nationalist Historiography

In all societies and in all ages visions of the past have been used to legitimate concerns of the present—and if the right vision of the past is not available it can always be created. Irish historiography, in particular, has been shaped by contemporary political concerns (at least) as far back as the earliest years of the Christian era. McCone (1991), for example, has shown how the historical accounts of Ireland's pagan past constructed by monastic authors during the fifth to the twelfth centuries—whether written in Latin or Irish, and whether concerned with ecclesiastical or secular matters—routinely presented a vision of that pagan past which met the needs of the Christian present. Irish historians in the modern period have done the same thing. Brendan Bradshaw (1993), for instance, demonstrates that Geoffrey Keating's well-known account of the early Irish Church (c. 1633) was little more than a projection backwards in time of the sort of Church being promoted (in Keating's day) by leaders of the Counter-Reformation. An even more recent example of the same phenomenon, and one directly relevant to our concerns here, is to be found in the nineteenth century, when a rising nationalist impulse led Irish historians to construct a vision of the Irish past that legitimated nationalist aspirations.

As Bradshaw (1989, 345) points out, "the controlling conception" of the nationalist historiography that rose to prominence in the nineteenth century (and which persisted well into the twentieth) was "the notion of a national past, of Irish history as the story of an immemorial Irish nation, unfolding holistically through the centuries, from the settlement of the aboriginal Celts to the emergence of the national polity of modern times." Central to this newly emergent vision of the Irish past was the view that Irish national identity was rooted most of all in a merger of Celtic experience and Irish monasticism that had occurred during the first centuries of the Christian era. In this nationalist vision of the past, then, an Irish national identity had been formed before the Anglo-Norman colonization of the twelfth century and had continued to exist despite this and all later colonizations. It was this continuing national tradition, formed from that early merger of Celtic society and Irish monasticism, that should determine both the contours of modern Ireland. Outsiders, and that included the Anglo-Irish elite, could become Irish but only by identifying themselves with this continuing national tradition (Graham and Proudfoot 1993, 7). The result was that, quite literally, "the character of Druidical Ireland was being treated as validating or invalidating, in some significant fashion, the early-nineteenth-century political and social order" (MacDonagh 1983, 2).[5]

The leading practitioners of this new nationalist historiography shared more than just a common vision of the Irish past; they also shared a methodological commitment to recovering that past using scientific procedures. This greater commitment to "scientific procedure" is evident in the increased concern, during the nineteenth century, with preserving (or at least cataloging) archaeological sites in Ireland (Cooney 1996). But "being scientific" also meant that historians should reconstruct the past using information from a variety of sources, so as to curtail the flights of fancy that had in the past resulted from a focus on one source alone. Writing in 1821, for instance,

The Rise of the "Celtic Origins" Hypothesis

George Petrie (1789–1866) stressed the special importance of merging antiquarian studies with the study of Irish historical manuscripts:

> The antiquities of a nation and its history are indissolubly linked, and to shine brightly each requires a reflected light from the other. . . . On the indispensableness of such a union, the literature of Ireland affords a striking example. We have had historians, who, knowing little or nothing of our antiquities, have given full scope to their imagination, and have substituted the wildest theories for historic truth; and we have had antiquaries who knew equally little of our history, and who have attempted to illustrate our ancient remains by bold assertion and fanciful conjecture, in the place of unprejudiced inquiry and historical research. (cited in Stokes 1868, 23)

It was precisely this attitude that gave rise to the work of the Ordnance Survey (of which Petrie would be an integral part), whose investigators carefully cross-checked material found in ancient manuscripts with information about antiquarian sites collected by investigators in the field.

But nationalist historiographers needed to do more than simply reconstruct the past. The nationalist vision required the existence of continuing traditions that linked the modern Irish to the ancient Celts in a direct and obvious way. One of those continuing traditions was obviously the Gaelic language itself, since by this time linguists had established with precision that modern Gaelic was a Celtic language. But the nationalist vision of the past would obviously be more convincing if other continuing traditions could be identified as well. As a result, nationalist historiographers were predisposed to accept the view, already a part of the Romantic tradition, that many of the folk practices found in the Irish countryside were the remnants of an ancient Celtic heritage. Folk practices that were more widespread in Ireland than elsewhere, like the gatherings at holy wells and the associated rounding rituals, were especially likely to be seen as continuing links to Ireland's Celtic past.

By the 1830s and 1840s, of course, it was obvious that holy well cults and rounding rituals were dying out. In the nationalist vision of the past, however, this was only to be expected. Unlike their predecessors in the Romantic tradition of the eighteenth century, the nationalist historians of the nineteenth century were not bound to a vision of Celtic society as necessarily superior. On the contrary, they were committed to a view of Irish society that was progressive and so consistently argued that the archaic devotions still being performed at a few holy wells and other sites could serve as a benchmark against which to measure how far Irish society (read: the members of their own class) had advanced. John O'Donovan, who took such an active role in the data-collecting activities of the Ordnance Survey, expressed the underlying orientation well: "Man looks with veneration upon every spot that has been hallowed by sincere religion be it ever so deluded and feels anxious . . . to preserve every trace by which the turas [pilgrimages] of the pilgrim and the progress of the human mind in art, religion or enthusiasm can be followed" (cited in Taylor 1995, 60).

In the end, then, a "Celtic origins" perspective on modern holy well devotions was doubly valuable to nationalist historiographers: it validated the nationalist claim that Ireland's national identity was rooted in archaic Celtic traditions and yet simultaneously suggested that this tradition was capable of progressive development, with certain savage customs (like rounding rituals) dying out and other, more civilized customs being assimilated to that tradition.

The Social Evolutionary Approach to Religion

In the latter half of the nineteenth century it became increasingly common, especially among British scholars, to explain social phenomena by appealing to the idea of cultural survivals. The nature of what a "survival" was is most clearly articulated by Edward Tylor (1871) in his influential textbook of anthropology. For Tylor, a survival was an institution or practice that had developed originally at one stage in the social evolution of a society, in response to conditions that characterized that stage, and which had persisted into a later stage even though that original condition no longer existed. Although the "survivals" concept was often invoked to explain the appearance of seemingly irrational practices in advanced societies, it was also regarded as a methodological tool that could be used to reconstruct the nature of ancient societies. W. Robertson Smith (1972 [1889]), for example, reconstructed the traditional religion of the

The Rise of the "Celtic Origins" Hypothesis

Semitic-speaking peoples of the ancient Middle East on the basis of "survivals" that he detected in the known religious traditions of later Semitic groups like the Israelites and Babylonians. Similarly, in his very popular work on myth and folklore, James Frazer (1987 [1892]) reconstructed on the basis of survivals a ritual (the regular and recurrent slaying of a divine king) that had once been central (he argued) to all human societies. But what social evolutionists like Smith and Frazer were doing was little different from what Celticists in both the Romantic and Irish nationalist traditions had been doing for quite some time. After all, from Macpherson on, "Celtic origins" scholars had been using contemporary folk practice to reconstruct the nature of Celtic society. The result was that the rising popularity of the social evolutionary perspective associated with the work of scholars like Smith and Frazer only served to reinforce even further the view that popular Catholicism in Ireland was rooted in ancient Celtic experience.

Though most textbooks dealing with the history of anthropological theory suggest that the social evolutionary perspective died out earlier in this century, social evolutionary thinking still pervades much anthropological thinking. In particular, Jane Nadel-Klein (1995) demonstrates that ethnographic accounts of village life in various areas of England, Scotland, and Ireland continue to set up an implicit contrast between the "countryside"—seen as a repository of outmoded and archaic traditions—and more cosmopolitan urban centers. In these conceptualizations "rural life is modernity's evolutionary precedent, surviving as an anachronism that shows us how far we have progressed" (Nadel-Klein 1995, 126)—which of course is exactly the same thought expressed by John O'Donovan in the passage just cited. The continuing persistence of social evolutionary thinking, of course, only serves to reinforce the "Celtic origins" approach to holy well cults and rounding rituals in Ireland.

The Modern Archeological Evidence

So far this chapter has been concerned with demonstrating two things: first, that the evidence cited by nineteenth-century investigators in support of the "Celtic origins" hypothesis concerning holy well devotions was weak if not nonexistent, and second, that this hypothesis was popular because it was so well suited to the needs of a number of intellectual traditions that rose to prominence during the eighteenth and nineteenth centuries. On the other hand, a great deal of archeological information on the ancient Celts has accumulated over the last hundred years, and some of that data does suggest that "watery sites" (notably rivers, springs, wells, lakes, and bogs) did indeed have a cultic importance for Celtic populations. However much we may criticize the process by which the early proponents of the Celtic origins hypothesis reached their conclusions, could they have been right after all?

The archeological evidence commonly seen as suggesting that water sites had a special importance in Celtic religion is of two sorts. First, there is abundant evidence that valuable objects were often deposited in rivers, lakes, and marshes in many areas of Celtic settlements. Although some scholars have indeed seen these objects as votive offerings being made to supernatural beings associated with these sites, other interpretations are equally plausible. Some scholars have suggested that the deposition of these objects was an act of conspicuous consumption designed to communicate information about the actor's wealth, while others have suggested that these depositions may have been associated with a rite of passage. Miranda Green (1995a, 133–34) provides a concise overview of the literature relevant to these various claims.

The second category of archeological data is more closely tied to springs (rather than to watery sites in general) and seems easier to interpret. The excavation of ancient spring sites in many areas of Europe has brought to light inscriptions and objects that explicitly associate these sites with Roman and/or Celtic deities. Also found at many of these same sites are objects (pins, coins, jewelry, figurines, body-part images, etc.) that are reasonably regarded as votive offerings tossed into the pools fed by these springs (see Green 1986, 150–66). All in all, there seems little doubt that in these cases the springs involved *were* the focus of cultic activity associated with particular deities. So doesn't this provide striking support for the "Celtic origins" view of Irish holy wells? Surprisingly, it does not.

During the nineteenth century, one of the implicit presuppositions characteristic of virtually all scholarly thinking about the ancient Celts was that Celtic society had been relatively homogeneous. It was this assumption of homogeneity that allowed nineteenth-

The Rise of the "Celtic Origins" Hypothesis

century scholars to, for example, take Caesar's remarks about the Celtic groups he encountered in Gaul as statements that were true of all Celtic populations. But it is precisely this assumption of cultural homogeneity that has been shattered by the archeological evidence. Michael Dietler (1994, 586), an archeologist specializing in the study of Iron Age Europe, provides a succinct summary of how modern archeology has changed our perception of the ancient Celts:

> Certain aspects of Iron Age material culture, such as the well-known La Tène art styles . . . exhibit considerable similarity over wide regions. However, much of the material culture shows a great deal of local variation over both time and space, and it would be misleading to speak of anything as homogeneous as a unified "Celtic culture" that could be linked isomorphically to a linguistic community or population. . . . It is more appropriate to think of ancient Celtic speakers in terms of a fluid network of autonomous societies speaking a set of related languages, linked by exchange, and differentially sharing certain cultural elements, but exhibiting considerable variation in political organization and other sociocultural structures and practices.

What makes all of this relevant to our concerns here is that a tradition of organizing cults around sacred springs seems to have been one of the things that varied from one Celtic population to another, and it did indeed vary across both space and time.

Virtually all of the archeological evidence suggesting that Celts engaged in ritual activity at sacred springs comes from Britain and (especially) from Continental Europe (Green 1986, 148–66; Webster 1995, 449–52); there is little if any such evidence from Irish sites. Just as importantly, this British/Continental evidence almost always dates from a period subsequent to when the Celtic populations involved came under Roman control. In her overview of the archeological evidence relating to Celtic sanctuaries and sacred places, Jane Webster (1995, 449–50) concludes that "archeological evidence for springs as pre-conquest cult foci is virtually non-existent" and therefore that such cults are most likely a "post-conquest phenomenon." A parsimonious way of explaining this pattern is on the hypothesis that Roman influence was critical in giving rise to a strong tradition of cults organized around sacred springs in Celtic areas.

The view that Celtic religion changed as Celtic areas fell under Roman control is not in itself novel. Green (1995b, 466), for instance, reads the archeological evidence as suggesting that the use of physical images to depict sacred beings or concepts only came into widespread use among Celtic populations with their exposure to Roman/Mediterranean traditions of iconography. Much the same thing could easily have occurred in connection with cults organized around sacred springs. Certainly, there is abundant archeological evidence suggesting that healing cults involving the use of ex-votos were widespread throughout the Italian peninsula during the middle to late republican period and that such cults were often localized at springs (see Comella 1981; Melis and Gigli 1982, 35; 1983, 6–9). These Roman healing cults, especially when merged with preexisting Celtic traditions about the sacredness of watery sites, could easily have given rise to a strong tradition of cultic activity at sacred springs as Celtic areas fell under Roman control.

But if Roman influence was critical in giving rise to cults organized around sacred springs, what would we expect in regard to Ireland, that area of the Celtic world upon which Roman armies never trod? Clearly we would expect that such cults would *not* have arisen in Ireland. While such a conclusion flies in the face of the Celtic origins hypothesis so frequently invoked by nineteenth-century scholars to explain modern (Catholic) holy well devotions, it is—remember—fully consistent with the evidence that we have been reviewing, showing that none of the hundreds of wells mentioned in the literature on early Irish saints are ever associated with Celtic religious rituals (save for the two overused examples of Patrick at the well of Slán and Columba at the Pictish well) and that all the archeological evidence for Celtic well cults comes from non-Irish sites.

The suggestion that there was little or no cultic activity associated with sacred springs in Celtic Ireland would also allow us to explain something that has puzzled earlier commentators on Celtic / early Christian Ireland and that has so far been unmentioned: the fact that such cults are not mentioned in the Irish vernacular literature.

Irish Vernacular Literature

One of the great difficulties in trying to understand Celtic religion has always been that the Celts themselves left few written records.

The Rise of the "Celtic Origins" Hypothesis

What we do have in the case of Ireland, however, is a vernacular literature set down by Christian scribes mainly during the seventh and eighth centuries. Even though the traditions preserved in this literature were undeniably filtered through a Christian grid, and even though we know the original works only through manuscripts that date from later periods, any number of Irish scholars have argued that this literature is a valuable source of information about the culture and society of pre-Christian Ireland (see Mac Cana 1991). Still, one of the things that has always puzzled scholars who take this view of the vernacular literature is that this literature does not lend any support to the claim that holy well cults were an important element in Celtic religion. Mac Cana (1987, 156), for instance, after reviewing the archeological evidence attesting to well cults in Celtic areas (outside Ireland) says:

> The abundant material [= archeological] evidence for this pan-Celtic phenomenon [well cults] is not matched by the early insular literary evidence: many Irish tales mention wells with preternatural powers and associations, but there is hardly anything about healing wells as such. Unless this is due to suppression by the monastic redactors of the literature, the only explanation would seem to be that the frequenting of healing wells had always been regarded, even in pagan times, as a popular practice to be distinguished from the more official tribal cults.

Since Mac Cana himself is thoroughly committed to the "Celtic origins" approach to Irish holy wells (see especially Mac Cana 1988), he accepts uncritically the premise that sacred springs must have had a special cultic importance in Celtic Ireland. Given this, the only way he can think to explain the failure of the vernacular literature to mention such cults is by suggesting that mention of such cults may have been suppressed by Christian scribes or possibly that they were overlooked by these same Christian scribes because such cults belonged to a "popular" rather than to an "official" tradition. But a simpler and much more straightforward way to account for the evidence is the hypothesis being offered here, that is, that there is little or no mention of cults organized around sacred springs in the Irish vernacular literature because such cults were of little or no importance in Celtic Ireland.

In summary, then, there is no compelling evidence suggesting that sacred springs had any special importance in Celtic Ireland and much evidence suggesting just the reverse. It is now time to consider the second half of the Celtic origins hypothesis, namely, that cults organized around sacred springs were absorbed into the Christian tradition during the early Christian period in Ireland and gave rise to a continuing tradition of holy well cult rituals that persisted into the modern period.

Holy Wells in Ireland after Christianization

If by "holy well" we mean a spring that was associated with a Christian saint and whose water was seen to have curative properties, then there is no doubt that a few such wells did exist in Ireland during the early Christian period. For example, just before relating the story of Columba at the Pictish well, Adomnán tells the story of another well. In this other story, Columba blesses a rock and causes water to pour out, and then uses that water to baptize a child. This story concludes with the line "and there even today [that is, in Adomnán's day] a spring is seen, that is potent in the name of St. Columba." Presumably this means that the well was dedicated to St. Columba and that its water had healing properties. In recounting the life of St. Findian, *The Book of Lismore* (Stokes 1890, 228) mentions a well dedicated to Findian in the district of Luigne and says that "whatsoever sick man shall go into that well will come healthy out of it." Similarly, *The Tripartite Life of Patrick* tells the story of a leper who sat under an elm near Clonmacnois and asked a man to pull up some rushes nearby. The water that broke forth from where the rushes had been, says the story, "is today the well of Ciarán" (Stokes 1887, 85). (I might add that a well dedicated to St. Ciarán still exists at Clonmacnois and that it is the first in the series of stations that are rounded by modern pilgrims doing the "Long Station" at this pilgrimage site; see Logan 1980, 23–24; figure 12 herein.) Also, the *Annals of Tigernach* are likely referring to a holy well under the entry for the year 757, which says that "Gorman, successor of S. Mochta of Louth . . . lived for a year on the water of Fingen's well in Clonmacnois, and died in pilgrimage at Cluain" (Stokes 1896, 258). On the other hand, although scattered textual references like these are evidence that a few sacred springs did exist in Ireland during the early Christian period, there is nothing in the documentary record to suggest that such springs were any more common in Ireland than elsewhere in the Christian world.

Remember, too, that a simple emphasis on the curative properties of water from a sacred spring is not what was most distinctive about Catholic holy well devotions in Ireland. On the contrary, as chapter 1 was at pains to make clear, what made holy well cults in the modern period most distinctive was their association with rounding rituals having penitential value. However, there is nothing in the documentary record to suggest that rounding rituals were assigned as penance in early Christian Ireland—and we know a lot of early Irish penances. Consider, for example, the testimony of the Irish penitentials.

The Irish penitentials were handbooks compiled by Irish clerics during the sixth, seventh, and eighth centuries that listed a great variety of sins and specified what penance should be associated with each.[6] In the Western Church the historic importance of these handbooks (along with similar handbooks produced in Wales and England) is that they helped popularize the idea of private and repeatable penances administered by priestly confessors in contrast to the public and nonrepeatable penances administered by bishops that had previously been the norm. The penances specified most often in these penitentials are fasting on bread and water and abstaining from meat and wine for various lengths of time, depending upon the seriousness of the sin involved. For example, in its considerations of sexual sins, the Penitential of St. Columbanus says that a layman who engages in homosexual activity should fast for three years and then abstain from meat and wine for another four; that a man who fornicates with a beast should fast for a year if he is married and for six months if he is single; that a man who wants to fornicate with a married woman, but does not do so, should fast for forty days; and so on. In the case of especially serious sins, fasting and abstinence could be supplemented by other measures. The Penitential of Finnan, for instance, says that a cleric who murders a man must (1) fast for four years and abstain for three, (2) spend ten years in exile, and (3) when he returns from exile, place himself in the service of the parents whose son he killed (Bieler 1963, 81). But although these penitentials did sometimes assign pilgrimage as a penance (see for example Bieler 1963, 267), they nowhere make reference to holy wells or rounding rituals and certainly say nothing to suggest that rounding rituals at holy wells had penitential value.

The Later Middle Ages

For the later medieval period, there is only one source that we can reasonably consult about Irish well cults, but it is a source that specifically concerned itself with springs in Ireland. This source is Giraldus Cambrensis's *The Topography of Ireland*, written originally sometime in the late 1180s. There is no denying that Giraldus's account of Ireland was shaped by a number of biases. Giraldus, after all, was a Welsh-Norman cleric with strong family ties to the Anglo-Norman adventurers who were colonizing Ireland in the late twelfth century. This alone would have predisposed him to depict the Irish (as he did) as a savage and uncivilized people who needed to be colonized by more civilized groups like his own. Secondly, Cambrensis was committed to the sort of Christianity that prevailed in England and on the Continent, and so was very much disgusted by the degree to which the laity and clergy in Ireland fell short of English/Continental practice. Finally, although Giraldus did undeniably visit Ireland (something that cannot be said of all the medieval authors who wrote on Ireland; see Rambo 1994), much of what he came to "know" about Ireland was derived from stories told to him by others. Like so many foreign visitors to Ireland over the last few centuries, he displayed a truly amazing willingness to accept at face value any number of tall tales about the Irish. The result is that a story about a fish with three gold teeth, one about Irish dust driving away poisonous animals when dispersed in foreign lands, one about talking werewolves, and so on—were all set down uncritically, right alongside his accounts of Irish topography, the animals found in Ireland, the state of the Irish Church, and so forth.

But in some ways Giraldus's biases are an advantage, since he was at pains to single out for special condemnation the ways in which the Irish diverged from the English/Continental view of what constituted good Christian practice. In discussing the laity in Ireland (90), for example, he tells us that they are "the least instructed in the rudiments of the Faith" of any Christian group; that they don't go to church; that they don't pay tithes or first fruits; that they don't contract formal marriages; and—worst of all—that they routinely com-

mit incest (by which he means marriage between prohibited categories of relatives) with impunity. Giraldus did give Irish clerics some
small praise for their celibacy and asceticism, but he was sharply
critical of their tendency to neglect their pastoral obligations (a neglect that Cambrensis attributes to the influence of the monastic tradition in Ireland). The clergy's lack of concern with preaching, in
particular, bothered him. Irish prelates, he says, make no effort "to
preach the word of God to their people, nor tell them of their sins,
nor extirpate vices from the flock, nor instill virtue" (97).

Given this sharply critical view of the state of Christianity in Ireland, it seems likely that Giraldus would have reported something
as unorthodox as the repetitive rounding of sacred springs dedicated
to Christian saints, especially if this were being done to discharge a
penance assigned by the clergy or to earn an indulgence. The fact is,
however, that Giraldus makes no mention of anything remotely resembling rounding rituals even though he does talk specifically about
Irish springs.

In a section entitled "The Wonderful Natures of Fountains" Giraldus describes six springs in Ireland, each of which he associates with
preternatural qualities. One fountain turns a person's hair grey. Another prevents a person's hair from turning grey. A third ebbs and
flows with the tides, even though it is located on a mountaintop. A
piece of wood dipped into the fourth turns to stone. Water taken
from a fifth is harmful to animals but not to humans. Finally, in the
case of the sixth and final fountain, should anyone touch or even
look at its water, the entire province is deluged with rain. As unusual
as these fountains might seem to modern readers, Giraldus himself
did not regard them as being distinctive of Ireland. On the contrary,
he very explicitly compares these Irish fountains to similar fountains
found in Wales, Norway, Brittany, and Sicily.

Most importantly, Giraldus does not associate these Irish springs
with ritual activities—with one exception. That one exception involves his sixth and final Irish fountain, the one that causes rain:
"The rain will not cease until a priest, who is a virgin in both mind
and body and specially chosen for the purpose, celebrates Mass in a
chapel not far from the fountain and known to have been erected
with this end in view, and appeases the fountain with a sprinkling of
holy water and the milk of a cow of one color. This is certainly a

barbarous rite, without rime or reason" (Giraldus 1951, 45). In this case there is a religious ritual associated with the spring, but that ritual is the Mass and has nothing to do with rounding. That Giraldus singles out this ritual for special condemnation only reinforces the argument that he would have mentioned rounding rituals at holy wells, especially if done to discharge a penance or acquire an indulgence, if he had heard about or observed such rituals.[7]

Sixteenth-Century Reports

Giraldus's account of Ireland was the basis of most other accounts written about early Ireland over the next four centuries. It is really only in the sixteenth century that we begin to encounter authors trying to provide some new "description of Ireland" that moves beyond Giraldus. One of the most valuable of these new accounts, at least for anyone interested in popular religion, is the one written by the English Jesuit William Good, who visited Limerick in the 1560s. Good's report is known mainly because it was incorporated into Camden's (1610) account of England, Scotland, and Ireland.[8]

As he went about his travels in Ireland, Good paid attention to precisely those things that were of concern to the Counter-Reformation Church. Thus, in his report he describes the ruinous condition of the churches; the foul appearance of the sacred vestments worn by priests; the torn missals and the poor quality of the chalices used in celebrating Mass. As well, he castigates the local clergy for their venality and sexual immorality ("The Priests minde nothing but gathering of goods and getting of children" [144]). In regard to lay religiosity, Good says that laypersons in Ireland fast extensively, especially the women, and are constantly making oaths that invoke the Trinity, God, St. Patrick, St. Brigid, their baptism, their Faith, their Church, and so on. He also describes a number of superstitions, many of which incorporated Catholic elements. For example, it was common, he says, for Irish parents to hang a written copy of the words that begin St. John's Gospel around the necks of their sick children. Similarly, the wise women to whom people went for cures were always careful to say a Pater Noster and an Ave Maria at the beginning and end of the many charms they dispensed.

Like so many other commentators over the centuries, Good was disgusted by Irish funeral practices, as much because of their apparent lack of concern with the Christian vision of salvation (the people around the dying person, he says, "never speake of God, nor of the salvation of his soule" [147]), as on account of the extreme nature of the lamentations offered when the person finally dies. Good even mentions a superstitious ritual that seems to involve something like rounding. Thus, he tells us, if a man falls on the ground, he gets up right away, walks around the spot in a rightward direction three times, and then digs out the turf (where he fell) with his sword or knife. If that man nevertheless gets sick within two or three days, a wise woman is sent to the spot to perform a magical ritual designed to appease the fairies who sent the disease.

Notwithstanding Good's attention to clerical laxity, popular religiosity, and various superstitious practices that invoked Christian imagery and involving rounding, he nowhere mentions holy wells and certainly nowhere associates wells with rounding rituals or any other form of cultic activity. Holy well cults and rounding rituals are similarly unmentioned in other reports from this same period that also paid special attention to religious practice. There is no mention of such cults or rituals, for example, in the "description of Ireland" written by the Jesuit David Wolfe, who served as papal nuncio in Ireland during the early 1560s.[9]

A Puzzle?

If there is no solid evidence attesting to the existence of holy well cults in Celtic Ireland nor any evidence that such cults were central to the Christian experience in Ireland through to the mid-sixteenth century, just when did these cults become central to the experience of Irish Catholicism? Certainly the practice of holding patterns at holy wells was well established during the seventeenth century, when these things came to be regulated by the synodal legislation discussed in chapter 1. Seventeenth-century commentators also make reference, at least occasionally, to rounding rituals. In 1644, for example, a French traveler in Ireland gave a fairly precise description of a station being performed at a site near the town of Wexford: "[At this site] are many ruins of old churches ... towards which the women have great reverence, and come there in solemn procession. The oldest march first and the others follow, then take three turns round the ruins, make a reverence to the remains, kneel and recommence this ceremony many times. I have noticed them at this devotion three and four hours" (Boullaye le Gouz 1837 [1657]). So the question remains: just when did holy well cults and rounding rituals become both widespread and central to the Catholic experience in Ireland?

The great difficulty in answering this question, as usual, is that the relevant documentary record quickly goes from meager to nonexistent as we proceed backward in time. On the other hand, there is one (but only one) pilgrimage site in Ireland that has been described on a regular basis from the twelfth century forward. Though not without its problems, the documentary record associated with this site allows us, as we shall see, to catch a glimpse of patterns and changes relating to popular religiosity in Ireland that would be difficult if not impossible to establish using other sources. It is a site well known throughout the Catholic world and associated with one of Ireland's greatest saints, even though he almost certainly never set foot there.

1. Glendalough (County Wicklow), which in the eighteenth century was identified as one of the four most important pilgrimage sites in Ireland.

2. St. Dolough's Well near Dublin as it appears in Hall and Hall's *Ireland: Its Scenery, Character, &c.* (1841–43).

3. St. Augustine's Well in Galway.

4. St. Kenny's Well in the city of Kilkenny.

5. Holy well (Tobernacogany) near St. Fechin's Church,
Fore (County Westmeath). The object in the foreground is a branch
of the ash tree that used to grow next to the well. Pieces of cloth
have been tied to the branch as votive offerings.

Croaghpatrick PILGRIMAGE

Every pilgrim who ascends the mountain on St. Patrick's Day or within the octave, or any time during the months of June, July, August & September, & PRAYS IN OR NEAR THE CHAPEL for the intentions of our Holy Father the Pope may gain a plenary indulgence on condition of going to Confession and Holy Communion on the Summit or within the week.

THE TRADITIONAL STATIONS There are three "stations" (1) At the base of the cone or Leacht Benain, (2) On the summit, (3) Roilig Muire, some distance down the Lecanvey side of the mountain.

1st Station - LEACHT BENAIN
The pilgrim walks seven times around the mound of stones saying seven Our Fathers, seven Hail Marys and one Creed

2nd Station - THE SUMMIT
(a) The pilgrim kneels and says 7 Our Fathers, 7 Hail Marys and one Creed
(b) The pilgrim prays near the Chapel for the Pope's intentions.
(c) The pilgrim walks 15 times around the Chapel saying 15 Our Fathers, 15 Hail Mary's and one Creed.
(d) The pilgrim walks 7 times around Leaba Phadraig saying 7 Our Fathers 7 Hail Mary's and one Creed.

3rd Station - ROILIG MUIRE
he pilgrim walks 7 times around each mound of stones saying 7 Our Fathers , 7 Hail Mary's and one Creed at each an finally goes around the whole enclosure of Roilig Muire 7 times prayin

6. Sign at the beginning of the path that leads up Croagh Patrick which describes the traditional way of rounding the various stations.

7. Leacht Benain, the first of the stations on Croagh Patrick.

8. Bell tower of the ruined abbey at Trim (County Meath), which contained one of the relatively few miraculous images found in pre-Reformation Ireland.

Plate XXXV

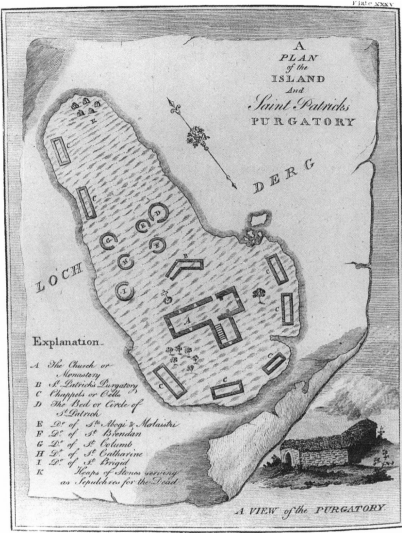

A
PLAN
of the
ISLAND
And
Saint Patricks
PURGATORY

DERG

LOCH

Explanation

A   The Church or
      Monastery
B   St Patricks Purgatory
C   Chappels or Cells
D   The Bed or Circle of
      St Patrick
E   Dᵒ of Stˢ Abogi & Molaistri
F   Dᵒ of St Brendan
G   Dᵒ of St Columb
H   Dᵒ of St Catharine
I   Dᵒ of St Brigid
K   Heaps of Stones serving
      as Sepulchres for the Dead

A VIEW *of the* PURGATORY.

9. Plan of St. Patrick's Purgatory,
from Edward Ledwich's *Antiquities of Ireland* (1790).
The structure depicted in the lower right corner is the famous cave.

10. Nineteenth-century pilgrims visiting St. Patrick's Purgatory.
Note the four "saints' beds" in the foreground.
(Courtesy of the National Library of Ireland)

11. Round tower and church ruins at Clonmacnois.

12. St. Ciarán's Well at Clonmacnois, the first station rounded by
modern pilgrims doing the "Long Station" at this pilgrimage site.

13. View of Monaincha, one of the most popular pilgrimage sites in eighteenth-century Ireland, from Edward Ledwich's *Antiquities of Ireland* (1790).

14. Drawing of a faction fight, from Hall and Hall's *Ireland: Its Scenery, Character, &c.* (1841–43). Note the tents in the background. These tents hosted the various secular activities (such as drinking, gaming, and dancing) that took place at a pattern.

15. The round tower at Ardmore (County Waterford). During the 1830s
Ardmore was the site of one of the most popular patterns in Ireland.

16. St. Declan's Stone at Ardmore (Country Waterford). During the annual pattern at Ardmore, pilgrims pulled themselves through the opening at the bottom.

17. St. Declan's Well at Ardmore (County Waterford).

18. St. Patrick's Well, Clonmel (County Tipperary)
in the nineteenth century.
(Courtesy of the National Library of Ireland)

Chapter Three

New Rituals for Old at Patrick's Purgatory

The first reference to St. Patrick's Purgatory appears in a work written about 1184 by Henry of Saltrey, a Cistercian monk living in the diocese of Lincoln (England). Henry tells the story, which he says he heard from another Cistercian, of an Irish knight named Owein who had gone on pilgrimage to St. Patrick's Purgatory in order to atone for his sins. Once there, Henry says, Owein entered a cave that proved to be an entrance to the otherworld and went on to have a series of adventures, the most colorful (and painful) of which involved his encounters with demons. Henry of Saltrey did not indicate where St. Patrick's Purgatory was located; writing only a few years later (c. 1188), Giraldus Cambrensis says that it was located on an island in a lake in Ulster. Giraldus's account is far shorter than Henry of Saltrey's but it also suggests that pilgrims regularly encountered demons and other horrible things:

> There are nine pits in that [island], and if anyone by any chance should venture to spend the night in any one of them—and there is evidence that some rash persons have at times attempted to do so—he is seized immediately by malignant spirits, and so crucified with such severe torments, and so continuously afflicted with many unspeakable punishments of fire and water and other things, that, when morning comes, there is found in his poor body scarcely even the smallest trace of life surviving. (Giraldus 1951, 43)

The one important difference between Henry of Saltrey's account and Giraldus's is that the latter mentions "nine pits" rather than a single cave.

St. Patrick's Purgatory would be described by nearly two dozen other authors over the next three centuries.[1] Although these accounts are not consistent among themselves in all details, they are consistent enough to give us the general structure of the pilgrimage experience. First, pilgrims were expected to appear before the Archbishop of Armagh to ask his permission to visit the site.[2] If permission was granted (and that never seems to have been problematic), the pilgrim proceeded to Lough Derg in County Donegal (Giraldus's "lake in Ulster") and sought out Saint's Island. This was one of the more than forty islands in that lake and was the location of an abbey belonging to the Canons Regular of St. Augustine. There he—and in all medieval accounts, the pilgrim is a "he"—applied to the prior for permission to visit the Purgatory itself. It was one of the conventions of the pilgrimage experience that the prior tried to discourage the pilgrim by warning him of the dangers associated with a journey to the otherworld. Assuming that this failed, the pilgrim fasted and prayed for fifteen days. During this time an Office for the Dead was said on the pilgrim's behalf. Eventually the pilgrim was taken to a smaller island nearby and led first to a chapel for prayer and then to the "cave" itself.

Giraldus Cambrensis aside, most later accounts make it clear that there was only one "cave" on the smaller island and that it was an artificial structure constructed of stone. It appears to have been something like fifteen feet long, two feet wide, and only three feet high (thus preventing anyone who entered it from standing upright). A movable stone allowed access to the interior, and pilgrims were shut inside for twenty-four hours. It was during this period that they had their otherworldly experiences.

In later centuries cynical Protestant commentators (see Jones 1647, 16–17; Boate 1652, 74–75) would suggest that the preparations forced on a pilgrim by the Augustinians—notably the dire warnings against danger, the fasting, the insistence upon treating the pilgrim as though already dead—were carefully calculated to predispose pilgrims toward hallucinations, especially once they were put into a darkened subterranean chamber. Whether intended or not, it seems likely that such preparations would have had just that effect.

Some of the surviving medieval accounts of the pilgrimage experience at St. Patrick's Purgatory are quite elaborate and were clearly meant to be read by literate audiences. The fact that manuscript versions of these longer accounts are found in a wide variety of locations in England and Continental Europe (de Pontfarcy 1988) is testimony to their popularity. Other accounts of the pilgrimage experience are quite brief and were likely intended to be used by the regular clergy in the course of their public preaching. There is, for instance, a brief account of St. Patrick's Purgatory in Jacobo de Voragine's *Golden Legend* (de Voragine 1993, 1:194–96). Compiled in the thirteenth century, this popular book contains a number of short stories dealing with various saints; it is now generally recognized that the book was intended as a manual for preachers (Ryan 1993). St. Patrick's Purgatory was also mentioned in collections of medieval exempla, the short stories that preachers included in their sermons in order to make a didactic point(see Tubach 1969, 307). Whether through the longer literary accounts that described the experiences of particular pilgrims or through the brief references that appeared in sermons (or both), St. Patrick's Purgatory became a pilgrimage site that was widely known throughout Europe. Its fame was such that on many medieval maps of Ireland St. Patrick's Purgatory figures more prominently than any other site (Leslie 1961).

Given the concerns of this book, however, what seems most striking about the various medieval accounts of St. Patrick's Purgatory is that they don't *feel* very Irish. First, all the authors of these accounts—without exception— lived outside Ireland, as did almost all the pilgrims. (Apart from the knight Owein in Henry of Saltrey's original account, only one other pilgrim is explicitly identified as being Irish.) Second, the Augustinians and the Cistercians, the two groups most involved in the early attempts to popularize St. Patrick's Purgatory, were recent arrivals in Ireland, having only established themselves there in the early twelfth century. Moreover, in the same period (the late twelfth and the thirteenth centuries) when these two groups were first actively promoting St. Patrick's Purgatory as a pilgrimage site, they were also involved in a general campaign to promote an acceptance of the recently emergent view that "Purgatory" was a distinct place (see Le Goff 1984). It seems likely, in other words, that the early Cistercian and Augustinian efforts to promote St. Patrick's Purgatory as a pilgrimage site were part of their campaign (throughout Europe) on behalf of "Purgatory" in general. Dorothea French (1994) suggests that is why the Augustinians at Lough Derg were especially concerned with attracting elite males from various European societies as pilgrims.

Irish Pilgrimage

None of the medieval accounts, I should note, make any mention of rounding rituals or stations, the elements that would be so central to the experience of popular Catholicism in Ireland in the centuries immediately preceding the Famine. The Italian merchant Antonio Mannini, who visited Lough Derg in 1411, does say that he was led in procession three times around the chapel before being led to the cave.[3] However, this detail is not mentioned in any other medieval account, and, as I have already noted, the practice of walking in procession around a church is found in a variety of European locations.

The general impression that results from these various considerations, then, is that during the Middle Ages St. Patrick's Purgatory was primarily a European pilgrimage site, which just happened to be in Ireland, and that the popularity of this site was tied to issues and processes that had more to do with what was going on in Europe generally than to anything happening in Ireland in particular.

This is not to deny that a few pilgrims going to Lough Derg were Irish. Apart from the two Irish pilgrims mentioned in the accounts already considered, the *Annals of the Four Masters* tell us that Bartholomew O'Flanagan, the prior of Devenish, died at Lough Derg in 1462 (O'Donovan 1854, 4:1019). Even so, Lough Derg is mentioned far less frequently in this and other annalistic sources than other pilgrimage sites like Glendalough, Armagh, Killaloe, and others.[4] During the Middle Ages, St. Patrick's Purgatory was not nearly as important, in Ireland, as it would become.

St. Patrick's Purgatory in the Modern Period

Jumping ahead to the early seventeenth century, the situation changes dramatically. Not only are Irish pilgrims now flocking to St. Patrick's Purgatory in large numbers, but once there, they are engaging in exactly the same sort of rounding rituals that would later be found to be associated with holy well cults. Table 3.1 presents my paraphrase of three accounts, all written in the early seventeenth century, each of which describes the rituals being performed at St. Patrick's Purgatory. The first is by the Franciscan Michael O'Clery, who compiled the *Martyrology of Donegal* and was one of the authors responsible for compiling the *Annals of the Four Masters*.[5] The second is derived from an Irish-language poem of the period that has been translated by Ní Chatháin (1988). The third account is taken from a

New Rituals for Old at Patrick's Purgatory

Table 3.1

Three Early-Seventeenth-Century Accounts
of the Ritual to Be Performed at St. Patrick's Purgatory

Michael O'Clery (from Harbison 1991, 62)	Irish-Language Poem (from Ní Chatháin 1988)	Henry Jones (1647, originally 1632)
Kneel in the church and recite a Pater, an Ave, and a Credo. Leave the church, kissing the door as you go. Visit and kiss the old Cross at the front of the Church, and then—moving rightwards—visit and kiss each of the stations around the church (which include various stone crosses and cairns, on one of which rest three fragments of Patrick's bell). Then walk seven times round the church.	Say a Pater, an Ave and a Credo at the great altar [of Patrick] . In the church say three Paters, three Aves and a Credo on your knees. Then say seven decades [of Aves] and with each decade say a Pater.	Pilgrims enter the church, kneel before the altar and pray a Pater, an Ave and a Credo. They then walk round the inside of the church seven times. Leaving the church, they kiss the door on their way out and proceed to the stone cross—called St. Patrick's Altar—between the church and the Cave and kiss it likewise. They then walk seven times around the outside of the church.
Next go to Brendan's Bed. Kiss the stone at the entrance. Then go sunwise three times round the outside of the Bed, reciting prayers, and three times sunwise round the inside, saying three Paters, three Aves and a Credo. Go next to Brigid's Bed, Catherine's Bed and Colum Cille's Bed, and at each repeat the same procedure. Then go to Patrick's Bed and kiss the stone at the entrance. The two Beds nearby, intertwined with Patrick's Bed, belong to Da-Bheog and Mo-Laisse. Go seven times around them all and after the last round say five Paters, five Aves and a Credo on your knees at the entrance to Patrick's Bed. Enter the combined beds of Mo-Laisse and Da-Bheog	Go to each of the seven penitential beds, starting with Brendan's and ending with Aibheóg's. At each bed go round the outside three times, saying three Paters, three Aves and a Credo; kneel at the entrance and say the same prayers; we enter the bed and round the inside three times on our knees, once again saying the same prayers.	Next they go to the six penitential mansions, called Beds or Cells of the Saints. These mansions are dedicated to Brendan, Bridget, Collum-Kille, Katharine, Patrick, Avogh, and Moleissay. The last two saints are placed in one Cell, which is joined to Patrick's. Pilgrims walk seven times around the outside of each bed barefoot, and similarly make seven circuits inside each bed on their knees.

(continued)

Irish Pilgrimage

Table 3.1 *(continued)*

Michael O'Clery (from Harbison 1991, 62)	Irish-Language Poem (from Ní Chatháin 1988)	Henry Jones (1647, originally 1632)
and divide them into two areas. Go round each area three times saying three Paters, Three Aves and one Credo each time.		
Go next towards the lake, across the sharp stones called An Chaorthannach, and walk round the stone where Patrick knelt. At the smaller stone nearby "where Patrick was" say a Pater and an Ave. Then go to another stone eastwards in the lake and say the same prayers.	Proceed across the sharp stones, through the water of the lake, to Patrick's stone. Walk around this stone saying five paters, five Aves and a Credo. Then kneel and say five paters, five Aves and a Credo. Move next to the stone with the footmarks where pilgrims refresh their feet and say one Pater, one Ave and one Credo.	Pilgrims then walk into the lake on the north-east end and go to the stone with the marks made when Patrick knelt there. They walk around this three times saying five Aves, five paters and one Credo. They then go further into the lake, to the stone called Lackevanny, which can heal feet made sore by going barefoot over the sharp rocks and stones. Here they stay for a quarter of an hour while saying one Pater, one Ave and one Credo.
Return to the cairn on the eastern side of the Church and kiss it. Go southwards to the other cairn and kiss it. Go to the church door and kiss it. Enter the church and say fifteen decades of Mary's Psalter on your knees, with a Credo every five decades. Do all this three times a day over nine days, taking bread and water only once a day.	Go back to the Great Altar of Patrick [near the church] and say one Pater, one Ave and one Credo on your knees. Enter the church and say a psalter on your knees.	After this they return to the church and pray the Lady's Psalter [the rosary] before the altar.
On one day you must spend twenty-four hours in either of the two caves, from morning to morning. After coming out of the cave, pilgrims should dunk	On one day, we spend twenty-four hours without sleep in Patrick's cave. We make the end of our journey with "three waves across the lake."	They do all this three times a day for seven days. On the eighth day, they double their circuits, so that they can spend the ninth in the Cave. On the ninth day,

Table 3.1 *(continued)*

Michael O'Clery (from Harbison 1991, 62)	Irish-Language Poem (from Ní Chatháin 1988)	Henry Jones (1647, originally 1632)
themselves three times under the water at Patrick's Pool.		nine persons are led in procession to the Cave and shut up there for twenty four hours. Exiting the Cave, they are led to the water's edge and dunk themselves under the water. Then they go to the church and give God thanks for the end of their penance.

book on St. Patrick's Purgatory written by Henry Jones, the Protestant bishop of Clogher (the diocese in which the pilgrimage site falls). Although Jones's book was published in 1647, his text makes it clear that he is describing the pilgrimage site as it existed just prior to 1632, when Protestant authorities landed on the island and uprooted the structures found there.[6]

All three of the seventeenth-century accounts agree in saying that there were three separate and distinct sets of stations that had to be visited by pilgrims. The first set consisted of the chapel itself and one or more stone structures set up in the immediate vicinity of the chapel. The second set consisted of a series of seven stone circles, or "penitential beds," each dedicated to a different saint. The third and final set of stations consisted of a series of stones at the north end of the island, at least one of which was in the water of the lake. The island itself, incidentally, is now explicitly called Station Island, a term that does not appear in the medieval accounts. All three accounts also indicate that the stations within each set had to be visited in a predetermined order and that each station had to be rounded a certain number of times. In short, stations and rounding rituals, unmentioned in the medieval accounts, are now not only present but central to the pilgrimage experience at Lough Derg.[7]

The three accounts do differ in some details. Both the poem and Jones, for instance, identify only a single station located in the immediate vicinity of the church (a cross called the Altar of Patrick), whereas O'Clery identifies four (the cross, two stone cairns, fragments of Patrick's Bell). The accounts also differ in regard to the precise number of roundings that had to be done at particular stations. O'Clery says that the first four saints' beds are to be rounded three times on the outside and three times on the inside, with a more complicated procedure being used for the final three (intertwined) beds; Jones suggests more simply that all the beds were rounded seven times on the outside and seven times on the inside. Finally, O'Clery mentions two caves on the island; the other accounts mention only one. This last discrepancy, however, provides a clue as to which might have produced these other discrepancies.

Jones (1647, 6) says that the great influx of pilgrims coming to Station Island had caused the authorities there to erect a second cave, and that one cave was used exclusively by male pilgrims and the other exclusively by female pilgrims. But, he adds, the change was unpopular and the second cave was dismantled; the sexes were subsequently kept separate by allowing males into the cave at one time and females at another. It would appear, then, that the three accounts in table 3.1 are capturing the rituals at Station Island at slightly different points during the early seventeenth century, with O'Clery's account describing the rituals during the period when two caves were being used.

The timing of these accounts can be pinned down even more precisely by considering a report (reproduced in Moran 1864, 309–10) written in 1624 by Thomas Fleming, the archbishop of Dublin. In describing St. Patrick's Purgatory Fleming says that "during twenty-four hours [pilgrims] are shut up in certain caves, like unto prisons, where they pass the whole day and night." Fleming's use of the plural here suggests that the two-cave arrangement was still in use at the time (1624) of his writing. Since Jones is describing the rituals as they existed before the destruction of the Purgatory in 1632, his account (which, remember, says that the second cave had been dismantled) must have been written sometime after 1624 but before 1632.

More than just the rituals on Station Island were changing during the early decades of the seventeenth century. There also appears to have been a dramatic increase in the number of pilgrims coming there, and that increase seems to have occurred in the relatively recent past. Jones, remember, cites an increased number of pilgrims as the reason for building two caves in the first place. In his 1624 report Archbishop Fleming also seems to be alluding to a recent surge in the number of pilgrims when he talks of the "pious and innumerable pilgrimages of the faithful" to Station Island in that year even though the pilgrimage had "almost been abandoned" following the onset of the persecutions launched by Protestants (Moran 1864, 309).

Numbers aside, the social composition of the pilgrims coming to Lough Derg was also changing in this period. Jones (1647, 9) tells us, for instance, that at the entrance to the island there were "four separate places" that were used to hear the confessions of pilgrims from Leinster, Munster, Ulster, and Connaught. Further, Jones's remarks regarding two caves, one for men and one for women, is evidence that both men and women were making the pilgrimage in large numbers —something that is not documented for the Middle Ages. In short, by the first few decades of the seventeenth century, St. Patrick's Purgatory was something it had not been in the Middle Ages: a pilgrimage site that was enormously popular with Irish Catholics, both male and female, from all parts of Ireland and distinctly Irish by virtue of the extensive rounding rituals performed there.

In 1632 Protestant authorities decided to demolish St. Patrick's Purgatory, and the decree authorizing this demolition (reprinted in Jones 1647, 229–30) took note of both its popularity and the "superstitious" rituals being performed there: "Forasmuch as the frequent and publicke resort of people in great numbers to that place or Island called St. Patrick's Purgatory, there performing superstitious ceremonies, pilgrimages, and offerings, is so ektreamely abusive and superstitious, as is not fit to be endured. . . . We have therefore adjudged it the best and fittest meanes to prevent and wholly take away the continuance of that abuse hereafter, that the place be defaced and utterly demolished." A few months after this decree was issued, James Spottiswoode, the Protestant bishop of Clogher, landed on the island with twenty men and proceeded to effect the demolition. Spottiswoode's account of actions (reprinted in Jones 1647, 132–34) makes it clear that he had been instructed to find out if the "cave" really did lead somewhere, just as the medieval accounts suggested:

The first thing I searched diligently after, was the Cave, wherein I remembered your Grace enjoined me to digge to the very foundations, and leave no corner unsought, and so I did: I caused to digge about it on all sides, til I cam to the Rocke, but found no appearance of any secret passage, eyther to the Chappel or to the Lough: neyther would the nature of the ground suffer it, in a word this Cave was a poore beggarly hole, made with some stones, layed together with mens hands without any great Art: and after covered with Earth, such as husbandmen make to keepe a few Hogs from the raine. When I could finde nothing there, I undermined the Chappel, which was well covered with shingles, and brought all down together. Then wee brake down the Circles and Saints Beds, which were like so many Colepits.

Presumably Spottiswoode took the trouble of demolishing the saints' beds (which were, remember, nothing more than low-lying circles of loose stones) along with the chapel and the cave, because these beds were just what commentators like O'Clery and Jones said they were, stations whose associated rounding rituals were central to the pilgrimage experience there.

Given the architectural simplicity of the structures on Station Island, it is not surprising that the site was rebuilt. Just when this happened, however, is not entirely clear. That it was rebuilt to some extent by the 1640s seems evident if only because we have references to a second demolition, this time by Puritan forces. Writing to the Holy See in 1649, for example, the papal nuncio Giovanni Rinuccini says of St. Patrick's Purgatory : "At present, the fury of the Calvinists has leveled everything with the ground, and filled up the cave; and as thus they destroyed every vestige of the spot, so do they seek to cancel every trace of its memory" (cited in Moran 1864, 336–37).

An even more graphic account of what appears to be the same event appears in a Jesuit report written in 1651: "The Parliamentary cavalry and foot soldiers were sent against this island in an infuriated attempt and with an irreligious mob they expelled the Franciscan friars who had care of the sacred place.[8] So that no insult might be wanting they profaned with filth the crypt itself or Purgatory and then filled it up with earth and stones" (cited in Millett 1964, 303). This second demolition, like the first, does not appear to have put an end to the pilgrimage experience for very long, if at all. In 1660, the archbishop of Armagh asked the Holy See to grant a plenary indulgence for pilgrims who visited twelve pilgrimage sites in Ireland, and St. Patrick's Purgatory was one of the twelve (Millett 1964, 304). This suggests that by 1660 at least a few pilgrims were still coming to this site.

Whatever was happening at St. Patrick's Purgatory in the last half of the seventeenth century, it was once again a major pilgrimage site in the early eighteenth century (see figure 9). The Penal Legislation passed in 1703, for instance, makes explicit reference not only to the large number of Catholics who gather at holy wells to celebrate patterns but also to the large numbers who flock to St. Patrick's Purgatory: "Whereas the superstitions of popery are greatly increased and upheld by the pretended sanctity of places especially of a place called St. Patrick's Purgatory in the county of Donegal, and of wells to which pilgrimages are made by vast numbers at certain seasons. All such meetings and assemblies shall be adjudged riots and unlawful" (cited in Burke 1969, 445). Moreover, and notwithstanding the penal legislation, an account of St. Kevin's life compiled in the 1730s identifies St. Patrick's Purgatory as one of the four most popular pilgrimage sites in all of Ireland (the other three being Croagh Patrick, Monaincha, and Glendalough; see Plummer 1968 [1922], 156).

In the eighteenth century, as in the seventeenth century, rounding rituals were central to the pilgrimage experience at Lough Derg. Writing in 1764, a Protestant visitor to Station Island described it this way:

> There are seven heaps of rude stone with each of them a cross at top, about five or six yards from one another. [Around each] is a circular row of the like stones not above a yard in height. . . . The pilgrim is obliged to foot it without shoes or stocking, nine times round the outside of each [circle] on a path consisting of very rough and sharp stones . . . and besides divide his attention from the Ave maries and Pater-nosters, whereof he is to mumble a certain number. . . . When this is over, he is sent to traverse on his bare knees the shorter paths within each [stone circle], and round the little heap nine times. . . . After this he is admitted into purgatory. (Anonymous 1766, 61)

This passage makes it clear, however, that a few of the details associated with these rounding rituals had changed. First, the number of times each saint's bed had to be rounded is now nine (rather than three or seven given in earlier accounts, like those summarized in table 3.1). This is just one more piece of evidence supporting the claim that the precise number of roundings associated with a station is less important than the general emphasis on repetition. Second, each of the stone circles (saints' beds) on Station Island has now acquired a stone cairn in its center. This feature establishes even more firmly the essential similarity between the rounding rituals performed at Lough Derg and those performed at local holy wells, where Irish Catholics also rounded stone cairns of this sort.

Pilgrims continued to flock to Patrick's Purgatory during the nineteenth and twentieth centuries, and all accounts from these periods attest to the continuing centrality of stations and rounding rituals (in addition to the accounts already cited, see Carleton 1867, 236–70; Fahey 1891; see also figure 10 herein). Indeed, stations and rounding rituals are still central to the penitential activities on Station Island (Lehrhaupt 1985). The "cave" that had been such an important part of the site's reputation during the Middle Ages was dismantled for safety reasons in 1780; subsequently pilgrims spent their twenty-four-hour period of isolation in a succession of "prison chapels." The last of these chapels was replaced by a basilica built on Station Island in the period 1926–31. By the early 1980s, Station Island was attracting on average twenty thousand pilgrims during the summer months ("J.E." 1984, 20). Taylor (1992, 175) estimates that the number is now more like thirty thousand.

I am not the first commentator to note that an emphasis on stations and rounding rituals, which is so much a part of the Lough Derg experience in the modern era, is entirely absent from medieval accounts of St. Patrick's Purgatory. On the contrary, this is something to which commentators writing in the early seventeenth century themselves called attention. Jones (1647, 11), for example, after presenting his readers with an account of the pilgrimage experience at St. Patrick's Purgatory as it appears in the "ancient" (i.e., medieval) manuscripts, notes explicitly that that experience has changed in the recent past, both because greater numbers are now coming to Station Island and because new "circumstances" have been added to their activities there:

New Rituals for Old at Patrick's Purgatory

Thus it [the pilgrimage experience] has been Anciently: by which it doth seeme that the Resort to this Purgatory was not then so frequent, and they that did come were not easily admitted: but by all (at least seeming) meanes to be diverted: The contrary to both which is now practised, no place more frequented; and the more the welcommer, which being considered, and that there is much more stirre in the later pilgrimages than formerly had been, with the Addition of many more circumstances; it will be necessarie to take a second view of the particulars.

The particulars that Jones goes on to describe, and which in his view have given rise to the "much more stirre" evident in the modern pilgrimage experience at St. Patrick's Purgatory, are the rounding rituals and ascetic practices summarized in column three of table 3.1.

But if stations and rounding rituals were not part of the medieval experience at St. Patrick's Purgatory, just when did they become central? Fortunately, what we have in the case of St. Patrick's Purgatory (and what we don't have in the case of the devotions at holy wells and other sites) is documentary evidence that allows us to assess the timing and sequencing of the changes that led to the emergence of these new rituals.

Moving Back a Bit

In 1481 the English printer William Caxton published his translation of the thirteenth-century French work *Image du Monde*. Following a passage describing the torments encountered by pilgrims to St. Patrick's Purgatory, Caxton felt compelled to insert the following comment:

> I haue spoken with dyuerse men that haue ben therin. And that one of them was a hye chanon of Waterford whiche told me that he had ben therin v or vi times. And he sawe ne suffred no suche thynges. He saith that with procession the Relygious men that ben there brynge hym in to the hool and shette the dore after hym. . . . And there he was all the nyght in comtemplacion & prayer, and also slepte there; and on the morn he cam out agayn. Other while in their slepe somme men hauve meruayllous dremes. & other thyne sawe he not.

Easting (1988, 80) cites Caxton's remarks to indicate that by the late fifteenth century the age of apparitions at St. Patrick's Purgatory was in decline—and likely that is correct. But equally significant, I think, and easily overlooked, is Caxton's remark that a cleric from Waterford, which is at the opposite end of Ireland, had been on pilgrimage to St. Patrick's Purgatory five or six times. What Caxton's remark indicates, in other words, is that by the late fifteenth century Irish pilgrims from as far away as Waterford were coming—and coming back —to St. Patrick's Purgatory even though they were no longer experiencing the visions so favored in medieval accounts.

In 1494 or thereabouts, an Augustinian friar from the Netherlands came to Ireland to visit the famous "cave" at Lough Derg. Not only (he would later report) was he beset at every point in his journey by clerics asking for money, but when he was eventually allowed to enter the cave he experienced no visions during his twenty-four-hour period of isolation. Upon his return to the Continent, the man made his way to Rome and lodged a complaint with Church authorities. After considering the matter, Pope Alexander V ordered the purgatorial cave dismantled. Whether the order was carried out or not is a matter of some debate.[9] We do know that within a decade St. Patrick's Purgatory was once again attracting pilgrims. In 1507, the prior of St. Patrick's Purgatory wrote a letter certifying that an Irish priest named Nylanus O'Ledan has "performed all the pilgrimages of the island of the said Purgatory and has stayed in the ditch of the same St. Patrick" (cited in Bieler 1958). The reference to a "ditch" (*fossa* in the original Latin) suggests that the cave, if indeed it had been dismantled, had been rebuilt. But perhaps the most important element in the prior's letter is his reference to "the pilgrimages of the island." This is the first documentary source which indicates that "pilgrimages" were being performed on the island itself. The prior's letter gives no indication as to what these "pilgrimages" involved, but a fairly detailed account of St. Patrick's Purgatory written only a few years later does.

Francesco Chiericati (1480–1539) had been sent as papal nuncio to the court of the young King Henry VIII in 1515. In July 1517, Chiericati traveled to Ireland with a group of pilgrims in order to visit St. Patrick's Purgatory. Returning to London a few weeks later, he found it seething with plague and left immediately for the Continent. His

New Rituals for Old at Patrick's Purgatory

account of his trip to St. Patrick's Purgatory appears in a letter he wrote to his friend Isabella d'Este of Mantua while traveling through the Spanish Netherlands. In this letter Chiericati says that his party made their way through various Irish towns and finally arrived at the shores of Lough Derg. There they were ferried over to the island containing the Purgatory by a servant of the Canons Regular of St. Augustine. The only buildings on the island—and Chiericati is clearly describing Station Island—were a small church (more "like an oratory" he says), two huts (one for the three resident canons and one for pilgrims), the cave itself, and "tre campane" (literally: "three bells") dedicated respectively to St. Brigid, St. Patrick, and St. Columba.

Chiericati's use of the term "tre campane" has always been problematic for translators. Julia Cartwright (1903, 178) renders *tre campane* as "three cabins" (possibly misreading *campane* as *capanne*). Mary Purcell (1987, 7) translates *campane* as "bell-shaped cells"—and maybe she's correct in guessing at what Chiericati was trying to convey. After all, beehive-shaped cells (which might very well be described as "bell-shaped") are commonly encountered at pilgrimage sites associated with the regular clergy in Ireland and could well have existed on Station Island. On the other hand, Chiericati's words may simply be garbled. In his later account Jones (1647, 7) says that the station called St. Patrick's Altar (near the church) was a "heape of stones" surmounted by a cross, on which lay "three pieces of a bell" carried by Patrick. Getting confused about pilgrims visiting these "three pieces of a bell" and their visiting three structures dedicated to Patrick, Brigid, and Columba might easily have led a foreign observer like Chiericati to say something about visiting "tre campane" dedicated to these three saints. Whatever the precise nature of the three structures visited by pilgrims in Chiericati's account, the fact that these structures were dedicated to three of the same saints (Patrick, Bridget, Columba) who would be found associated with the stone circles on Station Island a century later suggests that these structures were at least the precursors of those stone circles.

Chiericati did not take part in the penitential exercises at Lough Derg but he did describe them. He tells us that the experience lasted ten days and that for the first nine days pilgrims fasted by subsisting on bread and water. They were also required to visit the three saintly "campane" for several hours each day and while there to say a number of prayers ("hanno a visitare tante hore del iorno tutte tre quelle campane de sancti con dir alcun numero de orationi"; Purcell 1987, 4). Pilgrims also had to stand in the lake itself on a daily basis and pray. Some pilgrims, he says, immersed themselves up to their knees, while others immersed themselves up to their waists, and still others up to their necks. On the tenth day, pilgrims entered the cave itself as a group (in this case two pilgrims traveling with Chiericati entered with five other pilgrims) and were shut inside for the standard twenty-four hours. The cave itself now had a small window, a feature unmentioned in medieval accounts.[10] One of the canons stationed himself outside that window and constantly preached to the pilgrims inside so that they might not give in to diabolical temptations.

The significance of Chiericati's account lies in its being the first to tell us, in a clear and explicit way, that pilgrims to St. Patrick's Purgatory were visiting stations. Just as they would do a century later, the pilgrims observed by Chiericati went to the saints' beds several times throughout the day and also went out into the lake, and in each of these locations they said prayers. True, the stational emphasis seems less developed than it would become (there are no stations around the church, for instance, and there are only three saints' beds, not seven), but it is present for the first time.

It should be noted, however, that the stational emphasis which seems to have been emerging at Lough Derg in the early sixteenth century was not distinctively Irish. On the contrary, a stational emphasis can be detected in religious devotions that were becoming popular throughout Europe during this same period. The most well known example of this would be the Stations of the Cross. In this devotion each "station" is a picture depicting some event associated with Christ's Passion. Sometimes these pictures were affixed to the interior walls of a church; quite often they were affixed to freestanding structures (stone pillars, for instance) erected out of doors. Devotees move from station to station, meditate on the Passion event depicted, and pray some combination of Our Fathers and Hail Marys. Although there are fourteen stations in the modern form of the devotion, the number of stations in the earliest known version of the devotion was more usually seven or eight. The historical evidence (reviewed in Carroll 1989, 41–56) suggests that the Stations of the Cross emerged as a popular devotion in the German-speaking regions of Europe during the last half of the fifteenth century (which, remember, makes the emergence of this devotion more or less contemporaneous with the emergence of a stational emphasis at Lough Derg), and from there spread slowly to other parts of the Catholic world.

The Stations of the Cross aside, certain churches in the city of Rome had for centuries been "station churches," and people going in procession to these churches on designated days could earn an indulgence (Leclercq 1912). During the jubilee year of 1575 the guidebook prepared for the tens of thousands of pilgrims who visited the city from all over Europe made a special point of informing them about where these station churches were and what were the days on which indulgences could be earned. The title page of this guidebook (reproduced in Carroll 1992, fig. 15), for example, says specifically that it will tell readers where to find "the churches, stations and relics of saintly bodies." This is to say that the tens of thousands of pilgrims who flooded into Rome, especially during the 1575 Jubilee, were exposed to a devotion that had a strong stational emphasis, and it was a devotion associated with the most important religious center in Catholic Europe.

I am not suggesting that the Stations of the Cross or the practice of visiting stational churches in Rome served as models for the stational emphasis that was inserted into the pilgrim experience at Lough Derg. In the context of Catholic lay piety in the sixteenth century, my point is only that a stational emphasis was much "in the air" at a variety of European locations, and so the simple fact that the practice of visiting stations was now a part of the Lough Derg experience would not have struck observers of the time as distinctively Irish.

But if the stational emphasis emerging at Lough Derg was not distinctively Irish, other changes taking place there were. Here we need to focus on two other elements that are also mentioned for the first time in Chiericati's account. First, the "campane" on Station Island were said to be dedicated to St. Patrick, St. Bridget, and St. Columba. The choice of these three saints is hardly fortuitous: for centuries they had been regarded as the three "national" patrons of Ireland, and Church authorities in Ireland had in the past tried to make use of this fact when trying to co-opt the allegiance of Irish Catholics. In 1185, for instance, a mysterious light guided Malachi, the newly installed bishop of Down, to a particular spot in the Down Cathedral when he found the forgotten grave containing the bodies of these same three saints. Malachi immediately communicated news of the discovery to John De Courcy, the Anglo-Norman Lord of Down, and together they petitioned the pope to have the relics installed in a place of honor in the cathedral. The pope's permission was secured and the requested installation took place amidst much pomp and ceremony.[11]

Although not common in Ireland, the formula evident in this story ("mysterious light reveals hidden location of sacred object") was commonly encountered in connection with relic and image cults in Continental European societies during the Middle Ages. The bishop of Down was obviously importing this formula into Ireland in order to create a devotion that would secure the allegiance of Irish Catholics. In this case the stratagem did not work. As Taylor (1995, 46) points out, the relics of these three saints never did become the focus of a widely popular pilgrimage. Nevertheless, the fact that these same three saints (and only these three saints) are found associated with the "tre campane" at St. Patrick's Purgatory in Chiericati's account suggests that once again an attempt was being made to co-opt Irish national sentiment in aid of a popular devotion.

A second indication that the devotions at Lough Derg were becoming more distinctively Irish is evident in Chiericati's observation that after visiting the saints' beds pilgrims stood in the water of the lake to pray. "Standing in cold water" to pray was an ascetic practice that various medieval accounts had long associated with early Irish saints. St. Patrick in particular was supposed to have routinely stood in the cold waters of a spring or river to pray. *Fíacc's Hymn* (Stokes 1887, 2:407–8), for instance, says of Patrick that

> The weather's cold kept him not from staying at night in
> riverpools . . .
> In [the fountain] Slán, in the region of Benna Boirche, which
> neither drought nor flood affected,
> He sang a hundred psalms every night, to the angels' King he
> was a servant.

New Rituals for Old at Patrick's Purgatory

Likewise, the "Homily on St. Patrick" in the *Lebar Brecc* (Stokes 1887, 2:485) says that standing in cold water was one of the penitential activities that Patrick performed each night. The Irish pilgrims at Lough Derg who went into the cold waters of the lake to pray could hardly have failed to make a connection between what they were doing and what Patrick himself had done.

Despite the increasing "Irishness" of the rituals at St. Patrick's Purgatory that seems evident from Chiericati's account, it is once again necessary to take note of what is still missing. Chiericati makes no mention of anything resembling rounding rituals. Could pilgrims have been rounding stations and Chiericati simply have failed to report this? Although this is a possibility that can never be ruled out, a consideration of the man himself makes it unlikely.

Francesco Chiericati was a Renaissance diplomat used to the good life in various royal courts of Europe,[12] and his report reflects this. Thus, even after describing the rigors that pilgrims underwent for ten days (fasting, prayers, praying in water, being enclosed in the cave), he could still say to his friend Isabella d'Este that "nevertheless, the greater penance was mine" because he had had to wait around for those ten days, with nothing to do but consume the provisions his party had brought with them (see Purcell 1987, 4). Chiericati was also a humanist scholar in sympathy with the work of other humanist scholars, Erasmus in particular, who poked gentle fun at the excesses so associated with popular piety during this period. Indeed, on the very same day (28 August 1517) that he despatched his letter to Isabella d'Este concerning St. Patrick's Purgatory, Chiericati also sent a letter to Erasmus. In that letter (Erasmus 1975, 88–89) he expresses regret at having just missed the chance to meet Erasmus at Antwerp (Erasmus had been visiting there, but had returned to Louvain the day before Chiericati arrived) and affirms his admiration for Erasmus's scholarship and his willingness to be of service to him in any way he can.

At one point in his account of Lough Derg, Chiericati pokes gentle fun at the pilgrimage experience on Station Island in a manner that seems distinctly Erasmian. Chiericati tells Isabella that he talked to the pilgrims as they exited the cave. Only two reported anything out of the ordinary. One man came out nearly unconscious and said that he had been severely beaten, although by whom he did not know.

The second said that he had seen several women with gorgeous figures ("diverse donne de bellissima forma") who offered him food and shouted insistently that he should join them in general merrymaking. To Isabella d'Este and the other humanists in her circle at Mantua, the implications of such a passage would be obvious: the so-called visions at St. Patrick's Purgatory had less to do with the supernatural than with processes far more carnal and mundane. After all, it is hardly surprising that there might be some pushing and shoving when seven men who had been starved for nine days were subsequently squeezed into a small chamber for twenty-four hours, nor is it surprising that after nine days of fasting at least one of those men—all of whom were naked—might start thinking about food and sex.

Given his Erasmian predilections, it seems likely that Chiericati would have reported any devotional practice that would have struck his humanist friends at Mantua as unusual. This is presumably why he did report that Lough Derg pilgrims were regularly wading into the cold waters of the lake to pray. But he did not report rounding, even though the sight of pilgrims walking round and round the "campane" (or any other stations) on several occasions during the course of a day would certainly have qualified as unusual. Chiericati's silence with regard to rounding is, I suggest, best explained on the hypothesis that by the early 1500s rounding rituals were not as yet a part of the Lough Derg experience.

Reaching Conclusions

There is no denying that the various accounts of St. Patrick's Purgatory over the centuries are sketchy in regard to matters that are of paramount interest to modern investigators. Nevertheless, imperfect as they are, these accounts provide us with something that we have for no other location in Ireland: a continuous overview of devotional practice at this site over the course of eight centuries. What has emerged from the analysis of those accounts is that the pilgrim experience at St. Patrick's Purgatory underwent a series of transformations over the centuries.

When St. Patrick's Purgatory first emerges as important pilgrimage site (in the twelfth century) it is for the most part a European pilgrimage site that happens to attract male pilgrims, only a few of which were Irish, and the central experiences at the site were fasting, enclosure in the cave, and the experience of visions. By the end of the fifteenth century and the beginning of the sixteenth, however, this older pattern was being undermined. Irish pilgrims, both male and female, were coming to the site in larger and larger numbers, and many were coming on a regular basis. Moreover the medieval emphasis on the experience of otherworldly visions in the cave had faded, and the devotions performed there were coming more and more to be permeated both by the stational emphasis that was becoming popular in Europe generally and by emphases that were distinctively Irish (e.g., the association of stations with Irish "national" saints like Bridget, Columba, and Patrick, and the performance of ascetic practices associated with early Irish saints).[13]

A third and final phase in the development of the devotions at St. Patrick's Purgatory seems to have begun after the Reformation. Sometime in that confused period that runs from about 1520 to about 1620, when organizational structure of both the Catholic Church and the newly established Church of Ireland were in a weakened state, the stational emphasis seen emerging in the early 1500s became more pronounced (mainly through an increase in the simple number of stations), and rounding rituals became central to the Lough Derg experience for the first time.

A Hypothesis

If rounding rituals only became central to the Lough Derg experience after the Reformation, then an obvious hypothesis suggests itself: perhaps the repetitive rounding of holy wells and other stations in general, whether in the context of individual devotions or during the course of patterns attended by hundreds or thousands of people, was also a post-Reformation phenomenon. What I am suggesting is that the variant of popular Catholicism in which holy well cults, patterns, and so forth were central is every bit as much "invented tradition" as the kilts and tartans of Scotland, the Welsh mabsant, and the clachans along Ireland's Atlantic periphery—and that the invention of this particular tradition occurred in the post-Reformation era. If such a hypothesis is correct, this would mean that previous commentators have not only been incorrect in seeing this variant of Catholicism as deriving from a distant pagan-Celtic past, they have been wrong to see it as premodern.

One caveat: it should be kept firmly in mind that my argument is not about "origins." Holy well cults may not have been a feature of Celtic religion in Ireland, but—as already mentioned—some sacred springs dedicated to Christian saints have always existed in Christian Ireland, just as similar springs have always existed in many other areas of Christian Europe. Further, although there is no documentary evidence associating sacred springs with rounding rituals prior to the Reformation, it would be folkloric foolhardiness to state categorically that no one in any region of pre-Reformation Ireland ever thought to walk round a holy well, especially since occasional instances of rounding are found in a variety of religious traditions. The matter of "origins" aside, however, what I am suggesting is that holy well cults, patterns, rounding rituals, and so forth—in short, the whole panorama of elements that made Irish popular Catholicism before the Famine so distinctive—only become widely popular in the period following the Reformation.

My argument does require that the great majority of holy well cults found in post-Reformation Ireland were new creations, that is, that most of these cults sprang into existence in association with springs that had not previously been the focus of cultic rituals. Is this plausible? Is it plausible to suggest that holy well cults and rounding rituals could spring into existence ex nihilo at a particular location? In fact we have some documentary evidence indicating just how easily this could occur.

Hackett (1861–62, 268), for example, says that sometime around 1840 the Rev. John Power of Ballyhaloe died and that a year later

> on the very first anniversary of his death, a vast crowd of people assembled at this grave, not only from the immediate neighborhood but from distant parts of the country. This attracted the notice of two young clergymen, curates of the Catholic parish. On visiting the spot, they found the whole ritual of rounds going on just as it would do at any old established pattern; a certain number of Paters, Aves, and Credos being said at particular stations which appeared to be well known to the multitude. . . . The pat-

tern thus originating at Roscarbery has gradually increased every year, and is now as celebrated as any of the great sites of pilgrimage in Ireland.

In this case, of course, rounding rituals coalesced around a grave, not a well, but it does demonstrate the ease with which rounding rituals could be attached to a site only recently become "holy." In any event, there is other evidence suggesting it was not at all difficult to transform ordinary springs into holy wells that then became the focus of cultic activity.

Hackett (1861–62, 268) also reports that sometime around 1820 the location of a "hidden" holy well was revealed in a dream to a woman who was spending the night in the parish of Ballynoe (County Cork). With the help of some of the local inhabitants, the story continues, the woman subsequently found and uncovered the well and it became the center of a cult that attracted devotees from as far away as the cities of Cork and Waterford. Philip Dixon Hardy (1840, 64–65) reports a similar story. Sometime around the year 1795, he says, the parish priest in the parish of Marmalane, near Monkstown (County Cork) had a dream that a certain nearby well would prove to be miraculous. Upon awaking he promptly went to the well and blessed it and dedicated it to Saints Peter and Paul, whose feast was being celebrated that day. Very quickly, we are told, this well became the object of cultic devotions and "the usual observances followed on the part of the surrounding peasantry . . . similar to those which have heretofore been described in like places of superstitious fame" (by which Hardy is presumably referring to rounding rituals and votive offerings of the sort described elsewhere in his book).

Finally, writing in 1665, the Franciscan Anthony Bruodin (cited in Westropp 1911, 212) says that in 1632 the wife of one of his kinsmen living at Kilmihil (County Clare) had a dream in which the Archangel Michael appeared to her and told her to dig at a spot near a local church where rushes grew. Aided by her son and her parish priest, she did as she was told and uncovered a well. The story goes on to say that water from this well not only cured the woman herself of the gout from which she had long suffered but gave similar relief to other people. Even if the story is apocryphal, the more important point I think is that Bruodin appears not to have seen anything unusual in a holy well coming into existence in this way nor in the fact that a member of the local clergy was actively involved in establishing this particular well cult.

Most holy wells in Ireland are not associated with stories that locate their origin in the recent past, but then for most holy wells we simply have no information whatsoever on when and how they came into existence. I am suggesting that the process of "creating" holy well cults that seems evident in these stories was far more common than has previously been acknowledged.

The Silence of the Historical Record

Patrick Corish (private communication, 1996) has rightly cautioned against the dangers in making arguments about the history of Irish Catholicism "from silence," that is, from the absence of evidence. For a variety of reasons, the documentary record relating to Irish Catholicism prior to the Famine is scanty, and in many cases we simply will never know with any certainty what most Irish Catholics were doing (let alone what they were thinking) in the course of their daily lives. Professor Corish's point is well taken. But the silence of the historical record, I suggest, should be seen as an intellectually liberating condition. If we know so little, in other words, then we should be wary of a too rigid commitment to one particular view of history, like the view that Irish popular Catholicism has its origins in far-off Celtic mists, and be more willing to entertain alternatives, so long as those alternatives are equally consistent with the evidence that is available. One of those alternatives is the one being offered here: that the distinctive variant of popular Catholicism which flourished in pre-Famine Ireland was actually a post-Reformation phenomenon. Furthermore, as I now want to argue, an advantage of considering this particular alternative is that it allows us to detect patterns in the historical record that have been missed because of the scholarly over-reliance on the Celtic origins hypothesis.

Chapter Four

Ireland's Catholic Heartland

Some time ago Emmet Larkin (1972) argued that there had been a "devotional revolution" in Ireland in the aftermath of the Famine. The devotional revolution, he claimed, was most evident in connection with attendance at Sunday Mass. Whereas only about 33 percent of the Catholic population went to Mass before the Famine, this figure rose to well over 90 percent. But post-Famine Irish Catholics did more than just attend church more often. They embraced the whole gamut of devotions then being promoted by the Roman hierarchy as a way of standardizing Catholic practice throughout the world, including devotion to the Sacred Heart of Jesus, the Immaculate Conception of Mary, the Stations of the Cross, the Brown Scapular of Our Lady of Mt. Carmel, the Forty Hours, and others. There was also a dramatic increase in the use of rosaries, medals, novenas, retreats, triduums, and processions. The net result, Larkin claimed, was that within something very close to a single generation the majority of Irish Catholics became *practicing* Catholics for the first time.

Although Larkin's article continues to be cited favorably by many scholars (especially those who want to make a passing reference to Irish Catholicism in the context of discussing something else), specialists in Irish religious history have challenged his argument on several grounds. Some of his critics argue that what Larkin saw as a "revolution" taking place within a single generation was really an "evolution" that took place over a much longer time frame. Desmond Keenan (1983), for example, points out that many of the supposedly new devotions that Larkin noted had in fact been introduced in Ireland several decades before the Famine. Thomas McGrath (1991) makes a similar argument, suggesting that Larkin's devotional revolution is just the tail-end of a "Tridentine renewal" that began in the late 1700s, as the Church was freed from the debilitating effects of the Penal Laws and started to rebuild its organizational base in Ireland. Other critics have focused upon a relatively specific issue: the data used by Larkin to assess attendance at Sunday Mass.

Central to Larkin's argument is his assertion that rates of attendance at Sunday Mass jumped dramatically in the post-Famine period. In his original article he supported this claim using unpublished data on Mass attendance collected by David Miller (and subsequently published in Miller 1975). Patrick Corish (1985, 166–67) argues that Miller's estimates are systematically low because he did not take into account the fact that certain categories of people (such as children under seven and nursing mothers) were not under a canonical obligation to attend Mass. Just as importantly, Corish suggests, is the fact that there was great regional variation with regard to rates of Mass attendance. Miller (1975, 86) had himself pointed this out by noting that rates of weekly attendance at Mass were higher in English-speaking rural communities in eastern and southern Ireland than in Irish-speaking rural communities located in northern and western Ireland. Corish points out that rates of Mass attendance were highest (often coming close to 100 percent when allowances are made for those categories not under obligation to attend) in the towns and cities, a little lower in "rural English-speaking areas," and lower still in "rural Irish-speaking areas."

In the end, then, evidence has accumulated since the publication of Larkin's original article suggesting that the devotional revolution which he took to be a post-Famine phenomenon was already "in place"—at least in the urbanized and English-speaking regions of Ireland—by the 1830s. Still, although critics like Keenan, Corish, and McGrath are quite explicit in seeing their work as falsifying Larkin's argument, whether or not this is the case depends upon what we take Larkin's claim to be. If Larkin is arguing that the sort of Catholicism that became widely popular in Ireland after the Famine had not been established anywhere in Ireland prior to the Famine, then clearly he was wrong. On the other hand, if his claim is only that there was a dramatic change in religious practice in Ireland as a whole, then just as clearly he was right. After all, although Miller and Corish come up with different estimates for the rates of Mass attendance in particular areas, this should not blind us—as Miller (1986) himself points out—to the finding that is common to both of their studies: in pre-Famine Ireland rates of Mass attendance were substantially lower in some regions than in others. It is precisely this regional variation which vanished in post-Famine Ireland, when rates of attendance rose to over 90 percent of the Catholic population in all areas.

In summary, then, there *was* a dramatic change in the texture of Irish Catholicism after the Famine, at least at the national level, but the devotional style that defines this change did not emerge ex nihilo. On the contrary, a strong commitment to the rituals and practices of the official Church, including attendance at Sunday Mass, was very much in evidence in certain areas of the country, areas that we might reasonably call Ireland's "Catholic heartland." The already-cited figures on Mass attendance in the 1830s presented by both Miller and Corish suggest that this Catholic heartland was located mainly in the urbanized and Anglicized areas of Munster and Leinster. Subsequent research by other investigators indicates that this area had been a bastion of Tridentine Catholicism for centuries.

A Dynamic and Vibrant Culture

Kevin Whelan (1988; 1990a; 1990b; 1991) has used a variety of indicators to establish fairly precisely which areas of Ireland were most committed to Tridentine Catholicism during the eighteenth century. One of the Penal Laws passed in the early 1700s required "Popish clergy" to register with the government. As part of the registration process, priests were required to give the place of their ordination. Whelan suggests that the critical variable here is whether priests were ordained in Ireland or on the Continent. Since Continental-trained priests were far more likely than their Irish-trained counterparts to be committed to Tridentine ideals, he argues, the distribution of Continental-trained priests provides a rough measure of the degree to which local Catholic communities were exposed to these ideals. Plotting out the distribution of Continental-trained priests reveals a clear geographical pattern. First, there was a strong concentration of such priests in a broad band that stretches from Wexford in the east to Limerick in the west. Second, such priests were also concentrated in the Pale area (Dublin, northern Kildare, Meath, and Louth).

Whelan looks at several other indicators that might also be taken as measures of the degree to which Tridentine Catholicism was implanted in an area (e.g., the use of a parish register prior to 1775; birthplace by county of the regular clergy in Ireland). Whatever the measure used, these same two regions—the Pale area and that portion of east Munster / south Leinster falling widely on either side of a Limerick-Wexford axis—emerge as the areas of Ireland that were most committed to the Catholicism favored by the official Church. For the Dublin area specifically, Whelan's work supplements earlier studies which demonstrate that by the mid-1700s Dublin had a Catholic majority, a well-defined and well-organized parish structure, and relatively high rates of weekly attendance at Mass (see Corish 1985, 12–28; Burke 1974).

In short, it appears that those areas of Ireland that were characterized by relatively high rates of weekly Mass attendance during the 1830s were already bastions of official Catholicism during the eighteenth century. While such a conclusion, I suspect, will not surprise many readers, it is a point that must be made explicitly, if only because historians (see, for instance, Corish 1985, 187) have rightly cautioned against automatically assuming that patterns of religious behavior found in the 1830s were of long-standing duration.

A commitment to Tridentine Catholicism was not the only thing that made the Catholic heartland distinctive. This was an area characterized by the presence of Catholic big farms and the presence of established towns (i.e., towns that predated the seventeenth-century plantations) with large Catholic populations. Moreover, in Whelan's reconstruction, it was very much an area with strong ties to Continental Europe. In particular, Catholic merchants in the towns, especially the important port towns of the south (and here Whelan names Cork, Waterford, Limerick, and Dublin) were strongly linked to mercantile communities in Catholic Europe and so had access to Continental ideas and fashions. These same merchants were linked by ties of kinship and cultural affinity to large-scale Catholic farmers living elsewhere in the heartland. These dense social linkages meant that new ideas could and did move easily from Europe to Catholic elites in towns and cities, and from there to Catholic elites in the countryside. But influence flowed in the opposite direction—from rural to urban areas—as well. Whelan argues that the ties of kinship and cultural affinity between urban and rural Catholic elites produced a "symbiosis of town and country" which ensured that "urban consciousness [was attuned] to the rhythms and exigencies of rural life, perhaps to an extent unrivalled elsewhere in urban Europe" (1988, 259–60).

Generally, Whelan suggests, the Catholic heartland, especially in that broad band that lay astride the Wexford/Limerick axis, was a dynamic society which freely borrowed from a variety of traditions —Gaelic, Old English, and Continental European—in order to create new cultural forms that met modern needs. In his own words:

> [This] core area, then, was not just an anglicised modernising sector but one which had deep roots in the tradition of the area, which in turn was a product of the hybrid Norman [Old English]-Gaelic world which developed here in the late medieval period. . . . The Catholic core area [also] exhibited archaic and modern features cheek by jowl, in a form of radical conservatism, i.e., the ability to graft innovations onto traditional stock or to develop new solutions (administrative, technical) to old problems. (Whelan 1988, 271)

Whelan, remember, is here describing the culture of the Catholic heartland during the eighteenth century, but other investigators have reached much the same conclusions in considering this region during the seventeenth century.

The seventeenth century was a time of rapid social change in Ireland as ownership of most of the land was transferred from older Catholic owners to a new Protestant elite. This transfer of ownership is documented in a number of surviving records (the Civil Survey of 1654; the Down Survey; records of the 1660 poll tax; etc.), and William Smyth (1992) uses these sources in order to reconstruct a number of regional patterns in Ireland. For example, these seventeenth-century records show that east Munster and south Leinster (the same area identified as part of the Catholic heartland in Whelan's studies) was characterized by a relatively high concentration of townlands with an adult population of forty or more. Smyth (1992, 261–62) argues that such townlands would have ensured that this particular area of Ireland would have been characterized by a social heterogeneity and complexity not found in the more sparsely settled (and more purely Gaelic) areas of Ulster and Connaught. Similarly, using the evidence provided by naming patterns, he (1992, 250) concludes that this same area (east Munster and south Leinster) was characterized by a hybrid culture that merged elements from both Gaelic-Irish and Old English traditions. Smyth's analysis, in other words, complements Whelan's by suggesting that the culture that prevailed in east Munster / south Leinster during the seventeenth century was every bit as vibrant, and every bit as willing to borrow from both Gaelic and Anglo-Irish traditions, as would be the case in the eighteenth century.

Unfortunately, neither Smyth nor Whelan is much concerned with holy well cults, rounding rituals, pilgrimage, or any other aspect of popular Catholic practice. Smyth ignores popular Catholicism entirely, and Whelan, to the extent that he discusses religious practice at all, summarily contrasts the Tridentine Catholicism of the Catholic heartland with the Gaelic Catholicism of the north and west, with its emphasis on pilgrimage and on "a complex web of archaic beliefs and practices of a magical or naturalistic kind, dismissed as superstitious by the official Church" (Whelan 1988, 271). His suggestion here that Gaelic Catholicism rests upon a "complex web of archaic beliefs" is of course a veiled reference to the pagan origins hypothesis we have already considered in chapter 2. Whelan seems clearly to be suggesting that participation in popular Catholic rituals (like rounding) and participation in the rituals of the official Church (like Sunday Mass) were mutually exclusive.

What must be emphasized, however, is that neither Whelan nor any other investigator has ever brought forward any evidence whatsoever indicating that rates of popular participation in holy well devotions, rounding rituals, pilgrimages, and so forth were higher in the more purely Gaelic areas of Ireland than in the Catholic heartland. Previous commentators, including Whelan, have simply assumed a priori that the commitment of heartland Catholics to Tridentine Catholicism would have precluded their attachment to (and participation in) these popular rituals. In fact, if we put this a priori assumption aside and take a fresh look at the historical record, we catch sight of some evidence suggesting that for heartland Catholics participation in the rituals associated with these two variants of Catholicism—popular and official—went hand in hand.

Ireland's Catholic Heartland

Assessing the Popularity of Popular Devotions

The *Annals of the Four Masters* tell us that in the year 606 a pilgrim died at Clonmacnois (County Offaly), making Clonmacnois the oldest known pilgrimage site in Ireland (see figures 11 and 12). Generally, the various annalistic sources allow us to identify two dozen or so sites in Ireland that were the objects of pilgrimage before the thirteenth century, and these sites—which included Clonmacnois, Armagh, Cork, Lismore, Lough Derg, Cong, Tuam, Skellig Michael, and others (see Harbison 1991, 51–54, for a full listing)—were scattered across the entire island.

Another list of Irish pilgrimage sites appears in the ecclesiastical records associated with the already-mentioned pilgrimage of Heneas MacNichaill. Sometime around 1545 MacNichaill asked absolution of the dean who was administering the Archdiocese of Armagh. Since MacNichaill's sin was grave (he had killed his own son), the dean imposed a stiff penance: MacNichaill was required to do public penance at no fewer than fifteen different pilgrimage sites in Ireland. Here again, these fifteen sites were located in a variety of different regions.[1]

Pilgrimage, then, has been an established practice in Ireland since the early Christian period, and no one area of Ireland had a monopoly on pilgrimage sites. Nevertheless, the simple fact that a pilgrimage site exists is not in itself evidence that that site was a popular site, that is, frequented by relatively large numbers of Irish pilgrims. As indicated earlier, pilgrimage in early Christian Ireland was conceptualized primarily as an ascetic and mystical experience, and social isolation—and in particular the experience of separating yourself from kin—was an integral part of the experience. The fact that some Irish Christians sought out pilgrimage to a particular site as a mystical and ascetic experience is no more evidence that that site was widely popular with Irish Catholics generally than, say, the experience of the stigmata by some Italian mystics would be evidence that "experiencing the stigmata" was a widely popular religious activity for ordinary Italian Catholics. The fact is that prior to the Reformation (the case of St. Patrick's Purgatory aside) we know little or nothing about the numbers of people coming to particular Irish pilgrimage sites.

Irish Pilgrimage

One of the earliest documentary sources that does provide information about the relative popularity of different pilgrimage sites in Ireland appears at the beginning of the seventeenth century. In 1607 (or thereabouts) Paul V issued a brief to the "clergy, nobles and people of Catholic Ireland" in which he conceded a plenary indulgence to the faithful who visited certain popular pilgrimage sites (Hagan 1914, 260–64). Twelve such sites are named in this brief: Monaincha, Fore, Inishcealtra, Skellig Michael, Aran Islands, Croagh Patrick, Clonmacnois, Modreeny, Clane, Armagh, Clonmel, and Lady's Island. If we consider this list carefully in relation to the geography of Ireland, it becomes apparent that the sites fall roughly into two categories. First, several (notably Croagh Patrick, Aran of the Saints, and Skellig Michael) are located in sparsely settled areas of Ireland's Atlantic fringe and thus are relatively inaccessible, in the sense that they would have been difficult to access by anyone living any distance away. On the other hand, many of the sites listed in Paul V's brief (Clonmel, Our Lady's Island, Inishcealtra, Monaincha, Modreeny) were located in or very near the east Munster / south Leinster portion of the Catholic heartland. Counting the Pale area as part of the Catholic heartland, then Clane and Fore also fall into this "in or very near the Catholic Heartland" category. On the assumption that the crowds flocking to these pilgrimage sites were most likely to be from communities in the immediately surrounding region, it would seem that most of the "popular" pilgrimage sites in Ireland were popular because of their appeal to Catholics living in the heartland. Heartland Catholics, in short, were not just going to Mass at their local parish church in large numbers; they were going in large numbers as well to a variety of nearby pilgrimage sites.

A similar conclusion emerges from a consideration of a second list of "popular" pilgrimage sites, this one dating from the early eighteenth century. In an Irish-language life of St. Kevin transcribed around 1725, we are told that Kevin brought back some dirt from Rome and sprinkled it on his church at Glendalough in order to legitimize the church as an object of pilgrimage. Kevin's reputation for holiness, the account continues, ensured that Glendalough came to attract pilgrims from all over Ireland, and the result is that Glendalough "is one of the four great pilgrimages of Erin henceforth; to wit, the Cave of Patrick in Ulster [St. Patrick's Purgatory in Lough

Ireland's Catholic Heartland

Derg], Croagh Patrick in Connaught, Inis na m-Béo [Monaincha; see figure 13] in Munster and Glendalough in Leinster, where is Coemgen's [Kevin's] church" (Plummer 1968, 2:156). There are only four pilgrimage sites named in this second list, and two of these (St. Patrick's Purgatory and Glendalough) did not appear in Paul V's brief of a century earlier. Nevertheless, as short (and as different) as it is, this second list establishes the same geographical contrast established in Paul V's list: between "difficult to access pilgrimage sites located in sparsely settled areas of Ireland" (St. Patrick's Purgatory and Croagh Patrick) and "pilgrimage sites located in or very near the Catholic Heartland" (Monaincha and Glendalough).

It seems likely, then, that during the seventeenth and eighteenth centuries heartland Catholics were simultaneously embracing a Tridentine Catholicism imported from the Continent and flocking to nearby pilgrimage sites and (presumably) performing the rounding rituals that we know were associated with those sites. The upsurge in pilgrimage activity in Ireland following the Reformation did not go unnoticed by contemporary observers. Writing in 1611, for example, David Rothe, Bishop of Ossory, referred to "the fervour with which the faithful had begun of late years to visit the sanctuaries and hallowed pilgrimages frequented of old by their Fathers" (cited in Moran 1884, ciii). I might add that the Diocese of Ossory, which included County Kilkenny and the southeastern part of County Leix, was solidly a part of the Catholic heartland.

The dramatic increase in the popularity of pilgrimage that occurred during the early seventeenth century has not gone unnoticed by Irish historians; they simply have not devoted much attention to the phenomenon nor paid much attention to where in Ireland this dramatic increase was occurring. For instance, in his history of Ireland William Lecky (1913, 406) suggested simply that the Protestant prohibition of pilgrimages made these activities more appealing to Catholics. More recently Corish (1981, 50–51) acknowledges that the evidence for this surge in the popularity of pilgrimage activity is beyond question, but says only that a turning to traditional devotions "was only natural in times of such great strain." Summary judgments like these, however, hardly square with what we know about the Catholic heartland (which is, remember, where this upsurge seems to have occurred).

After all, the Catholic heartland that emerges from the work of Whelan and Smyth was a dynamic and heterogeneous society whose members borrowed from old and new traditions in order to create new cultural forms. We know that one of the traditions to which heartland Catholics turned during this period was the Tridentine Catholicism imported from Continental Europe. Indeed, it was a study of the distribution of Tridentine "markers" that first led Whelan to identify the boundaries of the heartland. But in the context of so dynamic and open a society, why assume that the upsurge in pilgrimage activity represents a "clinging to tradition" (as commentators like Corish would suggest)? The answer, of course, is that here again scholarly thinking has been shaped by an implicit commitment to the pagan origins hypothesis, that is, to the view that pilgrimage (and associated rituals, like rounding) are necessarily "traditional" activities inherited from a distant Celtic past. Putting this hypothesis aside, a much more plausible hypothesis is that the upsurge in pilgrimage activity following the Reformation, and the emergence (at least as far as the documentary record is concerned) of rounding rituals and holy well cults as truly popular activities during this same period, was a product of that creative impulse that we know (from the work of Whelan and Smyth) pervaded other aspects of heartland culture. This is the possibility I now want to explore, and the first step in that exploration involves challenging the view—also a legacy of the pagan origins hypothesis—that these popular rituals were first and foremost "peasant" activities.

The Social Composition of the Crowds at Popular Rituals

Which segments of the Catholic population in Ireland, particularly in the Catholic heartland, attended patterns and performed the rounding rituals at holy wells and other stations? Certainly most attendees were peasants—landless laborers and cottiers living in rural areas—if only because these groups constituted the bulk of the population. In addition, as already mentioned, we know that local priests were actively involved in these popular devotions, both because they assigned participation in these devotions as penances and because they themselves attended the patterns and said Mass, gave sermons, led the people in prayer, and so forth. But did other segments of the

population attend patterns on a regular basis? We have little information on this issue because few investigators bothered to record
the relevant information. Nevertheless, if we look carefully we find
some evidence suggesting that the social composition of the crowds
who participated in these popular devotions was more heterogeneous than has previously been acknowledged.

Writing in 1873, William Wilde described the annual pattern that
had been held at Glendalough, near Dublin, decades earlier:

> For many years I was in the habit of visiting "The Churches"
> [Glendalough] on the eve of the Pattern, or patron saint's day,
> and remaining until the faction fights were likely to commence,[2]
> about 3 o'clock P.M., on 23 June, when it was rather an unsafe lo-
> cality, unless a stipendiary magistrate and about 100 police could
> keep the combatants . . . separate. The scene was remarkable,
> and I and my friends often spent a large portion of the night,
> walking among the ruins, where an immense crowd had biv-
> ouaced, or were putting up tents and booths, or cooking their
> evening meal, gipsy-wise, through the space of the sacred enclo-
> sure. As soon as daylight dawned, the tumbling torrent over the
> rocks and stones of the Glendasan river to the north of "The
> Churches" became crowned with penitents wading, walking and
> kneeling up St. Kevin's Keeve, many of them holding little chil-
> dren in their arms. . . . The guides arranged the penitential
> routes. . . . Dancing, drinking, thimble-rigging, prick-o'-the-loop,
> and other amusements, even while the bare-headed venerable
> pilgrims, and bare-kneed voteens were going their prescribed
> rounds, continued. (449)

Although Wilde's description of the Glendalough pattern was only
made in passing (in the midst of his commentary on Gabriel Beranger's account of a visit to Glendalough in 1779), it is one of the most
detailed accounts we have of the secular activities staged on these
occasions. As a result, Wilde's account of the Glendalough pattern is
widely cited in the literature on Irish popular Catholicism. But no-
body, as far as I know, has called attention to what is likely the most
significant element in this account: the simple fact that Wilde and
his friends were in the habit of attending the pattern. Wilde was a

medical doctor and author in Dublin, and many of his friends were undoubtedly urban professionals like himself; certainly they were solidly middle class. Wilde himself was not Catholic, and I am not suggesting that he or any of his friends engaged in the penitential exercises; my point is only that this passage provides evidence that the Glendalough pattern did attract people from a variety of social strata.

Further evidence of social heterogeneity is found in Joseph Peacock's painting of the pattern held at Glendalough in 1813, which is—as far as I know—the only visual record we have of a pre-Famine pattern.[3] Peacock's painting was constructed by merging a series of separate scenes, each of which is concerned with one of the secular activities that was staged at Glendalough. W. H. Crawford (1986) presents an enlargement—and discussion—of each scene. Even taking into account that laborers often wore their best clothing to such functions, Crawford concludes, it seems clear that at least some of the attendees at the pattern were relatively well off. There is a knot of seven well-dressed men clustered around a fiddler, six of whom are on horseback (Crawford suspects that the seventh, on foot, is Peacock himself). In another scene, a group of five fashionable ladies are alighting from a four-horse landau driven by a coachman. Elsewhere two other fashionable ladies are sampling the sweetmeats and breads offered by a peddler. In a temporary ale house erected under a tent, two gentlemen and two ladies (or, says Crawford, possibly a gentleman and a lady and their personal servants) are dancing.

That members of the finer classes were attending patterns like the one at Glendalough would in itself have given these functions legitimacy in the eyes of the community at large. But did these middle- and upper-class attendees do more than just participate in the purely social (and secular) activities? Did any actually perform any of the penitential exercises? Generally, we don't know, because no one thought to ask the question. Even so, here too we sometimes come across fleeting references that suggest that they did. In an account of a pattern held on a summit of the Maamturk mountains (County Galway) in 1834, Inglis (cited in Hardy 1840, 95–96) tells us,

> It was about four in the afternoon and the pattern was in its
> height. . . . There were a score of tents or more . . . hundreds

in groups were seated on the grass, or on the stones. . . . Some
old persons were yet on their knees, beside the holy well, performing their devotions; and here and there apart, and half
screened by the masses of rocks which lay about, girls of the better order, who had finished their pastimes, were putting off their
shoes and stockings to trot homeward, or were arranging their
dress.

At the very least this passage provides evidence that "girls of the
better order" attended this pattern. Further, although the "pastimes"
mentioned here are possibly a reference to the dances and other secular activities that took place at patterns, it is also possible that these
"pastimes" included the holy well devotions mentioned in the immediately preceding part of the same sentence.

Another passage that might refer to the participation of the
middle and upper classes in the penitential activities at holy wells occurs in Hardy's account of the holy wells at Struel (County Down). After describing how pilgrims to these wells run up and then down a
hill at the site, Hardy (1840, 69) then says, "This they repeat three,
seven, nine or twelve times . . . according to the nature of their trans-
gressions. The more respectable among them keep their reckoning
by beads; while the poorer sort lift a pebble to make each ascent."
Here again it would be useful to know more precisely just who fell
into the "more respectable" category and here again we don't know;
but the possibility that the author was referring to members of the
middle and upper classes cannot be rejected.

In a few cases, observers were fairly explicit in calling attention
to the social diversity evident at patterns. In describing the parish of
Tracton Abbey (County Cork), Mason (3:472) says, "The great patron
day [of this parish] is that of St. John, on the 24th of June. . . . On the
festive day itself, and for the subsequent week, myriads of persons of
all ranks and ages, flock to the holy well of St. Zonoque . . . where
booths and tents are erected, and wondrous cures announced to be
performed by this miraculous water." Likewise, in discussing the parish of Shruel in County Longford, this same author (3:347) tells us
that "in the course of the summer, several individuals make pilgrimages, either to holy wells in the immediate neighbourhood of this
parish . . . or else to the more distant, but more celebrated, shrine of

Loughderg, in the county of Donegal. To which latter place many persons, in very affluent circumstances, have been known to walk barefooted as an act of penance for their sins."

In still other cases, observers recorded evidence of the social heterogeneity associated with popular Catholic devotions in a clear and unambiguous way, even though they themselves were often blind to what they were recording. A good example of this can be found in William Carleton's account of his visit to St. Patrick's Purgatory in 1829. Although Carleton's essay on Lough Derg was written when he was a young man, it was later incorporated into Hardy's (1840, 20–46) book on holy wells and Carleton's (1867, 236–70) own very popular book on Irish customs. In his essay, Carleton says he set out on foot to visit St. Patrick's Purgatory in Lough Derg and that for most of the trip he was accompanied only by two Irish women (who had mistaken him for a priest). But as he and his companions approached Petigo (a town just four miles from Lough Derg and the place where most pilgrims rested the night before going on to Station Island) the number of pilgrims increased substantially. Commenting on the gathering crowds, Carleton tells us that pilgrims "collected into little groups, of from three to a dozen each, with the exception of myself and one or two others of a decenter cast, having the staff and bag." Obviously "decent" (middle class?) individuals like himself were in a minority but they were present.

Once settled for the night in Petigo itself, Carleton "had now a better opportunity of examining [his fellow pilgrims] than while on the road" (252), and he proceeds to give a thumbnail sketch of a half dozen or so individuals. In most cases here Carleton is concerned wholly with character traits, and his characterizations border on allegory. One man is the "humorist," another is the "Pharisee," a third is the "miser," and so on. But in two cases Carleton gives us the specific occupations of his fellow pilgrims. One man is a tailor, he tells us, and the other is a "classical school master." He describes another man as "a battered rake," a characterization more likely to be applied to someone of gentry origin than to a landless laborer. In other words, although Carleton clearly considered pilgrimage to Lough Derg to be a "peasant" tradition (the title of his book, after all, was *Traits and Stories of the Irish Peasantry*), he just as clearly encountered individuals from social classes more closely resembling his own. Possibly these individuals caught his attention precisely because they were from his own social strata and so stood out from the majority of pilgrims, who were peasants. But, again, remember that the vast majority of the population in general were peasants. The issue is whether the social heterogeneity characteristic of the general population was reflected in the pilgrims who made their way to Lough Derg, and the scant evidence available suggests that it was.

Commentators like Wilde, Hardy, Mason, and Carleton wrote in the early part of the nineteenth century. What about earlier centuries? Who attended the patterns and holy well devotions that we know existed in the seventeenth and eighteenth centuries? Unfortunately, as murky as our understanding of popular Catholicism in Ireland is for the early nineteenth century, it becomes even murkier as we move back across the preceding two centuries. Nevertheless, even for these earlier centuries we sometimes come across references hinting at the social heterogeneity associated with popular Catholicism.

Social Heterogeneity in the Seventeenth and Eighteenth Centuries

In a report written in 1611 (and reproduced in Moran 1884, ciii and 298), David Rothe, the bishop of Ossory, says that Cornelius O'Devany, the bishop of Down and Connor, had visited the pilgrimage site at Monaincha (Tipperary) in 1610 but that age and infirmity had prevented O'Devany from participating in the penitential rituals there. Rothe's brief comments here are interesting mostly for what is only implicit. First, Rothe apparently saw nothing inappropriate about a Catholic bishop's making a pilgrimage to Monaincha, which we know was one of the most popular pilgrimage sites within easy reach of the Catholic heartland. Second, in saying that age and infirmity prevented O'Devany from participating in the penitential rituals (presumably roundings), Rothe seems also to be suggesting that participation in these rituals would have been quite legitimate otherwise. Rothe apparently approved of participation in the penitential rituals at Monaincha even though he had been educated on the Continent and—as bishop of Ossory—was strongly committed to the implementation of the Tridentine reforms in his diocese.[4] Rothe, himself, in other words, seems not to have regarded a commitment to Tridentine Catholicism as necessarily being in conflict with the rituals characteristic of popular Catholicism. If an impeccably Tridentine bishop like Rothe could hold this view, there is no particular reason not to believe that other members of his class (Rothe was from a wealthy mercantile family) might hold the same views.

Another reference hinting at the social heterogeneity of the crowds attending patterns in the seventeenth century, particularly in the heartland, appears in a description of Clonmel (County Tipperary) written about 1618 by Donatus Mooney. Clonmel was one of the popular sites listed in Paul V's brief, and Mooney had visited this site in his capacity as provincial of the Irish Franciscans. In describing Clonmel, Mooney says that "the church is frequently crowded with citizens. They pray here and their devotion is strong. On festival days and on Sundays, ruler[s] and citizens alike[5] assemble here and do the stations, as well as make offerings for the souls of the dead" (Jennings 1934, 78). Here again, in other words, the suggestion seems to be that it was the community as a whole, not just peasants, who gathered together and participated in the religious rituals at popular pilgrimage sites.

Additional evidence indicating that participation in popular penitential activities did not preclude a commitment to Tridentine ideals is to be found in John Lynch's biography of Francis Kirwan, written in 1669. Francis Kirwan was born at Galway in 1589 of an Anglo-Irish father and Irish mother. He was sent to Lisbon to be educated, returned to Ireland in 1614, was ordained a priest, and left again the next year to further his education. By 1618, he was teaching philosophy at Dieppe. In 1620, Kirwan returned to Ireland to assume the duties of vicar-general for the Archdiocese of Tuam,[6] a role that he would perform for the next sixteen years or so. As vicar-general, Kirwan very aggressively set out to implement the Tridentine reforms. Partly this meant instructing the laity in Church doctrine by employing effective preachers and using harsh penalties (including public denunciation from the pulpit and excommunication) to eliminate common vices, like the practice of common law marriage. Kirwan also sought to Tridentize the clergy. Young men were not allowed to be ordained until they had spent a year under Kirwan's tutelage, and Kirwan also instituted a program to educate older priests "not sufficiently acquainted with the ceremonies of the Church" (Lynch 1848, 49). Parish priests prone to bad habits, sexual improprieties, and gambling in particular were sent to remote areas until they mended their ways. Finally, Kirwan set out to implement some of the organizational reforms promulgated at Trent. He worked to ensure, for example, that individual priests had responsibility for only a single parish, rather than several (which had been common practice).

Kirwan, in short, was deeply committed to implementing the Tridentine reforms in his diocese. Even so, for him, as for David Rothe, his commitment to these reforms did not imply a rejection of the activities associated with popular Catholicism. On the contrary,

> that he [Kirwan] might not be wanting in any species of piety, he reverenced in his soul the custom of undertaking pilgrimages. Nor was he satisfied with visiting such places in Connaught [like] the rugged mountain, called Cruach Patrick, which he was wont to frequent, often ascending . . . [to] the very summit, covered with loose stones, and creeping on bended knees over the rough rock fragments. . . . Often too did he go into Ulster, to the far-famed Purgatory of St. Patrick, in which pilgrims are wont to abstain from meat for nine days, using no food, save a little bread, and water from the lake. During one of the nine days, they are shut up in the dismal darkness of a cavern, and therein fasting, partake of nothing, save a little water to moisten their throats when parched with thirst. At noontide and evening, they go on bended knees over paths beaten by the feet of saints, and strewn with sharp stones. In other quarters, they walk barefooted over rugged ways . . . for the expiation of sin. Sometimes walking, and some times on their knees, they advance to a considerable distance into the sea. . . . Thrice each day did Francis, with the other pilgrims, punctually perform these duties, and there did he apply himself to hearing confessions and preaching sermons. (Lynch 1848, 62–63)

The references here to "creeping on bended knees over the rough rock fragments" at Croagh Patrick and to going "on bended knees over paths beaten by the feet of saints" at Lough Derg suggest that Kirwan engaged in the rounding rituals that we know (from other sources) were being performed at these locations. In other words, here again we have evidence that someone thoroughly committed to Tridentine ideals saw nothing inappropriate in combining official activities like confession and preaching with the rituals and activities that lay at the core of the popular Catholic tradition in Ireland.

Clerics like Rothe and Kirwan aside, there is also some evidence, mostly from the eighteenth century, that lay elites also saw nothing inappropriate in supporting rounding rituals and other popular activities. For instance, in describing the inscriptions associated with St. John's Well near the Abbey of Killone (County Clare), Fitzgerald (1900, 245) says that a short distance from the well is a large altar of loose stones which incorporated the following inscription:

> This alter [*sic*] was
> built by Anthony
> Roch merchant
> from Ennis 1731

Such an inscription ties the religious activities at this holy well to the urban mercantile class in a particularly clear and obvious way. How many similar but unrecorded inscriptions exist (or existed) at well sites? And how many merchants used their money to sponsor religious activities at well sites without feeling the need to immortalize their participation in the manner of Anthony Roch from Ennis?

In some cases, eighteenth-century commentators were quite explicit in calling attention to the social heterogeneity of the penitents who flocked to holy wells. Describing the ceremonies associated with the holy wells at Struel (County Down), one Protestant commentator noted that "vast throngs of Rich and Poor resort [to these wells] on Midsummer-Eve, and the Friday before Lammas, some in hopes of obtaining Health, and others to perform Penances enjoined them by the Popish priests" (1744, cited in Reeves 1847, 42n). In other cases, eighteenth-century sources provide evidence of social heterogeneity but in ways that are not immediately obvious. Moran (1864, 3:337), for example, reproduces an account written in 1714 by Hugh M'Mahon, the bishop of Clogher, in which M'Mahon describes his visit to St. Patrick's Purgatory. As part of his account, M'Mahon tells us that he had traveled to this pilgrimage site and engaged in the penitential rituals there, disguised as a merchant from Dublin. Dr. Moran (1864, 3:357) himself presents this account as evidence that bishops during this period—when the Penal Laws were in full force —ran a great risk were they to be publicly recognized. But equally significant, I think, and easily overlooked, is the fact that adopting the persona of a merchant would not have been an effective disguise for M'Mahon unless merchants traveling from port cities like Dublin to St. Patrick's Purgatory were sufficiently commonplace as not to arouse the attention of the authorities. In other words, M'Mahon's disguise only "worked" because merchants from cities like Dublin *were* traveling to this pilgrimage site, and engaging in the rituals there, on a regular basis.

Thus far I have been cobbling together bits and pieces of evidence found in pre-Famine accounts of Irish religious practice which, taken collectively, support the view that crowds who were attending patterns and making rounds at holy wells and other stations were more socially heterogeneous than has previously been recognized and that this was especially true in the Catholic heartland. I concede that the amount of evidence here is not large, but this limitation has to be weighed against the realities encountered when investigating the Irish past. Simply put, there is very little in the documentary record that tells us *anything* about the religious practices favored by ordinary Irish Catholics between the Reformation and, say, the late eighteenth century. This presumably explains why Irish historians have had so little to say about Irish popular Catholicism prior to 1750, and why, when they do make summary judgments about this subject, they tend to use data from a later period.

For example, in his review of materials available to scholars studying Irish "Church history" during the sixteenth century, Colm Lennon (1991) does mention in passing that holy well cults were popular during this period. But the only evidence he presents in support of this claim is a citation to two articles by Kevin Danaher (1958; 1960) on holy wells in County Dublin. Anyone who takes the time to read Danaher's articles will discover that his account of these wells was very explicitly derived from nineteenth- and twentieth-century sources. As valuable as the Danaher studies are, how can they possibly be taken as saying anything about holy well devotions in sixteenth-century Ireland? The answer, of course, is that they can't. Nor is this an isolated slip. In his more recent and otherwise very informative monograph on sixteenth-century Ireland, Lennon does say—if only in passing—that "holy wells and other places associated with local saints were much frequented throughout the sixteenth century, pre-Christian folk traditions being carried on in some rituals" (132), but in this case he cites no sources whatsoever to support his claim. Note that Lennon's reference here to "pre-Christian folk traditions" suggests that his thinking is being shaped by the pagan origins hypothesis.

Partly, the problem facing Lennon is the problem facing anybody studying popular Catholicism in Ireland: there is so little information available. Benignus Millett (1991), for instance, makes no mention of holy wells or patterns in his review of materials available to scholars interested in studying the Irish Church in the seventeenth century. Even the well-known studies by Connolly and Corish, which specifically take "pre-Famine" Irish Catholicism as their focus, have surprisingly little to say about patterns and rounding rituals in the period prior to the late eighteenth century.

In the end, then, any study of popular Catholicism in Ireland between the Reformation and the late eighteenth century must inevitably rest upon bits and pieces of evidence; nothing else is available. In this situation, scholarly prudence demands that we remain open to all possibilities that are consistent with the meager historical record. One of those possibilities is the one that I have been advancing in this chapter, namely, that both lay and clerical elites in the Catholic heartland saw no inconsistency between participation in these popular activities and participation in the rituals favored by the official Church and that in fact heartland Catholics of all social levels and in large numbers did simultaneously embrace the rituals in both categories. I now want to consider some of the known historical processes that might plausibly have produced this situation.

The Bossy Thesis and the Heartland Experience

Some time ago John Bossy (1970) sought to reorient thinking on the Counter-Reformation by suggesting that scholars had for too long been studying the wrong thing. Traditionally, he argued, scholarly investigations of the Counter-Reformation had been concerned mainly with the reception given to Protestant doctrines by local populations. But for the vast majority of Catholics living in Italy and France (and in his original article Bossy was concerned only with these two areas), the Counter-Reformation was mainly about organizational change. The primary goal of the Counter-Reformation Church, Bossy argued, was to ensure (1) that all Catholics engage in a series of uniform religious practices (of which weekly attendance at Sunday Mass was especially important) and (2) that the local parish church be the locus of these activities.

There were, however, several obstacles to this drive for parochial uniformity. Among the most serious of these obstacles, Bossy suggested, were the various kin-based collectivities that had been allowed to flourish within the medieval Church. Partly, Bossy is referring here to the medieval Church's willingness to acknowledge and accommodate the norms of extended kin groups in regard to things like marriage, godparenthood, and feuding. But he was also referring to medieval confraternities, whose members were strongly bound together by ties of artificial kinship and which—as organizations—had been granted a substantial amount of autonomy by the Church. It was Bossy's contention that the Counter-Reformation desire for parochial conformity could only be implemented by neutralizing or eliminating these kin-based groups. This meant ensuring that Catholics participated in the Church as individuals, not as the members of a group—and this is just what happened in Italy and France. But there was a cost to all this. In breaking the link between Church membership and kin-based collectivities, the norms of these collectivities could no longer be co-opted to reinforce religious practice. This for Bossy is why so many Catholics (again, in Italy and France) were disaffected from the Church at the end of the ancien régime.

In a later article (1971), Bossy looked at the Irish case specifically within the context of his general argument. When the Counter-Reformation came to Ireland, he argued (158), it found a society dominated by kinship relations and one in which the primary method of articulating disputes between kin groups was the feud. The ill-feeling fostered between local groups by feuding made it impossible to implement one of the Counter-Reformation's most important goals, namely, ensuring that the entire community gather peaceably in one place (the parish church) on a regular basis (every Sunday) and engage in a common ritual (the Mass). One result, according to Bossy, was a predilection among Irish Catholics for masses and other religious rituals celebrated in domestic settings. This merging of religion with domesticity in Ireland drew much critical comment from members of the Church hierarchy. In particular it provoked a reaction of intense disgust from Cardinal Rinuccini, that "Tridentine bishop despatched in mint condition from Italy" (Bossy 1971, 169) who came to Ireland as papal nuncio in 1645. Nevertheless, it was precisely this failure to break the link between domesticity and religion which ensured, Bossy argued, that Irish Catholics would not become disaffected from the Church (as happened with Catholics elsewhere) and so ensured that Ireland would remain Catholic.

Taken collectively, Bossy's various arguments represent one of the most successful attempts to date to locate the Irish case within the context of the European Counter-Reformation. His suggestion that there was a tension between Counter-Reformation goals and the collectivist concerns of local Catholics is an insight that no student of the Counter-Reformation can now ignore. Furthermore, Bossy's analysis allows us to situate theoretically the strong "domestic" emphasis that was undeniably a feature of Irish Catholicism during the seventeenth century, as is evident—for example—in the tendency for Sunday Mass to be celebrated in homes. Yet for all its strengths, Bossy's is still an analysis implicitly informed by the standpoint of the official Church. Thus his primary concern (like that of the official Church) is whether or not the Tridentine reforms were implemented. If they were not implemented, as in Ireland, he (like the Church) wants to know why. Finally, in considering the alternative Catholicism that emerged in Ireland he focuses on precisely those things (like masses said in private houses) that struck members of the official Church as most inappropriate.

What happens if we remain sensitive to Bossy's insights concerning the conflicts between Counter-Reformation ideals and collectivist concerns but develop our analysis from the perspective that likely prevailed among lay Catholics living in the Catholic heartland during the seventeenth and eighteenth centuries? From Kevin Whelan's analysis we know that heartland Catholics (by definition) were more exposed to Counter-Reformation ideals than Catholics in other parts of Ireland. But we also know that the heartland, at least that part of the heartland that lay astride a Wexford/Limerick axis, was a dynamic and creative society whose members were predisposed to borrow freely from a variety of traditions—Gaelic, Old English, European—in order to create new cultural forms. How might such a society respond to the dilemma identified by Bossy, that is, to the conflicting demands of Counter-Reformation ideology and kin-based collectivities? Simply: by merging Counter-Reformation emphases with collectivist concerns in order to create hybrid forms of religious devotion.

With this prediction in mind (and that's all it is, a prediction) reconsider the matter of feuding, the one activity that Bossy saw to be such a barrier to the implementation of the Counter-Reformation's organizational goals in Ireland. Suppose heartland Catholics had set themselves the task of merging the traditional emphasis upon the feud as a method of articulating disputes with the Tridentine emphasis upon gathering the entire community together in one location to engage in uniform religious practices. What would be the result? One result, I suggest, might very well be the "traditional" pattern.

Patterns, after all, were held on a regular and recurrent basis in a well-defined location. True, a holy well was not a parish church, but like a parish church it was a gathering place not associated with any particular domestic setting. Furthermore, the evidence reviewed earlier in this chapter suggests that all social classes were represented at a pattern and patterns were indeed very much a community activity. The rounding rituals associated with patterns were also relatively uniform from region to region. Moreover, since the cult of the saints was rejected by virtually all Protestant groups, the fact that these rounding rituals were being performed at sites dedicated to a Catholic saint marked these rituals as distinctively Catholic.[7]

What I am suggesting, in other words, is that Counter-Reformation Catholicism was permeated by a set of very general emphases that could be (and were) used by Irish Catholics to shape religious practice even if they did not always embrace the specific forms in which the Counter-Reformation Church itself articulated these emphases in Continental Europe. Thus the Tridentine emphasis upon the community as a whole regularly gathering together in one location could be embraced without accepting the view that this location had to be the parish church; the emphasis upon uniform practices that were distinctly Catholic could be embraced without accepting that the Mass had to be central; and so on.

What about feuding, the one activity that more than any other— at least according to Bossy—prevented the members of a local community from gathering at their parish church? Why didn't that prevent these same communities from gathering together on the occasion of a pattern? The answer here is simple: feuding was embraced, not avoided, and made a ritualized part of the pattern experience. This was done by means of the faction fight. Whelan (1985, 243) describes a faction fight as "a ritualized method of settling disputes without recourse to external authority." What this definition fails to capture, however, is the strong emphasis on physical violence that was a central element in these encounters. Wakefield (1812, 2:752), by contrast, provides a less analytic but more complete account:

> Although quarrels here are very frequent, fighting single-handed is unknown. No one ever resolves to rely on his own personal courage or strength; when a man sustains an injury, or conceives himself affronted, he calls to his aid, not only his immediate relations and friends, but his neighbours and fellow parishioners, and sometimes the inhabitants of a barony. Whole districts thus become interested in individual disputes; the combatants marshal themselves under leaders distinguished for their prowess; *shillelas* are their weapons, and when a general engagement takes place, many are wounded on both sides. Bruised limbs and broken heads are the usual consequences of such encounters, but on some occasion they are attended with the loss of lives.

Although faction fights could be held on any social occasions, they were a regular part of the pattern (see figure 14). Peacock, for instance, depicted several dozen individuals rushing along with raised cudgels in his painting of the pattern at Glendalough (see Crawford 1986 for an enlargement of this detail). Remember too that William Wilde (in the passage cited earlier) says he was always careful to leave the pattern at Glendalough before the faction fight began. Since these fights did not usually involve fatalities, their outcome was rarely decisive and so the feud involved could last for years. One source (*Parliamentary Gazetteer of Ireland* 1844, 1:200), for instance, reports that two factions at Ballyvourney (County Cork) "had met annually for upwards of forty years to perpetuate their feud."

If (as I am arguing) faction fights came to be associated with patterns at holy wells when Tridentine emphases imported from the Continent were merged with elements of traditional Irish culture,

then the association of faction fights with patterns should have existed since the early seventeenth century (which was when the importation of Tridentine emphases reached a peak). Is this the case?
Although most existing accounts of faction fights, like most accounts
of patterns generally, date from the late eighteenth and early twentieth centuries, some limited evidence suggests that faction fights were
indeed a part of the pattern experience in the seventeenth century.
In an account of County Westmeath, Piers (1981 [1682]) describes a
chapel dedicated to St. Eyen which was the focus of ritual activities.

> This chapel is cut out of the natural rock . . . and hath long been,
> without a roof: it hath in it a curious purling brook of crystal wa-
> ter, which issuing out of the rock side of the chapel, traverseth
> it, [moving toward] the opposite side wall. . . . To this chapel, on
> the first Sunday in harvest, the natives pay their devotion in pil-
> grimages, which for certain stages they undertake barefoot . . .
> [and for] the remainder of their devotion on bare knees, all
> along to the chapel. . . . Their devotions performed, they return
> merry and shod . . . to a green spot of ground on the east side of
> the hill . . . and here men and women fall a dancing and carous-
> ing the rest of the day; for ale-sellers in great numbers have their
> booths here as in a fair. . . . Thus, in lewd and obscene dancing,
> and in excess of drinking, the remainder of the day is spent . . .
> and oftentimes it falls out that more blood is shed on the grass
> from broken pates and drunken quarrels, when the pilgrimages
> are ended, than was before on the stones from their bare feet
> and knees during their devotions.

Although Piers uses the term "chapel" in this passage, his reference to a "purling brook of crystal water" that issued from the rock
and flowed across the chapel floor makes it clear that he is describing a holy well of the "oratory" type (see chapter 1). Similarly, Piers
is clear in saying that pilgrims to this well first engaged in penitential
activities and then gathered to engage in a variety of secular activities of exactly the same sort that would be typical of patterns in the
early nineteenth century (compare Piers's account, for instance, with
Wilde's account of the pattern at Glendalough). Piers, in other words,
is describing a pattern, and, as far as I know, it is the only detailed
account of a pattern that we have from the seventeenth century. He

nowhere uses the terms *faction fight* or *feuding*, but his reference to "blood . . . shed on the grass from broken pates and drunken quarrels"—while it admittedly could refer to nothing more than random acts of drunken brawling—could also be a reference to faction fights. In short, the suggestion that faction fights were a part of the pattern experience when patterns first emerged as a popular activity is entirely consistent with what meager evidence is available.

In summary, then, if we choose to do so, we can view patterns in pre-Famine Ireland as a hybrid cultural form that only became truly popular in the post-Reformation period, when some very general Counter-Reformation emphases were merged with emphases that were central to Ireland's kin-oriented society.

One advantage of the argument that popular rituals at holy wells and Counter-Reformation Catholicism were mutually reinforcing, not mutually exclusive, is that it allows us to explain several historical patterns. It would explain, for example, the great surge in the popularity of "traditional" pilgrimage activities which occurred during the early seventeenth century and which so forcibly caught the attention of contemporary observers. The surge occurred at this time because this was the period during which Counter-Reformation ideals were being imported into Ireland. The same argument would also explain why so many of the most important pilgrimage sites in Ireland—sites at which rounding rituals were performed—were located in or near the Catholic heartland, which was that part of Ireland most exposed to Counter-Reformation ideals. Finally, the argument being offered here provides an explanation for some miscellaneous historical patterns that have otherwise puzzled earlier commentators. Consider, for example, the popular pattern at Ardmore.

Ardmore's Missing History

The village of Ardmore in County Waterford overlooks a bay situated along Ireland's southeastern coast (see figure 15). In the early decades of the nineteenth century, the pattern held at Ardmore on July 24 was one of the most well known and well attended patterns in all of Ireland. A relatively careful estimate made by someone attending that pattern in 1832 suggests that twelve thousand to fifteen thousand people took part in the devotions there (Hall and Hall 1841, 1:284).

As at all patterns, the central religious ritual at Ardmore was rounding. Hardy's (1840) account suggests that there were four stations at Ardmore that had to be rounded. The one that most attracted the attention of commentators was St. Declan's Rock (St. Declan being the patron of the festival). This was a large rock on the beach at Ardmore whose lower portion was exposed at low tide (see figure 16). Once the sand was cleared away, there was a space under the rock through which devotees might pull themselves. It was a tight fit and (much to the disgust of Protestant commentators) involved much rolling up and taking off of clothes:

> The men take off hats, coats, shoes and stockings, and if very
> large, waistcoats—they turn up their breeches, above the knee,
> then lying flat on the ground, put in hands, arms, and head, one
> shoulder more forward than the other in order to work their
> way through the more easily. . . . [Coming out the other side]
> they then proceed on bare knees over a number of little stones
> to the place where they enter again, and thus proceed three
> times. . . . The women take off bonnets, shoes, stockings, and
> turn their petticoats up above the knee, so that they may go on
> their bare knees. (Hardy 1840, 61–62)

After completing the devotions at St. Declan's Rock, pilgrims usually went to the holy well a little distance away (see figure 17). This well was adjacent to a ruined chapel, and pilgrims rounded the well/chapel complex three times. The other two stations at Ardmore were a round tower (of the sort found throughout Ireland) and a ruined structure called the Saint's House.

Despite the campaign that Irish bishops had supposedly launched to stamp out patterns in the late 1700s, it was still the case that the rounding rituals at Ardmore in the 1830s were being supplemented by quintessentially Tridentine rituals like the Mass. One observer reports seeing several thousand people attending a mass being said in the ruined chapel near the well and tells us that this was only one of three masses said on pattern day (Hardy 1840, 62).

Finally, just on the outskirts of the village, numerous tents were set up to dispense food and drink and to provide the sort of purely secular amusements (including cards, dice, and other games of chance) found at other patterns. The crowds who came to these tents, however, came mainly at night: "The tents, which throughout the day, the duties owing to the patron saint had caused to be empty, at evening became thronged with the devotionalists of the morning, and resounded till day-break with the oaths of the blasphemer and the shouts of the drunkard" (Hardy 1840, 59–60). This passage makes it clear that the secular activities at the Ardmore pattern did not serve an audience separate from the audience that rounded the stations. On the contrary, all the activities at the pattern—the rounding rituals at the various stations, crawling under St. Declan's Rock, attending Mass, and carousing—drew upon the same pool of participants and constituted a single, integrated experience.

In 1831 the village of Ardmore had a population of 414; by 1841 it was 716 (*Parliamentary Gazetteer of Ireland* 1844, 61). Obviously the thousands who attended the Ardmore pattern came from somewhere else. Many undoubtedly came from other communities in County Waterford and from communities in the eastern part of County Cork, including the city of Cork. But Ardmore also drew people from farther afield. One visitor to the especially well attended pattern held in 1832 reported that the "multitudes . . . there assembled [were] from all the neighboring districts, even from the county of Kerry, city and county of Cork, Limerick and Waterford" (Hackett 1861–62, 266). In short, the crowds who thronged to Ardmore in the early nineteenth century in order to pull themselves under St. Declan's Rock, walk round the Saint's House, and so on were from the western half of the Catholic heartland, precisely that area of Ireland that had been most exposed to Tridentine ideals during the preceding three centuries.

That a pattern like the one at Ardmore was so popular with Catholics of the heavily Tridentized heartland might in itself be considered a puzzle. But what has struck previous commentators as even more puzzling is the silence of the historical record. In commenting on Ardmore, Peter Harbison (1991a, 136) says that "there are, surprisingly, no early references to the pilgrimage here." He makes a similar remark in a later work (1991b, 195), pointing out that there are no historical sources attesting to pilgrimage at Ardmore prior to about 1600. But why should Harbison or anyone else find it surprising that Ardmore is not mentioned prior to the modern era? It seems clear that his surprise derives entirely from an implicit and a priori commitment to the hypothesis that Irish patterns were the continuation of archaic (Celtic) traditions.

By contrast, under the hypothesis being offered here, the silence of the historical record is not at all puzzling. I have argued that under the impact of the Counter-Reformation, heartland Catholics sought to merge some very general emphases associated with Tridentine Catholicism with the collectivist emphasis of Ireland's kin-oriented society. The result of this creative effort was the modern pattern. In some cases, heartland Catholics likely built upon existing celebrations at older pilgrimage sites that had always enjoyed some degree of popularity. But there was no particular reason not to create new sites for patterns, especially if these new sites were more easily accessible to large areas of the heartland than older sites. I am suggesting that Ardmore was one such site. There are no early references to the popular pattern at Ardmore, in other words, for the simple reason that that pattern did not exist until brought into existence by processes set in motion by the importation of the Counter-Reformation into Ireland.

Conclusion

In the end, I am suggesting that our view of the "traditional" pattern in Ireland must be revised in much the same way as our view of the "traditional" clachan in Ireland has been revised. Did patterns and their associated holy well devotions exist in Ireland before the Counter-Reformation? Possibly they did, just as clachans existed in certain areas in earlier centuries. But does this justify the view that patterns and their associated holy well devotions are best viewed as the remnants of an ancient Celtic tradition, to which Irish peasants "clung" in opposition to the Catholicism of the official Church? Not at all. Just as the view that clachans were the traditional form of settlement in Ireland led scholars to gravely misinterpret the dense cluster of clachans found in Ireland's western periphery during the early nineteenth century, so too has the "Celtic origins" view of patterns and holy wells led scholars to misinterpret the significance of the patterns that flourished in the Tridentized Catholic heartland until the early nineteenth century.

As a popular phenomenon, these patterns were a relatively recent cultural innovation, having only come into existence during the seventeenth century. It was the cultural creativity of heartland Catholics, in short, and not the remnants of some distant (and non-existent) Celtic past, which determined the shape of Irish popular Catholicism between the Reformation and the Famine.

Chapter Five

The Two Devotional Revolutions

If I am correct in my interpretation of Irish history, there have been (at least) two devotional revolutions in Ireland. The first occurred sometime around the beginning of the seventeenth century, mainly in areas of Munster and Leinster, when the laity and local clergy merged a number of general Tridentine emphases imported from Continental Europe with local communitarian traditions. The result of this merger was a variant of popular Catholicism in which holy wells, rounding rituals, and patterns became central to the experience of "being Catholic." The second devotional revolution occurred during the early nineteenth century and is the one described by Larkin. In this case, the variant of Catholicism that became popular was one in which the local parish church was the focal point of Catholic religiosity and in which confession and the Mass were the most important ritual activities. Just as important, this new variant of popular Catholicism held that "true" Catholic rituals like the Mass and confession should now be disassociated from those very things —notably, holy well cults, rounding rituals, patterns—that had been central to the Catholic experience since the first devotional revolution.

Two questions remain in connection with the argument I have been developing. The first, and the easiest to answer (if only because much of the answer has already been presented in the last chapter) is why the first devotional revolution occurred at all. The second question is why the variant of popular Catholicism born of this first devotional revolution fell into disuse. Finding the answer to both questions requires that we go back and rethink the historical event that is central to any understanding of Irish Catholicism.

Irish Pilgrimage

Back to the Beginning: The Reformation in Ireland

The Reformation was formally implanted in Ireland in 1536, when the Irish parliament declared Henry VIII to be the supreme head on earth of the Irish Church. In theory, there were now two churches in Ireland, one Catholic and one Protestant, and similarly two hierarchies, two sets of clergy, and two groups of laity. In practice, the distinction between "Catholic" and "Protestant" would remain blurred for decades.

This blurring of the two religions resulted in part from the fact that the Reformation in Ireland, like the Reformation in England, did not—at least initially—result in any dramatic shift in the thinking and practice of ordinary laypersons. As any number of commentators have noted, the Henrician Reformation was relatively conservative in regard to matters of devotional practice. True, the monasteries were dissolved in Ireland as in England, and a few Reformation bishops in Ireland—notably George Browne, Archbishop of Dublin—carried out the same sort of campaign against images as was being carried out in England. There is no evidence, however, that these things had any dramatic effect on popular religiosity. Further attempts at liturgical reform were made during Edward's brief reign, in Ireland as in England, but Alan Ford (1986) is almost certainly correct in suggesting that the ease with which Catholicism was reestablished during Mary's reign is evidence that these reforms did not change the thinking or practice of Irish Catholics in any fundamental way—which is the same point that Duffy (1992) makes in regard to England.

In Ireland, language clearly played a role in minimizing the experience of change for many of the laity. An important element of the Reformation in England was the development of a vernacular liturgy, and that meant a liturgy in English. Finding clergy who could speak English was often a problem in Ireland. This is why the Act of Uniformity passed during the second year of Elizabeth's reign specifically directed clergy who could not speak English to use the Latin version of the Book of Common Prayer. To lay audiences in Ireland, a Protestant service in an incomprehensible language would probably not have seemed dramatically different from a Catholic service in that same language. Indeed, even Catholic historians have conceded that the use of Latin would have been seen by many Irish Catholics as the one sure sign of orthodoxy (Moran 1864, 61).

But the continuing use of Latin was not the only thing that would have made it difficult for ordinary people to distinguish clearly between "Protestant ministers" and "Catholic priests"; lifestyle and pastoral behavior also contributed to the confusion. This is made clear in an account of Church of Ireland clergy written by Andrew Trollope in 1587:

> Most ministers [of the Church of Ireland] are stipendiary men, and few have £5 a year to live on. . . . In truth such they are as deserve not living or to live. For they will not be accounted ministers but Priests. They will have no wives [though] they will have Harlots. . . . And with long experience and some extraordinary trial of these fellows, I cannot find whether the most of them love lewd women, cards, dice or drink, best. And when they must of necessity go to church, they carry with them a book in Latin of the Common Prayer set forth and allowed by her Majesty. But they read little or nothing of it or can well read it, but they tell the people a Tale of our Lady or St. Patrick or some other saint, horrible to be spoken or heard, and intolerable to be suffered, and do all they may to dissuade and allure the people from God and their prince, and their due obedience to them both, and persuade them to the Devil the Pope. (cited in Brady 1868, 118)

To Irish laypersons, the fact that a "Protestant" minister was unmarried, using Latin, preaching about St. Patrick, recommending pilgrimages, and promoting obedience to the pope would have been less a cause for criticism (as it was for Trollope) than clear evidence that nothing much had changed.

The confusion that surrounded the local clergy often surrounded Irish bishops as well. True, many dioceses were claimed both by a Protestant bishop and a Catholic bishop, and to some extent this "pulled apart" the two churches. But there were many cases in which the distinction between Catholic and Protestant bishops was less clear-cut, if only because some bishops seemed to move so easily back and forth across the Protestant/Catholic divide.

The career of George Dowdall is a good example of just how fluid the boundary between Catholic and Protestant could be. Dowdall had been prior of the monastery of the Crutched Friars at Ardee until it was suppressed in 1539. Four years later he was appointed by Henry VIII to be archbishop of Armagh, and in that capacity Dowdall acknowledged Henry's supremacy. Even so, and despite the existence of a rival claimant to Armagh put forward by Rome, Dowdall was firm in his commitment to Catholic tradition. Thus, when instructing his representatives on what they should look for during the course of a pastoral visit in 1546, Dowdall showed concern for precisely the same things that would later be of concern to Counter-Reformation bishops in Italy and France: the practice of clerical celibacy, the regular celebration of the Mass, and the recitation of the Divine Office, maintaining the local church and its sacred objects in good condition, and so forth (see Gwynn 1946, 272–73). It was also, incidentally, during his tenure as the *Protestant* archbishop of Armagh that Dowdall granted absolution to Heneas MacNichaill after MacNichaill had completed the pilgrimages assigned as penance for his having killed his son (see chap. 4). Eventually, Dowdall did retire from his position and flee Ireland. In early 1553, during Edward's reign, Dowdall was once again appointed archbishop of Armagh but this time by Pope Julius III. Upon Mary's accession, Dowdall returned to Ireland and fulfilled his duties as the Catholic archbishop of Armagh for most of her reign. Was Dowdall Protestant or Catholic? Whatever the legalities involved, it is not a question that would have been easily answered by ordinary Catholics living under his jurisdiction.

The confessional ambiguities that surrounded some Irish bishops was further enhanced (if I can use that word) by the fact that both Protestant and Catholic authorities themselves often paid less attention to a candidate's formal affiliation than to more pragmatic matters in deciding who should administer a diocese. In 1536, for instance, the Dublin government appointed Richard Nangle bishop of the Diocese of Clonfert. It soon became clear that the papal appointee, Roland de Burgo, had stronger local support, and so in 1541 Dublin dropped Nangle and confirmed de Burgo, who thus administered his diocese with the approval of both churches (Martin 1979, 40). Similarly, in 1561 the papal nuncio to Ireland, David Wolfe, suggested that Christopher Bodkin, the Protestant archbishop of Tuam, was probably better suited to the governance of the diocese than the papal appointee, since Bodkin was "skilled in administration and has great influence with the gentry of the district," and so Wolfe recommended that the Holy See accept the resignation of the papal claimant and confirm Bodkin (Moran 1864, 86). In other cases, we are less certain why particular bishops came to be accepted by both Catholic and Protestant authorities, and know only that they were. Alexander Devereux, for example, was made bishop of Ferns during Henry's reign and remained in office during the reigns of Edward, Mary, and Elizabeth; his tenure was brought to an end only by his death in 1566 (Walshe 1989, 353).

This blurring of the organizational boundaries separating the two churches continued well into the 1570s. In 1577, for example, Sir William Drury, Lord President of Munster, complained of several Catholic prelates operating in the Waterford area. After naming three prelates who openly preached against the Protestant religion, Drury comes to a fourth, who seems to have taken a different tack: "The fourth is Chaunter Walsh of Waterford, one that hath procured dispensation of the Pope to use the English service, to receive benefits from the same, and to abjure himself without hurting his conscience. He came over last March. He preached praying to saints and going on pilgrimages" (cited in Brady 1868, 23). Whether this particular prelate truly had papal permission to use the English service is less important than that he was simultaneously using this service, proclaiming his allegiance to Elizabeth, and promoting devotional forms that were impeccably Catholic.[1]

The Emergence of Catholic Ireland

It was only in the last two decades of the sixteenth century that the confusion between "Catholic" and "Protestant" began to dissipate as the two traditions became more sharply differentiated in Ireland. This differentiation was most of all evident in the steady rise in recusancy (that is, in the steadfast refusal to participate in ceremonies associated with the Church of Ireland) that began in the 1570s and 1580s. This rise in recusancy was initially associated with Anglo-Irish mercantile and gentry families in southern cities like Dublin, Cork, Limerick, and Galway (Lennon 1989; Bradshaw 1988), but it quickly became the norm among the general population as well. In some

cases, the wholesale abandonment of the established religion, especially on the part of social elites, occurred within a remarkably
brief period of time, and contemporary commentators were often
fairly precise in dating the decline. For example, writing in 1590,
Adam Loftus, the Protestant archbishop of Dublin, had no doubts as
to when recusancy in the pale had escalated: "Yet, this general recusancy is of but six years' continuence at the most. . . . Before which
time, I well remember and do assure your lordship, there were not
in the pale the number of twelve recusant gentlemen of account; but
since then they have grown to such obstinacy and boldness, that it
is to be feared (if some speedy remedy be not provided), upon pre-
tence of religion, they will shake off all duty and obedience" (cited
in Moran 1864, 151). Similarly, in 1596 William Lyon, who by that
time had been the Protestant bishop of Cork and Ross for the past
fifteen years, complained that "within these two years so far, that
where I had a thousand or more in a church at sermon, I now have
not five; and whereas I have seen 500 communicants or more, now
are not three" (*Cal. S. P. Ire.* 1596–97, 14). By 1604 the Protestant
bishop of Cork, Cloyne, and Ross could say that not a single Protestant marriage, christening, or burial had taken place in his diocese
during the previous eleven years (Ford 1986, 58).

This general turn toward recusancy in the closing decades of the
sixteenth century was accompanied by the increasingly open profession of Catholicism at all levels of Irish society. In the same 1596
report just mentioned, for instance, Bishop Lyon indicated that Catholic priests walked openly in the streets with the aldermen and other
officers of the city of Cork. He also suggested that many Protestant
ministers were forsaking "their benefices to become massing priests,
because they [massing, or Roman, priests] are so well entreated, and
much made of among the people" (15). But perhaps the one incident
that most of all epitomizes the revitalized Catholicism that came to
predominate in the urbanized areas of southern Ireland occurred in
1603, when, following the death of Elizabeth, Catholics in Waterford,
Cork, Kilkenny, Wexford, and Clonmel took over (if only temporar-
ily) their local churches and reestablished the Mass (on this episode
see Corish 1985, 89, 95).

By 1610 there was no longer any confusion about who or what was
Catholic and who or what was Protestant, nor any confusion as to

the religion that prevailed. Writing in 1613, the papal internuncio in Brussels could brag:

> The people in this kingdom [Ireland] are in general Catholics, and almost all of them profess their Catholic religion quite openly. . . . Only in the cities, and mainly in those cities involved in commerce, are a part of the people infected by heresy. But even in such cities heretics are greatly outnumbered by Catholics. Throughout the countryside the inhabitants are all Catholics, even if they are for the most part wrapped in a deep and blind ignorance of the faith they profess. Among the highest rank of the nobility, you might with great effort find three or four that were heretics and the same could be said of the gentry. Because their zeal and constancy in holding to the ancient faith has been so great, it has been easy to maintain among them a great number of priests, and these in turn have been able to cultivate that faith even more. (cited in Hagan 1914, 300–301)

In sum, by the early seventeenth century Ireland was clearly and unequivocally a Catholic nation.

The Centrality of the Anglo-Irish

Anglo-Irish merchant and gentry families in Leinster and Munster played a key role in this revitalization of Catholicism. As mentioned, they took the lead in openly absenting themselves from Church of Ireland services and in patronizing distinctively Catholic services. Just as importantly, this group became increasingly willing to use the financial resources they controlled to support the Catholic Church. Most of the monasteries dissolved in 1534–37 had been located in Munster and Leinster,[2] for instance, and much of the property associated with these monasteries had passed into the hands of local Anglo-Irish elites (Lennon 1986, 84; Bradshaw 1988, 454–55). These same elites often had rights to the tithes and other ecclesiastical dues collected in different parishes and controlled as well the income and properties belonging to religious confraternities (Lennon 1989, 126–27). When these Anglo-Irish elites pulled away from the established church in the late 1500s, they could—and did—use these financial resources to support a distinctively Catholic clergy.

But the Anglo-Irish of Leinster and Munster committed more to the Catholic cause than just their wealth; they committed their sons as well. Starting in the 1570s (and so simultaneous with their turn toward recusancy) Anglo-Irish mercantile families increasingly chose to send their sons to Continental Europe, rather than to England, in search of a university education (Hammerstein 1971). It was this influx of Irish students that eventually fueled the establishment of the Irish colleges. Between 1590 and 1610 Irish colleges were established at Salamanca (1592), Lisbon (1593), Douai (1594), Bordeaux (1603), Toulouse (1603), Paris (1605), Santiago de Compostella (1605), Lille (1610), and Rouen (1610)—and others would be established later in the century.[3] These colleges provided more than just a Catholic education; they were seminaries, and their stated goal "was to produce virtuous and well-educated priests who would be intellectually equipped to preserve and spread the catholic faith in Ireland" (Cregan 1979, 107). Most of the Irish students coming to these colleges, in other words, were expected to become priests imbued with Counter-Reformation ideals who would bring those ideals back to Ireland, and the available evidence suggests that most students did return to Ireland upon completion of their studies (Silke 1976, 624). Over the period 1590–1615 the Irish colleges at Douai and Louvain alone produced about three hundred priests for the mission to Ireland (Cunningham 1991, 16).

What needs to be explained, of course, is why the Anglo-Irish elites of Leinster and Munster increasingly withdrew from the Church of Ireland during the period 1580–1610 and why they increasingly embraced—by their open profession of Catholicism, by the act of directing the resources they controlled toward the support of a Catholic clergy, by their decision to send their sons to Catholic seminaries abroad—a distinctly Catholic tradition. Some commentators (Canny 1975; 1976) have suggested that the Anglo-Irish rejection of the established church and their turn toward Catholicism was in both cases a response to their increasing feeling of alienation from English institutions in Ireland.

Although Irish historians seem generally agreed that the Anglo-Irish did indeed feel increasingly alienated during the latter half of the sixteenth century, these same historians are divided on the likely cause of this alienation. For most Irish historians, Anglo-Irish alienation derived from the fact that as a group they were increasingly

being excluded from governance (both civil and ecclesiastical) in favor of the "New English" (i.e., English who had come to Ireland since
1530). Bradshaw (1988, 469) provides a concise summary of this view:
"As the sixteenth century progressed the crown's favor came to rest
increasingly on a new colonial coterie, the New English, as the in-
struments of its programme of reform in church and state. And the
programme came gradually to evolve into a policy of conquest and
colonization. None of this was to the benefit of the older colonial
community and their mood of resentment and alienation became
increasingly manifest in political protest of various forms." More recently Brady (1994) has suggested that alienation of the Anglo-Irish
has less to do with their exclusion from governance (which, he argues, has been exaggerated) and more to do with the increasing financial burdens they were being asked to bear. Whatever its cause,
there seems little doubt that starting in the middle of the sixteenth
century the Anglo-Irish did increasingly come to feel alienated from
English institutions.

Still, as Bradshaw (1988, 468) points out, the "increasing alienation
of the Anglo-Irish" hypothesis—even assuming it is true—really only
explains why the Anglo-Irish rejected the established church; it does
not explain why they turned toward Catholicism. Indeed, since there
is much evidence to suggest that the resentment of the Anglo-Irish
was directed at English authorities in Ireland and not the English
crown (to which they were consistently loyal; see Canny 1976, 137–53;
Brady 1994), it is not at all obvious why they would have adopted an
ideology (Roman Catholicism) that was so strongly associated with
England's Continental enemies.

For some Irish historians, then, the Anglo-Irish turn toward Catholicism is a puzzle that can never be solved. Patrick Corish (1985,
78) suggests that "it will always probably remain something of a mystery why they did not accept some reasonable form of Anglicanism
when the pressure came on them during the reign of Elizabeth—and
there can be little doubt a very reasonable Anglicanism would have
satisfied the Queen." Others, however, have sought to explain the
Anglo-Irish turn toward Catholicism by suggesting that it derived
from the essentially conservative nature of this group. In this view,
the Anglo-Irish remained attached to the traditional society that had
prevailed in Ireland (and in England for that matter) before the Ref-

ormation, and Catholicism had been a part of that traditional society. Catholicism was, to use Lennon's (1986, 82) words, "the faith which they had inherited from their ancestors and which had remained relatively untouched by reformation ideas." This traditional faith, Lennon argues (82), was for the Anglo-Irish a "fund of religious experience of the community—worship, institutions, devotions, civic piety—[that] became a legacy to be cherished in the face of innovation and change." In this line of thinking, then, the Anglo-Irish turn to Counter-Reformation Catholicism was an attempt to "conserve" a traditional identity that they felt was being undermined by innovations and changes taking place around them.

It is this last interpretation—which sees the Anglo-Irish turn toward Catholicism as a conservative response—that I now want to consider carefully, since I think that it epitomizes a common way of thinking about religion in sixteenth-century Ireland that misreads in a very fundamental way the cultural dynamics that caused post-Reformation Ireland to become a Catholic nation.

Conservatism or Innovation?

What needs to be emphasized, in order to make the argument I want to make, is that the Counter-Reformation Catholicism to which Anglo-Irish sons were exposed on the Continent was dramatically different from the variant of Catholicism that had likely prevailed in pre-Reformation Ireland. (I say "likely" because most of what scholars infer about pre-Reformation Ireland is based on information obtained in the sixteenth century.) There is lots of anecdotal evidence, for instance, suggesting that Catholics in sixteenth-century Ireland were as woefully ignorant of key Church doctrines as Catholics in other areas of the Catholic world (Bossy 1971, 157–58), and there is no particular reason to believe that things had been much different in the fifteenth century. Even the already-cited report of the papal internuncio written in 1613, which is generally so positive about the state of Catholicism in Ireland, suggests that Irish Catholics in the countryside were "wrapped in a deep and blind ignorance of the faith they profess." The available evidence also suggests that pre-Reformation laypersons were generally unfamiliar with the sacrament of confession, and were certainly not confessing at least once a year as would be required by Trent (Bossy 1971, 166). Finally, although Catholics in pre-Reformation Ireland almost certainly attended Mass on special occasions, there is absolutely nothing to suggest that they did what Counter–Reformation Catholicism would come to regard as central: attend Sunday Mass on a regular basis in the local parish church.

Recognizing that Counter-Reformation Catholicism was quite unlike what had previously prevailed in Ireland permits—I suggest—a gestalt shift in our conceptualization of what happened among the Anglo-Irish in the late sixteenth century. In particular, it permits us to see the Anglo-Irish turn toward Counter-Reformation Catholicism as something quite innovative rather than as something that derives from a backward-looking conservatism. During the late sixteenth century the Anglo-Irish were reaching out to a variant of Catholicism that was new and quite unfamiliar rather than trying to revivify some older variant that might have been familiar to their grandparents. Do I mean thereby to deny the recurrent characterization of the Anglo-Irish as conservative? Not quite.

What I am suggesting is that the conservatism of the Anglo-Irish lay not in any attachment to those devotional practices that had prevailed in the pre-Reformation era (which, I suspect, had played only a very small role in the lives of the Irish laity) but rather in their commitment to a set of societal values that characterized traditional societies throughout Europe. Preeminent among these were the values identified by Bossy and discussed in the last chapter: an emphasis on collectivities bound by kinship, on feuding as a method of dispute resolution, and on communal experiences characterized by the merger of the sacred and the profane.

I have already suggested that Bossy was correct in arguing that these traditional values were at variance with many of the activities required by Trent, and that as a consequence the Tridentine reforms could not be implemented in most areas of Europe until these traditional values had been eroded. But I also suggested that Bossy had overlooked the possibility that some groups might respond to the conflict between these traditional values and Tridentine Catholicism in a highly creative way. The essence of this creative response was to take from the specific prescriptions mandated by Trent a set of emphases that were sufficiently abstract that they could be merged with these traditional values. The result of this merger, I have argued, was that variant of popular Catholicism in which holy wells, patterns, and rounding rituals were central and in which Tridentine rituals like the Mass were present but incidental.

Gaelic Ireland

What about the Old Irish? What role did Gaelic Ireland play in the emergence of this first devotional revolution? Certainly, the Old Irish were slower to turn to Counter-Reformation Catholicism. Even though an Irish college specifically intended for Ulstermen had been founded at Alcalá (Spain) as early as 1590, Nicholas Canny's (1987) review of the Gaelic-language religious literature produced over the period 1580–1750 suggests that Old Irish elites had little understanding or interest in Protestantism or Counter-Reformation Catholicism prior to the contact with Continental Europe fostered by the rebellion in Ulster that took place in 1594–1603. It was, Canny argues, the exodus of Gaelic lords and soldiers provoked by the English victory in that rebellion that led to a similar exodus of Gaelic scholars, many of whom found their way to the same Continental seminaries to which their Anglo-Irish counterparts had come decades earlier.

In thinking about the ties between "Gaelic Ireland" and the Continental seminaries, however, we must (as always) pay careful attention to geography. Where in Ireland, for example, were the Old Irish students who went to the Continent from? Some information on this issue can be gleaned from the oaths required of students entering the Irish college at Salamanca. The oaths taken from a hundred students over the period 1595–1619 have survived (see O'Doherty 1913), and in his own analysis of these oaths Corish (1985, 94) points out that at least a third of these students were Gaelic Irish. By my count, in fact, forty-one of these hundred students had (or likely had) Gaelic surnames.[4] But these same oaths identify the diocese or province of origin for each student, and it turns out that over 70 percent of these Gaelic students (twenty-nine of forty-one) were from Leinster and Munster. In short, at least during the period surveyed, the vast majority of Gaelic students were from the same areas of Ireland as their Anglo-Irish counterparts.

It might be argued that where the Gaelic students attending Continental seminaries were from is less important (given that our concern is with dissemination of Counter-Reformation ideas in Ireland) than where they ended up. Looking only at Irish bishops, it might seem that graduates of the Continental seminaries made their way into all corners of Ireland. Donal Cregan's (1979) study of the thirty-seven bishops appointed to Irish sees in the period 1618–57 indicates that almost all of them had been educated on the Continent, and that this was as true for the seventeen men appointed to dioceses in (or mainly in) Connaught and Ulster as for those appointed to dioceses in Leinster and Munster. The problem here, of course, is that a bishop's having a Continental education tells us little if anything about the educational background of the local clergy in his diocese.

In fact, we know that Continental-trained priests were relatively scarce in northern dioceses. Remember that the geographical distribution of Continental-trained priests in 1704 was one of the indicators used by Whelan (1988) to establish the boundaries of the Catholic heartland in Leinster and Munster, as was the geographical distribution of parishes keeping a parish register (as required by Trent) prior to 1775. What Whelan's data suggest, in other words, is that to the extent Gaelic students trained in the Continental seminaries did bring the Counter-Reformation back to Ireland, they—like their Anglo-Irish counterparts—brought it back almost solely to those particular areas of Leinster and Munster that would become (by these very efforts) Ireland's Catholic heartland.

What all this means, incidentally, is that scholarly attempts to decide if "Gaelic piety" or "Anglo-Irish piety" is the wellspring of Irish Catholicism (see, for example, Miller 1975) are misconceived. On the contrary, the analysis that I have been developing here suggests that it was the dynamic and creative culture that prevailed in areas of Leinster and Munster which was ultimately responsible for Ireland's first devotional revolution, and this culture was in the end shared by both the Anglo-Irish and the Gaelic Irish living in these areas.

An Aside: Cultural Studies and Irish Historiography

Some time ago K. Bottigheimer (1985, 205) suggested that there had been few if any attempts to develop a "sociology" of the Reformation or Counter-Reformation in Ireland, mainly because Irish historians have generally held to the view that religious matters are determined not by "society" itself but rather by the actions and decisions of its leaders. Nothing much has changed over the intervening years. Most studies of the Reformation and Counter-Reformation in Ireland are still very much concerned with individual personalities, that is, with asking who did what on what date and how did somebody else respond. What I am suggesting here, by contrast, is that "culture"— not personalities—was decisive in ensuring that Ireland remained (or, more accurately, became) a Catholic nation. Specifically, I am arguing that it was the dynamic and creative culture that prevailed in areas of Leinster and Munster that was decisive in making Ireland Catholic. I claim no originality in pointing to the simple existence of this culture; the work by Whelan and Smyth has already done that. What is novel is only the suggestion that this culture was "in place" during the late sixteenth century and that it was responsible not just for the importation of the Counter-Reformation into Ireland but also for that great surge in supposedly "traditional" activities (involving holy well cults, patterns, rounding rituals, etc.) that has been documented for the early 1600s.

It is now time to consider the second of the questions posed at the beginning of this chapter, namely, why did the variant of popular Catholicism born of this first devotional revolution, in the early seventeenth century, come to an end?

Transformations Misconstrued

All commentators are agreed that the period from the late eighteenth through the early nineteenth centuries was a time of transition for Irish Catholicism. It was during this time that the popularity of holy well cults and patterns declined dramatically and rates of attendance at Sunday Mass in the local parish church increased. However, scholarly opinion has always been divided on two questions: (1) Was the rise to prominence of the new "romanized" Catholicism, in which attendance at Sunday Mass was the central ritual activity, relatively sudden (emerging mainly in the post-Famine period) or gradual, and (2) What was the underlying cause of this religious transformation? I have already reviewed the answers given to the first question by Larkin and others; I now want to consider the answers usually given to the second question.

In his original article, Larkin (1972) suggested that the devotional revolution resulted from three things: (1) the population decline caused by the Famine, which substantially improved the ratio of priests to people (and thus the degree to which the clergy could promote adherence to Tridentine norms), (2) the fact that Catholicism provided Irish Catholics with a clear national identity at a time when their language and culture were being Anglicized, and (3) the efforts of particular individuals to promote a Romanized Catholicism (Larkin singles out Paul Cardinal Cullen as having been especially important in this regard).

Canny (1979) proposes a slightly different explanation of the (second) devotional revolution. His central contention is that during the sixteenth century a fairly substantial minority among the Anglo-Irish elite in Ireland were in fact won over to the Reformation cause and that the use of coercion initially ensured that most of the general population also became at least nominal members of the established church. Up to this point, then, the Reformation experience in Ireland was not that much different from the Reformation experience in those areas of Europe that would eventually become Protestant. What subsequently happened in those other areas, however, is that early Protestant successes among social elites and the forced conversion of the masses were quickly followed by a campaign of mass evangelization that produced a genuine and widespread commitment to Protestantism. This next step, mass evangelization, never took place in Ireland. But this does not mean that the Counter-Reformation triumphed. On the contrary, Canny (450) argues, the "majority of the native population remained outside the structure of the rival churches and clung tenaciously to pre-tridentine religious practice." Only in the late eighteenth century, in the face of a sharply increasing population in Ireland, were Protestant authorities driven to mount the attempts at mass evangelization they had failed to mount centuries earlier. But this Protestant campaign provoked a counter-reaction from a newly revitalized Catholic hierarchy. As part of this counter-reaction, the Catholic hierarchy mounted its own campaign of mass evangelization, and it was this campaign, Canny concludes, that eventually led to the triumph of Tridentine Catholicism in Ireland.

Whereas Larkin and Canny are concerned mainly with explaining the increased appeal of Tridentine Catholicism during the late eighteenth and early nineteenth centuries, other investigators have provided explanations for the diminishing appeal of holy well cults and patterns during this same period. David Miller (1975) argues that these popular traditions had always been permeated with "magico-religious" significance and that peasants remained wedded to these traditions only as long as they seemed to "work." What the Famine demonstrated was that these popular traditions did not work, that is, that the rituals associated with these traditions could not be relied upon to secure a good harvest, to cure disease, or ensure good health.[5] In a book that has since become a basic reference work in the study of Irish Catholicism, S. J. Connolly (1982) also stresses the magico-religious significance of the rituals surrounding holy well cults and patterns, suggesting that these rituals (and a wide range of other activities) met certain psychological and emotional needs of Irish peasants. Primary among these needs, he suggests, was the need for peasants to believe that they could exert some control over what happened to them in life. For Connolly, the Famine did indeed bring an end to these popular traditions. This was not because the Famine showed these traditions to be ineffective (as suggested by Miller) but rather because the Famine, through death and forced emigration, devastated the peasant class that had always been the mainstay of these popular traditions.

For Desmond Mooney (1990) the decay of "folk practice" in the early nineteenth century was linked most of all to the rapid growth of educational institutions, mainly local schools. Mass education, Mooney argues, led inevitably to a decline in the use of the Irish language. Since the Irish language had been "the repository of the concepts, stories and beliefs which were an integral part of folk practices" (210), its decline led inevitably to a decline in those practices.

Although different in many of their particulars, all of these theories—by Larkin, Canny, Miller, Connolly, Mooney—share in common a number of implicit assumptions, namely, that the variant of popular Catholicism that prevailed in pre-Famine Ireland was pre-Tridentine in origin; that it was associated mainly with Gaelic traditions; and that it appealed mainly to peasants. Each of these assumptions, however, has been called into question by the evidence and analysis presented in this book. This, for me, necessitates a fresh look at the second devotional revolution and its likely causes.

The Two Devotional Revolutions

Dating the Decline

When, exactly, did holy well cults and patterns cease to be truly popular activities in Ireland? Although Larkin and Connolly allow for some decline in the popularity of these activities in the pre-Famine period, they both see the Famine as being a pivotal event, and I suspect that that view is shared by many readers. Yet the evidence of the OSL, it seems to me, establishes with near certainty that patterns and holy wells had long since ceased to be widely popular activities by the 1830s. Although the OSL do occasionally report that rounding rituals were still being performed at some particular holy well, it is far more common to find them saying that such rituals "used to be performed" at some well or that there is "no report of rounding rituals being associated with" some particular well. Much the same is true of patterns. A few wells were still associated with patterns in the 1830s but the overwhelming majority were not, even though it is common to read that a pattern "used to be held" at a particular site within living memory. In the end, then, evidence from the OSL suggests that the variant of popular Catholicism we have been considering went into sharp decline sometime during the period 1760–1830, and so it is to events of this period—not to the events of the 1840s and 1850s—that we must look in order to understand the cause of this decline.

At least one cause, I think, has been "hidden in plain sight" for some time, by which I mean that it involves a historical trend that is very familiar to Irish historians but whose significance in regard to popular Catholicism has been missed.

The Declining Ratio of Priests to People

Ireland's population increased dramatically during the eighteenth and early nineteenth centuries. One estimate suggests that it went from less than 2.5 million in 1753 to 4.4 million in 1791 to 6.8 million in 1821 to almost 8.2 million by 1841 (Clark and Donnelly 1983, 26). During the same period the supply of available priests increased only slightly, and so the net result was a steady deterioration in the ratio of priests to people among the Catholic population. Connolly (1982, 33) reports that this ratio was 1:1,587 in 1731, 1:2,676 in 1800, and 1:2,996 in 1840. In little more than a century, in other words, the ratio of people to priests nearly doubled. While virtually all previous commentators have taken note of this fact, they have invariably taken it as supporting the view that the pre-Famine Church lacked the resources to promote a wider acceptance of Tridentine rituals (see Larkin 1972; Connolly 1982, 31 f.; Corish 1984, 159; Whelan 1985, 218–19; Keogh 1993, 7). But how would this worsening priests-to-people ratio have affected the popularity of holy well cults and patterns?

At least implicitly, most commentators take it for granted that the unavailability of priests was one of the conditions that allowed such popular devotions to flourish (see especially Whelan 1985, 218–19). As reasonable as such a view might seem, we should remember that it is inconsistent with the historical evidence. As already noted, the same period that witnessed an increasing shortage of priests relative to the Catholic population also witnessed a dramatic decline in the popularity of holy well cults and patterns. In other words, it would appear that as priests became relatively scarce, holy well cults and patterns became less popular.

I suspect that this correlation has been ignored in earlier commentaries on Irish Catholicism because it does not "make sense" from the perspective of the official Church, which is the perspective that Irish historians (whether they chose to admit it or not) have so often adopted when studying Irish Catholicism. After all, in the view of the official Church, priests are agents of Tridentine Catholicism whose job it is to woo ignorant peasants away from superstition and error. Given this, it makes no sense to predict that decreasing the relative supply of priests should lead to a decline in the popularity of "superstitious" practices. Such a correlation, however, does make sense given the perspective that has been developed in this book.

I have argued that popular Catholicism is a variant of Catholicism which develops within a set of broad constraints and that one of those constraints is that for a belief or practice to be seen as "Catholic" it must be legitimated by at least the local clergy. Indeed, the local clergy in Ireland did initially (and for a long time thereafter) legitimate the holy well cults and patterns that emerged in the wake of the Reformation, and I have argued that this was a major factor in explaining the popularity of those devotions. Now: all else being equal, a declining number of priests relative to the Catholic population would impede the ability of the local clergy to legitimate holy well cults; that is, there would be fewer priests available to send Irish Catholics to holy wells in order to discharge a penance and fewer priests available to attend patterns and participate in the rituals there. The fact that the local clergy was increasingly unable to legitimize holy well cults would have undermined the popularity of such cults. Given this reasoning, the expected result is that a worsening ratio of priests-to-people would be associated with a decline in the popularity of holy well cults—which is precisely the correlation that we do in fact observe in the historical record.

Class Matters

To the Ordnance Survey investigators who went into the field during the 1830s, the cause—at least the proximate cause—of the declining popularity of patterns and holy well cults seemed obvious: the local clergy had finally decided to discourage these popular practices. After describing the stations performed at a site in County Roscommon, for instance, John O'Donovan took note both of the role of the local clergy and the relative recency of their efforts in this regard: "The Priests, I am very sorry to see and to say, inclining very much in this Century to Protestant notions, are putting an end to all those venerable customs [like performing stations]. But I would wish they had delayed their reformation for six years longer till I had the Territories traversed" (OSL, 1837, Co. Roscommon, vol. 1)—and any number of other passages in the OSL make a similar point. In this same period Protestant commentators also called attention to the fact that Catholic clergy were now, finally, working to eradicate the superstitious practices associated with holy well cults (see, for instance, Hall 1841–43, 1:279–80). It would appear, then, that during the early decades of the nineteenth century, not only were there fewer priests available to give legitimacy to holy well cults and patterns, but among those who were available, an increasing number were actively turning against these activities.

Surprisingly, the issue of why the local clergy turned against such popular traditions has not attracted much attention from Irish historians. Most discussions assume that the opposition to patterns and holy well cults which was increasingly voiced by the hierarchy from the late 1700s onward eventually filtered down to the local level. But this view presupposes that "official Church policy" would have been —and was—the thing that most influenced the attitudes of the local clergy. Likely this was not the case.

In a careful study of local priests in County Tipperary over the period 1850–91, James O'Shea (1983) shows that these priests were overwhelmingly from the well-off tenant farmer class and that their attitudes and priorities in regard to pressing issues of the day—including landlordism, evictions, republicanism, agrarian violence, the Land League, support for Parnell—were shaped more by their class background than by their seminary training or theological knowledge. While O'Shea's study is limited to the post-Famine period, there is no reason not to believe that class origin would also have been critical as well in shaping the attitudes of the local clergy in the pre-Famine period.

What were the social origins of the local clergy during the pre-Famine period? Although hard evidence is difficult to come by, most commentators seem agreed that this clergy was drawn primarily from the same group identified by O'Shea, the wealthy tenant farmer class, and to a lesser extent from merchant and artisan families in the cities. Historically, of course, the costs associated with sending a son abroad to be educated at one of the Continental seminaries in itself ensured that priests would come from well-off families. But it would appear that the class origins of the local clergy did not change even with the establishment of the Irish seminary at Maynooth in 1795 (Corish 1985, 160–62). To understand why a clergy recruited from relatively well off middle-class families might turn against holy wells and patterns in the period 1750–1830, we need to understand the cultural history of this class during this period.

Eugene Hynes, a Sociologist among Historians

The late eighteenth century was a time of relatively rapid social change in Ireland. In the rural areas of Ireland, in particular, the rapidly increasing population and the commercialization of agriculture produced a number of class-based cleavages within the Catholic community. One of the most important of these was the cleavage that emerged between Catholic "strong farmers," that is, Catholic tenant farmers whose holdings were substantial enough to allow them a comfortable living, and the Catholic "poor," a mixed group that included tenant farmers with smaller holdings, cottiers, and landless laborers. Usually, Irish historians who discuss the divergent class interests that came to characterize strong farmers and the rural poor, respectively, are concerned with relating these divergent interests to the agrarian violence that occurred over the period 1760–1830 (see Clark 1979, 21–104; Roberts 1983; Donnelly 1983; Power, 1993). Less attention has been paid to the effect that this newly emergent social cleavage in the Irish countryside had upon the shape and texture of popular Catholicism. The one exception here is Eugene Hynes, and Hynes's work will serve as the foundation for the argument that I want to develop here.

Hynes (1978; 1988; 1990) argues that the living standards of the Catholic strong-farmer class improved dramatically during the late eighteenth century, mainly as a result of (1) the relaxation of the Penal Laws, (2) the commercialization of Irish agriculture, and (3) the growing demand for Irish foodstuffs in Britain. A psychological consequence of this improvement in living standards, Hynes argues, was that Irish strong farmers came to be characterized by a "great hunger" for land, that is, by an intense desire to control enough land to maintain their newly acquired standard of living. This, in turn, gave rise to a desire among strong farmers to avoid the fragmentation of family farms and to prevent the dissipation of the capital that might be used to maximize the profit from such farms. For these reasons, Catholic strong farmers increasingly adopted the stem family system. Under this system, only one son within a given family inherited and the marriage of this son was arranged with the daughter of some other strong farmer. Authority was concentrated in the hand of the father, at least until the father turned over control of the family farm to the inheriting son. The system of impartible inheritance and concentration of authority in the hands of one person guarded against the fragmentation of land and capital that threatened the lifestyle of the strong-farmer class.

This turn toward the stem family system brought along with it a set of cultural values. The most important of these stressed family solidarity, obedience to a single authority (necessary if the family head was to exert sole control over the family capital), and sexual restraint (in order to reduce the number of mouths dependent on a given family farm). For Hynes, the emergence of these cultural values within the strong-farmer class during the late eighteenth century proved to be of critical importance in the history of Irish Catholicism since it happened that, for an entirely separate set of reasons, the Church hierarchy in Rome was coming to emphasize precisely these same values. It was this affinity between the cultural values of the strong-farmer class and the values then being promoted by Rome which ensured that this class in Ireland increasingly became staunch supporters of "official" Catholicism.

Like most other investigators, Hynes sees holy well cults, rounding rituals, and patterns as folk traditions associated for the most part with cottiers and landless laborers. As a result he sees the changing pattern of religious practice in Ireland during the nineteenth century as reflecting the demographic changes induced by the Famine. In particular, Hynes—like Connolly—argues that "Romanized" Catholicism triumphed mainly because the Famine killed off or drove off cottiers and landless laborers while hardly affecting the strong-farmer class at all. In short, for Hynes, the religion of the strong-farmer class did not change as a result of the Famine; the Famine simply ensured that this class—and therefore the official Catholicism they preferred—would come to predominate in Ireland.

Before suggesting a modification of Hynes's theory, I should note that his work has had an odd fate in the literature on Irish Catholicism. Among American and Canadian scholars, his work is well known and generally respected. Larkin (1984, 6–11), for instance, singles out Hynes's 1978 essay for special praise, even though a large part of that essay was devoted to criticism of Larkin's original article on the devotional revolution. Irish scholars, by contrast, have generally ignored Hynes's work. Hynes is not cited, for instance, by either Connolly (1982) or Corish (1985), even though his account of the devotional revolution is obviously relevant to (and at times quite compatible with) their own. My suspicion is that Irish scholars studying Irish Catholicism have ignored Hynes's work partly because he is American but mainly because he is a sociologist and as such is seen to be an interloper in a domain almost invariably (at least in Irish scholarly circles) reserved for historians.

I find Hynes's explanation of why Catholic strong farmers increasingly turned to official Catholicism from the late 1700s onward to be eminently plausible and an explanation that accords well with the historical evidence. Moreover, since Hynes is not concerned with the variant of Catholicism favored by the Catholic strong-farmer group prior to the mid-eighteenth century, there is no inconsistency between his argument and the claim being made here, namely, that from the early 1600s to the late 1700s holy well cults, rounding rituals, and patterns enjoyed the support of all social levels in the Catholic community (including Catholic strong farmers). The only part of Hynes's argument that needs to be modified (but not, as we shall see, by much) in light of the analysis presented here is his account of why holy well cults, rounding rituals, and patterns declined in popularity among cottiers and landless laborers.

For Hynes, as for Connolly and others, these activities were folk traditions to which the rural poor "clung" and which fell into disuse because this class was devastated by the Famine. As already indicated, this view seems falsified by the evidence suggesting that the popularity of these activities declined precipitously in the decades preceding the Famine. My own argument is that these activities fell into disuse because the local clergy turned against them and in so doing deprived such activities of the legitimacy that was a necessary precondition of their popularity. What Hynes's theory does, however, is to provide us with an answer to the question posed at the end of the last section, namely, why the local clergy turned against holy well cults and patterns.

The local clergy, remember, were drawn disproportionately from the strong-farmer class and so would have shared those cultural emphases—upon family solidarity, upon obedience to authority, and upon sexual restraint—that increasingly came to characterize this class. While these values would indeed (just as Hynes suggests) have predisposed the local clergy toward the Catholicism of the official Church, these same values would have predisposed them against the variant of popular Catholicism in place since the first devotional revolution. The ethos that pervaded holy well cults and patterns, after all, was far more "communitarian" than "familial," and many of the activities associated with patterns (notably faction fights and the secular activities that intermingled the sexes) clearly negated, rather than affirmed, the emphases upon "obedience to a central authority" and "sexual restraint." In short, the local clergy who turned against holy well cults and patterns starting in the late eighteenth century did so less because they had finally become imbued with the spirit of Trent and more because they were guided by the cultural values that had recently emerged within the strong-farmer class from which they were drawn.

One advantage of seeing the local clergy in Ireland as increasingly being guided by the values that were emerging within the strong-farmer class during the late eighteenth century is that such a perspective helps us to better understand a devotional practice that first makes its appearance during this same period—and which has always presented something of a puzzle for scholars concerned with the history of the second devotional revolution.

The Rise of a New Kind of Station

Commentators in the early nineteenth century who wanted to present the general public with an account of the religious practices prevailing among Irish Catholic peasants invariably pointed out that there were two quite different meanings of the term *station*. On the one hand, the term referred to the rounding rituals performed at some particular site (a holy well, a pile of stones, a stone circle, etc.). But the term *station* was also used in connection with a practice that had nothing at all to do with holy wells or rounding rituals. Basically, this second sort of station involved a priest visiting each of a series of private homes in an area, and at each home hearing confessions and saying Mass for those members of the community who attended. Hardy (1840, 77) drew the distinction between the two kinds of station in this way:

> The reader is to understand, that a station in this [second] sense
> differs from a station made to any particular spot, remarkable,
> for local sanctity. There, a station means the performance of a pil-
> grimage to a certain place, under peculiar circumstances, and the
> going through a stated number of prayers and other penitential
> ceremonies . . . here, it simply means the coming of the parish
> Priest and his Curate to some house in the townland, on a day
> publicly announced from the Altar for that purpose on the pre-
> ceding Sabbath . . . to give those who live within the district in

which the station is held an opportunity of coming to their duty, as frequenting the ordinance of confession is emphatically called.

Because hearing confessions was central to this new kind of station, the practice was often called "stations of confession."

In the post-Famine period, leaders of the Irish Church, like Paul Cardinal Cullen, suggested that holding stations of confessions at private homes was a practice that had emerged in response to the restrictions forced on Irish Catholics by the Penal Laws passed in the early eighteenth century, and some modern scholars continue to endorse this interpretation (see Larkin 1980, 209). At least two considerations, however, make such an interpretation unlikely. First, even in the early part of the eighteenth century, when the enforcement of the Penal legislation was most intense, Catholic Mass-houses (makeshift structures used to say Mass and vacant the rest of the time) were allowed to function even though their precise location was usually well known to authorities. There was, in other words, no need to "conceal" a mass by having it said in a private home. Second, and more important, the first certain evidence that stations of confessions were a popular practice does not appear in the documentary record until the 1780s, that is, during the period when the Penal Laws were being eased. In light of such considerations, I suspect that many commentators would likely concur with Corish's (1985, 134) suggestion that the origins of this practice are obscure.

What is puzzling about these "newer" sort of stations—the stations of confession—is that they were so much at variance with the Catholicism of the official Church. The practice of holding Mass in private homes, after all, had been specifically condemned by the Council of Trent. Furthermore, both Roman authorities and leaders of the Irish Church like Paul Cardinal Cullen actively discouraged stations of confession. Yet the practice flourished in Ireland well into the 1860s (and in some areas, well into the twentieth century)—and this was true despite the general turn toward "Romanized" Catholicism that otherwise constitutes the devotional revolution. The puzzle, in other words, is why Irish Catholics in the immediate post-Famine period, who were so loyal to Rome on other issues, broke with Rome on this one particular issue.

What no one seems to have taken note of, as far as I can tell, is that this "newer" way of doing stations first appears in the documentary record during precisely that same period of time (the late eighteenth century) when the popularity of the "older" way of doing stations (involving holy well cults and rounding rituals) began to decline dramatically. Certainly no one has previously suggested that these things proceeded from the same cause. That, however, is precisely the argument I now want to make. Specifically, I want to suggest that the same cultural values which predisposed the local clergy against holy well cults and patterns predisposed them toward the practice of making stations of confession.

An Occasion for Social Display

A concise summary of the full sequence of events, both religious and secular, that transpired during a station of confession appears in a report critical of this practice that was sent to the Vatican in 1870:

> On Sunday, the parish priest announces from the altar that tomorrow, Monday, there will be a station at the house of such, Tuesday at the house of such other, and so on for Wednesday and Thursday. On the said day the parish priest and his curates go early in the morning to the designed house, and there the people from the surrounding neighborhood set themselves to hear the confessions of the men and women; finished hearing confession, one of the priests celebrates the holy mass and the people receive communion; then the owner of the house gives a dinner to all the priests and to some of the more respectable of the faithful. The dinner over there begins the drinking of their "whisky" and it continues until the reverends must be carried drunk to their house. (cited in Larkin 1996, 8–9)

Stations of confession were usually held sometime around Christmas and Easter, and priests used the occasion to collect the dues they were owed by the members of their flock. In some parishes the number of stations held during a single year could be quite large. Writing in 1800, for instance, the bishop of Kildare and Leighlin (dioceses in mid-Leinster) suggested that "the stations, in large populous parishes, generally exceed, sometimes considerably, one hundred in the year" (Vane 1849, 4:15).

The Two Devotional Revolutions

Stations of confession were generally rural events and in principle could be held at any house in the countryside. Certainly stations must have been held, at least occasionally, in homes belonging to cottiers or landless laborers. Nevertheless, most stations were held in homes belonging to what the bishop of Kildare and Leighlin, writing in 1800, called "the upper sort of [the] inhabitants" (Vane 1849, 4:154). Generally, this meant that stations of confession were held in homes belonging to Catholic strong farmers. Furthermore, it seems clear that the strong farmers who hosted a station saw it as occasion for social display, that is, as an occasion for demonstrating that they were associated with a particular lifestyle, as much as they saw it as an occasion for confession and Mass. William Carleton's (1867, 145–80) account of a station of confession, though fictionalized, is one of the most detailed accounts available of what went on during these events, and provides a good sense of the link that existed between this practice and the strong-farmer class.[6]

The central character in Carleton's story is Phaddhy Seamus Phaddhy, who, Carleton tells us, had inherited a farm and a large sum of money (what Phaddhy several times calls "a stockin' of guineas") upon the death of his rich brother. He was, in short, a strong farmer, and he relished the thought of holding a station precisely because it would confer upon him "a personal consequence" (150) in the eyes of his neighbors. As well, true to the pattern typical of the strong-farmer class, one of Phaddhy's sons was intended for the priesthood and allusions to this son's eventually studying at Maynooth appear often in the conversations that Carleton re-creates.

In the days before the station, not only was Phaddhy's house and all its furnishings scrubbed and put into good repair, but new suits were ordered from the local tailor for Phaddhy and each of his six sons. Every effort, in short, was expended to ensure that those attending the station would come away with a positive opinion of Phaddhy, his family, and his house. But it was the dinner at the end of the station day that presented the greatest opportunity for social display.

At one level, a station was a community event. Everyone in the neighborhood was welcome to attend, including cottiers and landless laborers. As a result, it was not uncommon for more than a hundred people to attend a given station (Fitzpatrick 1861, 1:97–98). Dinner, however, was always reserved for a more select group that included the farmer himself and his family, the priests involved, and what the 1870 report quoted earlier called "the more respectable of the faithful." The dinner, then, provided a farmer with an opportunity for demonstrating to the people that counted that he and his family enjoyed the lifestyle to which the strong-farmer class as a whole aspired. At the station dinner described by Carleton, more than two dozen people sat down to eat, and these included Phaddhy, his family, the two priests who officiated, the local landlord, other strong farmers, and nephews of the two priests.

As an author, Carleton himself emphasizes the importance of the station dinner as an occasion for social display by having the officiating priest play upon Phaddhy's insecurity. Thus, Carleton says, the priest inspects Phaddhy's larder and finds that while it contains "an abundance of fowl, and fish, and bacon, and hung-beef" it does not contain any mutton. Accordingly, the priest mentions casually to Phaddhy that at the last station he attended some unnamed persons had suggested that Phaddhy was miserly and so predicted that he would not likely stage a particularly bountiful dinner—and then suggests to Phaddhy that a good leg of mutton and a good bottle of wine, added to what was already available, would certainly put the lie to that charge. Phaddhy, though he knows perfectly well what the priest is up to, cannot take the risk of appearing to be less "dacent" than those of his neighbors who had hosted a station, and so promptly sends for the mutton and wine.

The dinner that followed was a great success. Phaddhy himself reflected upon the day's events this way:

> How could he be otherwise than happy?—he had succeeded to
> a good property, and a stocking of hard guineas . . . he had the
> "clargy" under his roof at last, partaking of a hospitality which
> he felt himself well able to afford them; he had settled up with
> his Reverence for five years arrears of sin [five years being the
> time since his last confession] . . . he was training up Briney [his
> son] for the Mission, and though last, not least, he was far gone
> in his seventh tumbler! (Carleton 1867, 178)

In summary, then, Phaddhy was a strong farmer, with the recognizable lifestyle of a strong farmer, who interacted with the clergy as a social equal and who would soon be linked to the clergy by kinship—and all this had been made clear during the course of the station.

Carleton's account is semifictional. That stations of confession were costly affairs, however, mainly on account of the costs associated with the station dinner and the spirit of rivalry that prevailed among those hosting these events, was something noted by several contemporary commentators (see Newenham 1809, appendix 40–41; Fitzpatrick 1861, 1:98).

I am suggesting, then, that the practice of holding stations of confession became popular because it was a practice that incorporated and expressed the values and interests that pervaded the thinking of the strong-farmer class in the late eighteenth century. The emphasis upon family and family solidarity, for instance, was reflected in the simple fact of holding the station in a family home. A station of confession also provided an opportunity for a strong farmer to demonstrate to the community at large that he enjoyed the lifestyle to which the members of his class aspired. Finally, by establishing a distinction between the "respectable sort of faithful" who were invited to stay for dinner and everyone else, a station of confession gave clear expression to the class consciousness that was an increasingly important element in day-to-day thinking of strong farmers from the late eighteenth century forward.

Seeing the popularity of stations of confession as deriving from the fit between this practice and the cultural values of the strong-farmer class allows us to understand several empirical patterns that were associated with this practice. First of all, it would explain why stations of confession were popular with the strong-farmer class despite the opposition of Church authorities and despite the strong support given by the strong-farmer class to the official Church in most other areas. Second, it would explain why there are no documentary references to stations of confession until the late eighteenth century (i.e., whatever its exact origins, the practice only became popular with the strong farmer with the emergence of the cultural values described by Hynes, and that occurred in the late eighteenth century). Finally, it would explain the geographical pattern associated with this devotional practice.

Stations of confession first appear in the documentary record during the 1780s in association with dioceses located in east Munster

(Corish 1981, 108; Brady 1965, 245–47). Even by the mid-nineteenth century, although there is abundant evidence that the practice had spread to most areas of Ireland, it was still the case that the practice was most strongly entrenched in Munster, east Munster in particular. This is why the Munster bishops, almost unanimously, continued to endorse and encourage stations of confession at the same time that Paul Cardinal Cullen and other Irish bishops were working to eliminate this practice in the 1850s (see Larkin 1980, 209–10). Why east Munster? In fact, this is an area of Ireland in which Catholic strong farmers were especially numerous and influential during the eighteenth century (Whelan 1988) and so is an area where we would expect a practice so suited (under the hypothesis being offered) to the interests of the strong farmer to emerge and become deeply rooted.

Summary and Conclusion

One of my goals in this book has been to convey in a clear and concise manner a sense of the rituals and beliefs that were central to the experience of "being Catholic" in Ireland over the period that runs, roughly, from the Reformation to the Famine. I have also endeavored to induce a gestalt shift in how pre-Famine Catholicism is conceptualized. The prevailing view has long been that the holy well cults and patterns central to popular Catholicism in pre-Famine Ireland were traditions inherited from a distant pagan past and that Irish peasants continued to cling passively to these traditions until such time as the official Church had the manpower, the organization, and the will to win them over to Tridentine Catholicism. I have challenged this view in several ways.

To repeat once more the central contentions of this book: the distinctive variant of popular Catholicism that prevailed in pre-Famine Ireland emerged after Trent (not before); it was a variant of Catholicism most of all associated with the dynamic Anglo-Irish/Gaelic culture which flourished in areas of Leinster and Munster (not simply a diffuse Gaelic tradition); and it was a variant of Catholicism that enjoyed the support of all social levels in the local community (not just peasants). I have also argued, in this chapter, that what most of all caused this variant of Catholicism to decline was the fact that starting in the late eighteenth century the local clergy—guided by

The Two Devotional Revolutions

the values of the social class from which they were drawn—increasingly turned against holy well cults and patterns and in so doing deprived these activities of the legitimacy that had always been a necessary precondition of their popularity.

Generally, the Irish Catholics who emerge from the analysis developed in this and earlier chapters are not passive automatons who cling to traditions inherited from a dim Celtic past and who occasionally absorb beliefs and rituals passed down from on high by Catholic bishops. Whether talking about the Anglo-Irish and Gaelic communities in Leinster and Munster who were responsible for the first devotional revolution or the strong-farmer class in the late eighteenth century (also concentrated mainly in Leinster and Munster) that was responsible for the second devotional revolution, we are talking about people—both laypersons and clerics—who actively synthesized several different traditions in order to forge new and distinctive ways of "being Catholic." In both cases this new synthesis was a highly creative response to changing social conditions, and in both cases it is something that merits recognition and admiration.

At this point, my analysis is generally complete and I am tempted to end the book here. Unfortunately, there is one question that remains unanswered and which I find difficult to put aside: why were rounding rituals, in particular, so central to pre-Famine Catholicism in Ireland? The historic origin of these rituals is not problematic. As indicated in chapter 2, while there may be no evidence that such rituals had any special religious significance in Celtic Ireland or early Christian Ireland, it *is* the case that occasional instances of rounding in religious contexts occur spontaneously across a wide variety of societies and historical periods. That such rituals might therefore have occurred—occasionally—in Ireland, and so have been "available" for use in constructing a new variant of popular Catholicism, is entirely possible. What needs to be explained—and this for me is the nagging question that remains—is why rounding rituals became so popular in post-Reformation Ireland. This is the question that I feel I must address in a final chapter.

Before proceeding, I should issue a warning. Explaining the popularity of rounding rituals inevitably involves exploring the psychological appeal of these rituals. Moreover, investigating the psychological appeal of a ritual in which penitents visit wells and shapeless piles of stone in order to walk round these objects a determinate number of times, always in the same direction, inevitably leads (at least it leads me) to the one psychological tradition in which discussion of behaviors like this is commonplace. That tradition is psychoanalysis. Readers who like their history devoid of psychology, and, in particular, readers for whom a good cigar is—under all circumstances and all conditions—never anything more than a good cigar, may or may not wish to continue on to the next chapter.

Chapter Six

The Psychology of Pre-Famine Catholicism

In the decades following his death in 1939, Sigmund Freud has become something like Hollywood's version of Count Dracula: no matter how many times the Van Helsings of academia pronounce Freud discredited, falsified, outmoded, rejected, or downright silly, he keeps coming back, in the sense that his work continues to be a touchstone of inspiration for countless scholars. Many of these scholars have a clinical orientation and are concerned mainly with psychoanalysis's usefulness as a therapeutic tool. Many others, however, following Freud's lead, continue to use psychoanalysis as a tool for the interpretation of cultural patterns. Even feminist scholars, who would seem to have a clear basis for rejecting Freud's work given the androcentric bias that undeniably pervades some of his analyses, are increasingly coming to give Freud, or at least psychoanalysis, a second chance (see Chodorow 1989; Barrett 1992; Kurzweil 1995).

For myself, I have always found psychoanalysis to be particularly well suited to the study of popular Catholicism. After all, taken at face value the Catholic tradition is awash with individuals who have supposedly talked face-to-face with motherly madonnas come down to Earth to give messages of reassurance or threat. It is also a tradition populated with individuals who have bled from their hands and feet in imitation of Christ's crucifixion; lived years without food; levitated; appeared in two places at once. Similarly, popular Catholic cults have coalesced around saints whose corpses have been preserved incorrupt and around statues depicting Jesus and Mary wearing their physical hearts on the outside of their bodies.

Italy, a Catholic society with which I am especially familiar, was for centuries a land where paintings depicting some particular madonna holding her infant son suddenly started dispensing supernatural favors; where ritual flagellation was a popular practice, even among children; where "tongue dragging" and "falling down" were a routine part of the pilgrimage experience at many sanctuaries; where the dried blood of long-dead saints liquefied (and liquefies still) on a regular and recurrent basis; and where the living petitioned favors from the skulls of people who had died en masse in some long-ago plague.

Generally, the imagery associated with Catholic beliefs and practices of the sort that I have listed here bears a strong similarity to the imagery commonly encountered in connection with those phenomena—like hallucinations, dreams, neuroses, hysteria, sexual fetishism, etc.—whose study has always been central to the psychoanalytic enterprise. As a result, some portion of each of my previous studies of popular Catholicism has been devoted to demonstrating that what otherwise seems problematic about popular Catholic beliefs and practices becomes intelligible when these beliefs and practices are viewed through a psychoanalytic lens. I have no hesitation, then, in turning that same psychoanalytic lens toward a variant of Catholicism in which the central ritual act requires devotees to walk endlessly around pools of running water and shapeless piles of stone.

Ritual Misunderstandings

Freud's view of religion varied somewhat, depending upon whether he was talking about religious belief or religious ritual. He explained religious belief by borrowing directly from his theory of dreams (Freud 1900). In essence he argued that a particular religious belief would be popular to the extent it allowed for the disguised gratification of an unconscious wish. His best-known application of this argument (certainly the one most often cited) was first presented in his *The Future of an Illusion* (1927) and subsequently repeated in *New Introductory Lectures on Psychoanalysis* (1933, 158–84). As adults, Freud argues, we inevitably confront a world permeated with hostile and threatening forces over which we have no control. The resulting feeling of helplessness, however, is not unfamiliar to us; it inevitably reminds us of the helplessness we experienced as children. In that earlier situation our feeling of helplessness was assuaged by the presence of powerful parental figures who protected us, and so we come to long for a similar sense of protection in the present. The result: as adults we are predisposed to believe in a powerful god (or gods) modeled upon the parental imagos buried in our unconscious. This "wish fulfilment" approach to religious belief was to prove popular with several of Freud's students (see, e.g., Jones 1951; Rank 1959) and continues to be used by more recent investigators (in addition to my own work, see Dundes 1987, 1988; Paul 1985).

Freud's view of religious ritual (as opposed to religious belief) was a bit more complicated and as a result has given rise to a fair amount of confusion. In his first extended essay on religious ritual, Freud (1907) very explicitly rejected the common-sense view that people cling to religious rituals only because these rituals had been transmitted to them from the previous generation. Such a view, he felt, seemed incapable of explaining the strong and continuing compulsion to engage in ritual that so obviously drives religiously minded individuals. For him, this sort of compulsion could only be explained on the hypothesis that it was being fed by strong unconscious impulses or desires. In this same essay Freud also made the observation that would prove to be central to all of his subsequent work on religious ritual: these rituals seemed similar to the ceremonials carried out by individuals suffering from obsessional neurosis. In both cases, he said, there is a feeling that the ritual or ceremony has to be performed upon pain of something bad happening; in both cases the ritual action is kept isolated from other activities, in the sense that it must be performed without interruption; and in both cases there is a strong insistence that the actions that define the ritual must be performed in a particular order. Finally, it is the case that religious rituals—like obsessional ceremonies—are often characterized by the stereotypical repetition of the same action a set number of times.

The similarities between religious rituals and the ceremonies of obsessional neurotics led Freud to hypothesize that perhaps both phenomena were produced by a similar process. His clinical investigations had already led him to conclude that obsessional ceremonies were shaped by two equal but opposing forces: a strong unconscious sexual desire and an equally strong (and conscious) prohibition of that desire. Obsessional ceremonies are constructed in such a way as to honor the demands of the conscious prohibition while simultaneously allowing for the disguised gratification of the prohibited unconscious wish. Given the similarities that existed between these ceremonies and religious rituals, Freud hypothesized that perhaps religious rituals were shaped by a similar sort of compromise.

Unfortunately, subsequent commentators have often interpreted Freud's argument here as suggesting that religious rituals are a *form* of obsessional neurosis. Some have even gone as far as to suggest that for Freud religion generally is a form of mental illness (see, e.g., Stark and Iannaccone 1991). Although such interpretations are undeniably facilitated by Freud's inexact use of language in some places, the fact is that even a cursory reading of either his original article or his later work makes it clear that he was as much concerned with the differences between religious rituals and obsessional ceremonies as with the similarities. In particular, he was at pains to make clear that the unconscious desire that gave rise to obsessional neuroses was in the usual case qualitatively different from the unconscious desire that fueled religious ritual.

Obsessional ceremonies, Freud felt, were almost always fed by a repressed sexual desire, whereas religious rituals typically sprang from aggressive impulses in the unconscious whose open expression would impede the smooth functioning of human society. In *Totem and Taboo* (1913) Freud gives several examples of the sort of impulses that fueled religious ritual. In a section entitled "The Taboo upon Rulers" (41–50) he discusses a variety of prohibitions that surround chiefs, kings, priests, and other rulers in different societies. In some societies, he says, subjects may not touch the ruler or objects (including food) that belong to the ruler; in others the ruler is not allowed to go outside his home; in others he cannot stay in certain towns on certain days; in still others he is never allowed to touch the ground and so must be carried aloft everywhere. Ostensibly, the purpose of these taboos is to exalt the ruler above his subjects and protect him from danger—and they did serve that purpose. But, Freud argues, they served a second purpose as well. The great number of restrictions placed on the ruler make his life "an intolerable burden" and so in effect constitute "a revenge taken on [rulers] by their subjects" (51). Since the ruler is a father surrogate, what all this means is that enforcing these prohibitions (and so making the life of the ruler burdensome) allows for the disguised gratification of the hostility toward the father that lies buried in the unconscious of all adults. That religious rituals were fueled by repressed hostility toward the father was sufficiently important to Freud that he regularly called attention to this conclusion even when presenting extremely brief summaries of his work on religious ritual (see Freud 1924; 1925, 66–68).

Apart from a difference in the nature of the underlying impulse or desire that gives rise to religious rituals and obsessional ceremonies, respectively, these two phenomena are different in other ways as well. A defining feature of an obsessional ceremony, and one of the things that makes the behavior neurotic in the first place, is that it is *unwanted* and yet the individual involved feels compelled to engage in it nonetheless. Moreover, the compulsiveness and anxiety associated with obsessional ceremonies often interferes with the individual's ability to function as a member of a social group. Neither of these two things is true of religious rituals. On the contrary, religious rituals are valued activities within a group; so not only is their performance desired by individual members of the group but, more importantly, participation in such rituals enables individuals to become more (not less) integrated into the social life of the group.

In short, it seems fairly evident that there is nothing in Freud's account that requires us to see religion as a form of mental illness, and authors who make that claim are likely simply giving vent to their own personal hostility toward psychoanalysis. Still, as different as they are in the ways just delineated, there is a common emphasis upon repetition, orderliness, and isolation, and this needs to be explained.

Repetition, Orderliness, and Isolation

Freud's suggestion that both obsessional ceremonies and religious rituals are pervaded by an emphasis on repetition, orderliness, and isolation has been substantiated by any number of later investigators (for some recent examples here, see Dulaney and Fiske 1994; Paul 1996). Freud himself consistently argued that in the case of obsessional ceremonies, this particular cluster of emphases had its origin in the infantile experience of anal-eroticism. I recognize that any reference to "anal-eroticism" usually evokes—and has always evoked—a strongly negative reaction from nonpsychoanalytic audiences. Freud (1908, 171n) himself, for instance, in commenting on the reaction to his 1905 essay on infantile sexuality, noted that it had been his remarks on infantile anal-eroticism that most scandalized his readers. Ernest Jones (1955, 295–96) makes a similar point, noting that Freud's remarks on anal-eroticism routinely elicited intense derision from doctors working in psychiatric facilities. Nothing much has changed over the intervening decades, and arguments that invoke infantile anal-eroticism as an explanatory concept continue to evoke a strongly negative and peremptorily dismissive response from social scientists (see, e.g., Stark 1991, 249). Nevertheless, if we approach Freud's remarks about anal-eroticism with the recognition that our aversion to "anality" is culturally determined, then what Freud had to say is fairly straightforward and eminently plausible.

Freud suggested that young children derive physical pleasure from the release that is an intrinsic component of urination and defecation, and they derive pleasure as well from the warmth experienced when newly expelled urine and feces are kept close to their bodies. "Anal-eroticism" is simply the term he used to denote the diffuse experience of physical pleasure that the young child associates with these activities. In the course of time, the young child's experience of anal-eroticism inevitably runs up against our strong cultural aversion to anality. The result is that children are required by powerful parental figures (either the parents themselves or parental surrogates) to regulate and control their urinary and excretory activities, to isolate these activities from other activities, and—as much as possible—to avoid, not seek, contact with urine and feces. In the usual case, this intervention is successful. Children come to exert the control over excretion and urination that ensures their behavior will conform to parental demands, and the original desire for the unregulated experience of anal-eroticism comes to be repressed. But the repression of this desire is an ongoing process and one that involves a variety of defense mechanisms.

The key to understanding the most important of the defense mechanisms used to maintain the repression of anal-erotic desires lies in recognizing that a blurring of boundaries is central to the experience of anality.[1] Urine and feces by their very nature are substances that blur the boundary between the body and the outside world (since they originate inside the body but pass outside). Moreover, fecal matter is a substance that smears easily and (just as easily) attaches itself to whatever it comes into contact with—and this too reinforces the conviction that the anal world is one characterized by a lack of boundaries.

Since anality involves a blurring of boundaries, an emphasis upon the maintenance of boundaries can be an effective aid in the continued repression of anal-erotic desire. Translated into behavior, an emphasis upon the maintenance of boundaries becomes a desire to isolate one activity from another and to divide up any particular activity into a number of separate and discrete acts that collectively must always be performed in a certain order. The resulting behavioral emphases—upon isolation and orderliness—will to some extent be found in almost all individuals but will be most pronounced in those individuals whose early anal-erotic desires had been especially intense, since such individuals will have a relatively greater need to maintain the repression of their anal-erotic desires. This for Freud (see especially Freud 1908; 1917) explains the origins of the "anal" personality type.

Freud linked anal-eroticism and the anal character to obsessional neurosis when he discussed the "problem of choice of neurosis," that is, why a particular person develops one form of neurotic behavior rather than some other (see especially Freud 1913b). Individuals whose experience of anal-eroticism is particularly intense develop a fixation to the anal-erotic stage. Later in life, when such individuals are faced with a repressed sexual desire (of any sort) that is threatening to burst into consciousness, this fixation predisposes them to respond to this new threat by using the very same defense mechanisms—involving an emphasis upon isolation and orderliness—that proved so useful in maintaining that first repression of (anal-erotic) sexual desire. The result is an obsessional ceremony that is pervaded by an emphasis upon isolation and orderliness. But while such a ceremony does function to maintain the repression of the forbidden desire, the desire itself remains and the threat of its bursting into consciousness continues. For Freud, this explains why obsessional neurotics feel compelled to repeat their ceremonies over and over again. Unfortunately, it is at this point that we encounter a lacuna in Freud's argument.

Although Freud was clear in explaining why obsessional ceremonies would come to be pervaded by an emphasis upon isolation, orderliness, and repetition, what he never got around to doing, as far as I can tell, was to explain why these same emphases should be associated with religious rituals. Certainly he nowhere suggests that particularly intense anal-erotic experiences during infancy (something, remember, that he does see as predisposing individuals toward the "choice" of obsessional neurosis) are necessarily implicated in the genesis of religious rituals. On the other hand, Freud's view of obsessional neurosis has come to be modified somewhat by subsequent investigators, and these later formulations allow us to see a link—that Freud himself missed—between the process that gives rise to obsessional neurosis and the process that gives rise to religious ritual.

As mentioned, Freud originally argued that the unconscious desire which gave rise to obsessional behavior was usually sexual in nature, and he was still advancing this view in his *Introductory Lectures on Psychoanalysis* (1916, 286–319). Subsequent investigators, by contrast, have come to de-emphasize repressed sexual desire in explaining obsessional neurosis. In particular, it is now more common to suggest that obsessional neurosis derives from repressed feelings of hostility and in particular from the repressed hostility that results when a demand for subordination is unwanted but ultimately accepted (see, e.g., Ostow 1972; Schneiderman 1986, 89–115; Giovacchini 1987; Silverman 1996). Mortimer Ostow (1972, 325) provides a succinct summary of this later view: "In obsessive-compulsive neurosis the major issue is subordination, that is, accepting one's subordinate place, originally with respect to one's father within the family, and subsequently to one's superiors within the community." In other words, these more recent formulations suggest that the conflict that commonly gives rise to obsessional neurosis is the conflict between (1) a conscious recognition that you must accept a subordinate position and (2) an unconscious unwillingness to do just that. In this situation, individuals regress to the anal stage, since this is the stage "wherein they first accept[ed] self-control in deference to authority" (Ostow 1972, 325). This regression permits them to use those same defense mechanisms (involving an emphasis on isolation and orderliness) that were so useful in responding to that first act of subordination, in order to handle the hostility engendered by this new demand for subordination.

In the end, then, Freud was correct in perceiving a link between the anal-erotic stage and obsessional neurosis, but wrong in his account of the nature of this link. Obsessional neurosis does indeed involve a regression to the anal-erotic stage, but not because the individual had experienced particularly intense anal-erotic experiences. Rather, this regression occurs because it is at the anal-erotic stage that we are first required to subordinate our desires for pleasure to the demands of external authority. It is thus the stage to which we regress as adults when faced with a demand for subordination that— like that very first demand for subordination—is unwanted but with which we feel obliged to comply.[2]

The recognition that obsessional ceremonies are often (if not usually) fueled by the unconscious hostility that results from the experience of unwanted (but accepted) subordination helps us to understand the fact that so fascinated Freud: the obvious similarity between obsessional ceremonies and religious rituals.

Religion and Subordination to the Sacred

Some time ago Emile Durkheim (1912) suggested that a common feature of all religious rituals was the fact that they bring people into closer contact with sacred objects, that is, objects that must be treated with reverence and respect because of their association with a powerful force. In some societies, this powerful force is associated with a single god, in others it is associated with several gods, and in still others this force is not localized in beings having identifiable personalities at all but rather in a series of impersonal forces that permeate different aspects of the natural world. Whatever specific form it takes, what is common to all (or at least, almost all) conceptualizations of this sacred force is that it is seen as something that transcends human existence and that constrains human behavior. From Durkheim's discussion, it is clear that in talking about "constraints" he is thinking less about morality than about the behavioral prohibitions that surround sacred objects (the fact that they must only be used in certain ways; the fact that they can only be approached at certain times, etc.).

Although Freud was aware of Durkheim's work (he cites several of Durkheim's publications on religion in *Totem and Taboo*), he nowhere, as far as I know, commented on Durkheim's conceptualization of the sacred. Had he done so, it seems likely that he would have regarded the transcendent and coercive force that lies at the core of all conceptualizations of the sacred as a projection of the parental imagos buried in the unconscious of all human beings. Durkheim, of course, saw this force as deriving from the psychic effervescence experienced during social interaction among like-minded individuals and from the experience of external constraint induced in us by societal norms.

Whatever might be the origin of the transcendent and coercive force generally associated with the sacred (and certainly neither the psychoanalytic nor the Durkheimian view exhausts possible answers to this question), it seems reasonable to suggest that coming into closer contact with such a force—as happens during the course of a religious ritual—should at the very least evoke parental imagery. From the child's point of view, after all, parents are transcendent (if only because adults seem unrestricted by the limitations that typically apply to children) and are also authoritative and coercive. But to the extent that the experience of "coming into contact with the sacred" does evoke unconscious memories of our infantile experience with our parents, it must inevitably evoke as well those unconscious feelings of rage and hostility engendered in us when we had to subordinate ourselves to parental demands. Since these feelings of repressed rage and hostility are sharply inconsistent with the conscious reverence and respect that we owe to the sacred, keeping such feelings repressed becomes especially important, and so we—like obsessional neurotics—make use of those emphases upon isolation and orderliness that were so useful in maintaining the hostility engendered by our first experience of subordination (at the anal-erotic stage). The result: religious rituals, like obsessional ceremonies, come to be pervaded by an emphasis on isolation and orderliness. Because the repressed hostility toward our parents that fuels these rituals is never eliminated, we are driven to repeat these orderly and isolated rituals over and over again.

One of the great strengths of psychoanalysis has always been its ability to order a range of seemingly disparate and quite unrelated elements into a coherent pattern. What I now want to demonstrate is that the psychoanalytic perspective on religious ritual just presented helps us do just that in connection with popular Catholicism in pre-Famine Ireland, that is, it helps us to see the underlying (psycho)logic that ties together those seemingly disparate elements—notably rounding rituals, holy wells, stone piles, the need to visit stations in a particular order, etc.—that were so central to this variant of Catholicism and that made it so distinctive and possibly unique.

Going to Extremes

From a psychoanalytic point of view, what is most immediately noticeable about the rounding rituals that were so central to the experience of "being Catholic" in the two centuries or so following the Reformation in Ireland is that these rituals incorporate to an extreme degree those emphases—upon isolation, orderliness, and stereotypical repetition—that are to some extent found in religious rituals generally. Rounding rituals, after all, require that devotees move from one station to the next, always in a particular order, and at each station to walk around the station a precise number of times, always taking care to move in the same direction (rightward) and all the while saying a set number of prayers. Finally, all this must be done without interruption. The most parsimonious way to account for the fact that these emphases were particularly intense in the Irish case (at least within the logic of the psychoanalytic argument presented earlier) is on the hypothesis that the repressed feelings of rage—deriving from unwanted subordination—which fuel religious ritual generally were especially strong in this case. In fact, I think there are solid historical grounds for believing that such rage would indeed have been especially strong in post-Reformation Ireland.

A caveat: in most scholarly accounts of post-Reformation Ireland, a discussion about "subordination" would likely be concerned with the subordination of the Irish—both the Gaelic Irish and the Anglo-Irish—to English rule and with the ascendancy of the New English. This is not what I will be talking about here, if only because there is no particular reason for believing that the resentment over these forms of subordination would have been repressed, that is, driven into the unconscious. Given the psychoanalytic argument sketched above, what we must look for in the case of Irish Catholics is a demand for subordination that was unwanted but regarded by them as legitimate, since only a demand of this sort would have been repressed—and I think that Bossy's (1970; 1971) already-cited work points us toward a demand for subordination that was of precisely this sort.

The core of Bossy's argument, remember, is that the most important changes promulgated by the Counter-Reformation Church were organizational rather than doctrinal. In particular, the Counter-Reformation Church sought to promote a uniform code of religious observance—mainly having to do with attendance at Mass and participation in the sacraments—that was to be enforced at the level of individual parishes. But the successful implementation of this goal was inextricably bound up with another: to establish a hierarchical structure in which the pope had authority over local bishops, local bishops had authority over the priests in their dioceses, and priests had authority over the laity in their parishes. Although such a rigidly hierarchical Church was clearly envisioned in the decrees passed at the Council of Trent, it was a type of Church that was largely unfamiliar to the great mass of European Catholics. In Bossy's (1971, 156) words, "the pre-Reformation Church, in practice and at the popular level, was not a hierarchically ordered structure but a conglomerate of autonomous communities"; by "autonomous communities" he means monastic communities, confraternities, kinship groups, and the like.

In effect, then, the Counter-Reformation Church demanded that individual lay Catholics accept an unfamiliar system of religious subordination in which they were at the lowest rung of a rigidly defined hierarchical structure. This demand for subordination posed no problem for those willing to reject it outright (by rejecting Catholicism). It did however pose a problem for those individuals who wanted (for whatever reason) to remain Catholic, if only because "remaining Catholic" meant at the very least being acknowledged as Catholic by Church authorities. In this case, accepting the legitimacy of the Counter-Reformation Church's demand for subordination— as unfamiliar and unpalatable as it might be—was the price of maintaining a Catholic identity.

Although Bossy's characterization of the pre-Reformation Church (as consisting of a nonhierarchical conglomeration of autonomous communities) is valid to some extent for most areas of Western Europe, it is a characterization that seems especially applicable to Ireland. One of the distinguishing features of the early Irish Church, after all, had been the near absence of anything resembling true diocesan organization. The focal points of ecclesiastical organization were the great monasteries and the lands they controlled, and the importance of these institutions only increased under the impact of the Viking raids of the ninth and tenth centuries. Bishops did exist, of course, and they were often entitled to a portion of the monastic revenues. But a "bishop" in Ireland was conceptualized, even among educated elites, far more as a simple functionary whose job was to consecrate priests than as the ultimate source of spiritual authority within a precisely defined diocese.[3]

Several attempts were made to reform the Irish Church during the eleventh and twelfth centuries, and much of this reform effort was directed at establishing in Ireland the sort of diocesan/parish system favored by Roman authorities. In the end, however, these efforts had only a very limited impact on particular areas of the island, and even these limited successes came to be undermined by developments in the early modern period. In particular, diocesan organization came to be undermined by the fact that the links between the organizational structure of Church and local kinship groups—always strong —became even stronger.

By 1500, for example, most diocesan and parochial lands, at least in Gaelic areas, were administered and maintained by coarbs and erenaughs (Ellis 1985, 186). These were generally laymen, or, at best, individuals who had taken minor orders. Generally, a coarbship or erenaughship was vested with a particular kin group, and the office had to be filled by a male from that group. Although in principle accession to a coarbship or erenaughship was subject to episcopal approval, the need to appoint from among the members of a given kin group gave bishops little leeway (even if they had wanted to exercise it) in selecting candidates.[4]

The matter of coarbs and erenaughs aside, kinship came to pervade the Irish Church in other ways as well. The transmission of both clerical office and Church property, for instance, increasingly flowed along from one kinsman to another. As Stephen Ellis (1985, 187) remarks, "The pre-Reformation clerical profession [in Ireland] was increasingly hereditary in character, despite the work of the twelfth-century reform movement." Bishops, in particular, were often related by blood to earlier bishops and to the leaders of local kin groups. Then too, Church property often fell under the de facto control of local families because Irish priests often lived openly in common-law relationships and raised families who regarded the local parish church as their patrimony. In his already cited report on the state of religion in Ireland, for example, William Good says that "the Priests Lemmons and their bastards, abide within the circuit of a Church, drinke until they be drunke, lie together, shed blood, and keepe up their cattell there. . . . The priests minde nothing but gathering of goods and getting of children. . . . They have their children to succeed them in their Churches, for whose illegitimation they are dispensed with" (cited in Camden 1610, 144–45). Although Good's characterization dates from the 1560s, it seems likely—given the evidence we have of clerical laxity in the fifteenth century—that it would have applied equally well to the pre-Reformation period.

In the end, individuals at all levels of the Irish Church during the early modern period—from lay administrators to bishops to local priests—came increasingly to be subordinated to the interests of local kin groups. Lateral attachments of this sort, between the organizational Church and local kin groups, worked to undermine that hierarchal ordering (with bishops having authority over priests and priests having authority over laity) that is the foundation of a diocesan system.

Quite apart from the increasing influence of kinship on ecclesiastical organization, diocesan organization in early modern Ireland was weakened by the great resurgence of the mendicant orders that occurred during the fifteenth and early sixteenth centuries. Far more than in England, the Observant reforms (which had originated on the Continent) had proved popular in Ireland, especially with the Dominicans, Franciscans, and Augustinians (Bradshaw 1974, 8–16; Ellis 1985, 188–89). Since an integral part of the Observant reform was a renewed commitment to public preaching, the mendicant orders in Ireland were brought into close contact with the general public, and the Irish public seems to have regarded their efforts favorably. Certainly there is documentary evidence from the sixteenth century that friars occupied a privileged position in the eyes of the laity and as a result were often called upon to settle disputes. A government report from 1534, for example, suggested that the Observants "were feared, obeyed, and almost adored, not only by the peasants but by the lords, who held them in such reverence as to endure from them blows with a stick" (Bradshaw 1974, 11). The mendicant orders in pre-Reformation Ireland (as elsewhere) were generally in competition with the secular clergy, both for the allegiance of the laity and in regard to more practical matters, like burial fees. As a result, the great popularity of the mendicant friars functioned to undermine the position of the secular clergy, the local parish church, and, by extension, whatever system of diocesan/parochial organization might have been in place.

In short, while problems having to do with the nonresidence of bishops, their moral character and education, their involvement in secular pursuits, and so forth were widespread throughout Europe, what made Ireland distinctive (not unique, perhaps, but distinctive) was that the very "idea" of a bishop and a diocese in the Tridentine sense were far less a part of established tradition, even among educated elites, than in most other areas of Europe. Pre-Reformation Ireland, then, is justly regarded as an extreme version of the sort of society described by Bossy. Specifically, it was a society in which a variety of semiautonomous groups—including monasteries, the mendicant orders, the secular clergy, various civil authorities, local kin groups, etc.—negotiated with each other (and sometimes with Rome itself; see Quinn and Nicholls 1976, 30) in order to achieve a variety of secular and religious goals.

In the Irish situation, then, the intensely hierarchal vision favored by the Council of Trent—in which "pope," "bishop," "parish priest," and "laity" were arranged in a precisely defined order of diminishing authority—should have been (and, I argue, was) particularly unpalatable, and yet we know that the Irish did undeniably embrace the organization that was promoting this unpalatable vision. The reason for this apparent contradiction is not problematic. For a variety of reasons (some of which have already been discussed; for a more comprehensive account, see Corish 1968), both the Anglo-Irish and the Gaelic Irish in the post-Reformation period increasingly turned to Catholicism as a way of building a distinctively Irish national identity. "Being Catholic," in other words, increasingly became central to "being Irish." Since it would have been impossible to maintain a Catholic identity while simultaneously rejecting outright the legitimacy of the organizational reforms being promulgated by the Counter-Reformation Church, these reforms—and in particular the demand for episcopal supremacy within a rigidly defined diocesan/parochial structure—were accorded legitimacy.

In the end, my reconstruction suggests that two things happened in post-Reformation Ireland: (1) the demands for ecclesiastical subordination made by the Counter-Reformation Church did engender a substantial amount of hostility among Irish Catholics (because these demands were so much at variance with established tradition) but (2) the legitimacy accorded these demands (on account of the increasingly central role played by a Catholic identity in the maintenance of an Irish national identity) caused this hostility to be repressed, that is, driven into the unconscious. Given this, Irish Catholics were especially predisposed to make use of those defense mechanisms—involving an emphasis on isolation, orderliness, and repetition, respectively—that are so useful in maintaining the repression of the resentment generated by unwanted (but accepted) subordination. This explains (or so I am suggesting) why the religious rituals that became so popular with Irish Catholics during the early Counter-Reformation were pervaded to such an extreme degree by the emphases that pervade religious rituals generally.

One of Freud's central insights was that religious rituals, like obsessional ceremonies, are the result of a compromise, that is, these rituals maintain the repression of an unconscious desire while simultaneously allowing for the disguised gratification of that same desire. Thus far I have been considering the ways in which the rounding rituals popular with post-Reformation Irish Catholics functioned to maintain the repression of unconscious hostility. It is now time to consider the other side of the compromise, namely, how these rituals functioned to allow for the disguised gratification of this same hostility.

Anal-erotic Imagery and Religion

For many readers, I suspect, the strong aversion to anality that prevails in our culture will make any discussion that mixes terms like *anal imagery* and *religion* seem odd and inherently implausible. Yet if we put this cultural aversion to anality aside (yet again), it seems evident that relatively overt anal imagery appears in a number of religious contexts and that when it appears it is usually associated with concerns about authority. Robert Paul (1985), for instance, discusses the relatively overt references to defecation that appear in the biblical book of Samuel's account of the contestations between David and Saul for the kingship of Israel. Martin Luther's very explicit use of scatological imagery in attacking papal authority is well known and has been the subject of several analyses (see in particular Dundes 1989, 59–62).

The use of overt scatological imagery in the face of unwanted demands for submission to authority is by no means limited to religious contexts. Claude Gandelman (1996), for instance, provides abundant evidence demonstrating that the same sort of scatological imagery which pervaded attacks on the papacy during the Reformation in the sixteenth century came also to pervade attacks on the authority of the monarch during the French Revolution. Scatological imagery can also emerge in response to demands for submission that emanate from purely cultural processes. European folktales centering on the character of Till Eulenspiegel, for example, are pervaded with explicit references to excrement (Dundes 1989, 49–50). Ronald Glasberg (1990) has noted that these tales first became widely popular in the early sixteenth century, and he suggests that this is because the anal themes constituted an act of popular defiance against the "civilizing process" of the early modern era, a process that required individuals to exert more affect-control during the course of their increasingly complex dealings with others.

Why anal themes should be associated with defiance in the face of unwanted demands for submission to authority, in so many different contexts, is unproblematic. In the mind of the child, feces (and urine) are initially associated with pleasurable erotic experiences and so come to be positively valued. Indeed, as Freud (1905, 185–93; 1917) suggested, this initially positive evaluation of feces gives them the quality of "gifts" that can be offered to parental figures. Only under the impact of the cultural attitudes associated with the parental demand for control and regulation of excretory and urinary activities do feces and urine come to acquire the negative evaluation that is more familiar to the adult mind. Even so, precisely because this very first demand for submission to external authority requires a repudiation of anality, an emphasis upon anality becomes a prototypical way of expressing defiance against unwanted authority. In other words, just as the defense mechanisms which develop at the anal-erotic stage are especially likely to be used later in life to repress the hostility engendered by unwanted demands for submission to authority, an emphasis on anal imagery can function—in the mind of the adult as in the mind of the child—as a way of expressing this same hostility.

In the case, say, of a Luther, the hostility associated with the demands for submission to (papal) authority was conscious and overt, and so the anal imagery used in defying this demand could be overt as well (as it was in Luther's writings). By contrast, when the hostility engendered by a demand for submission to authority is repressed (as was true in the case of Irish Catholics), anal imagery needs to be disguised before it can serve as a way of expressing defiance. What form would such a process of disguise take? One possibility here was outlined some time ago by Sandor Ferenczi (1914).

In Ferenczi's reconstruction, the most objectionable attribute associated with feces within the logic of prevailing cultural attitudes is their odor, and so the (mental) process of disguise proceeds first by transforming feces into odorless substances, like mud and clay, that have a similar consistency. A further step in the process of disguise involves deleting both odor and consistency. Under the impact of this transformation, objects that are odorless and hard but still similar to feces in the homogeneity of their composition can serve as a feces symbol. For Ferenczi, this is why stones, and in particular small stones, could so easily serve as feces symbols. Using a similar reasoning, it seems clear that water—running water in particular—can serve as a disguised representation of urine. Certainly, it seemed evident to Freud that in dreams running water could function as a disguised representation of urination (see for example his analysis of the "French Nurse's Dream"; Freud 1900, 367–68).

The matter of simple symbolism aside, anality can also be expressed, as already noted, by blurring boundaries. In his already cited study of the Eulenspiegel tales, for instance, Glasberg (1990, 426) suggests that a common motif in these tales is "Eulenspiegel's habit of mixing up what should be kept separate or logically distinct." This blurring of boundaries, Glasberg suggests, is just as much an act of defiance in the face of the demands for affect-control made by the "civilizing process" as Eulenspiegel's more overtly excremental activities.

All of the objects and emphases that previous commentators like Ferenczi, Freud, Glasberg, and others have taken as reflecting anal/urinary imagery are objects and emphases that were central to the experience of Irish popular Catholicism. Certainly there was an emphasis upon stone in this variant of Catholicism. Stones, stone circles, and piles of small stones, after all, were routinely encountered at the sites associated with holy wells, and, more importantly, were commonly the focus of the rounding rituals performed at these sites. Running water was also routinely incorporated into these rituals, if only because the "holy well" that served as the most important of the stations at some particular site was usually a pool fed by a running spring. Finally, these rituals were associated with "shapelessness" (and so with the absence of boundaries) not only by virtue of the fluidity associated with spring water but also by virtue of the stone cairns that so often served as stations. Indeed, as mentioned earlier, it was the blatant and overt "shapelessness" of those cairns that routinely attracted the attention of disdainful Protestant commentators. Even now, the stone cairns that continue to serve as stations at particular sites exude a strong sense of "shapelessness"(see for instance the first station at Croagh Patrick in figure 7).

The hypothesis being offered here, then, is that the psychological appeal of rounding rituals derived at least in part from the fact that the emphasis on stone, running water, and shapelessness that were everywhere associated with the rounding rituals at holy wells and other pilgrimage sites functioned as the disguised expression of anal/urinary imagery. This meant that participation in these rituals allowed for the disguised gratification of the repressed hostility that had been engendered in Irish Catholics by the Tridentine demand for ecclesiastical subordination.

I am not, of course, saying that shapeless piles of stone and pools of running water are everywhere and always disguised representations of feces and urine; I am simply saying that they can function in this way and that is how they did function in the mind of Irish Catholics.

Closure

I concede fully that to some extent the practice of organizing Catholic rituals in Ireland around springs and piles of stone was a matter of convenience. Deprived for the most part of their church buildings by Protestant authorities, it was likely inevitable that Irish Catholics would gather, at least occasionally, around some particular feature of the local landscape to engage in religious rituals. Even so, I am suggesting that the immense popularity of the rounding rituals at holy wells (springs) and elsewhere can be explained on the hypothesis that the particular character and structure of these rituals resonated in some very fundamental way with the dynamic changes that were taking place in the thinking of Irish Catholics in the post-Reformation period. Thus part of their appeal is that the rituals provided a way of operationalizing the general Tridentine emphasis upon the entire community meeting together at a particular location on a regular and predictable basis and engaging in a standardized set of rituals that were distinctively Catholic. But another part of their appeal, and perhaps the most important part, derived from that juxtaposition of elements that I have been discussing in this chapter.

My argument, in short, is that rounding rituals were popular in post-Reformation Ireland because they effected precisely the sort of compromise that is central to all religious rituals. On the one hand, the intense emphasis on isolation, orderliness, and repetition helped to maintain the repression of the unconscious hostility engendered in Irish Catholics by the Counter-Reformation Church's demand for strict submission within a rigidly hierarchal system of ecclesiastical authority. On the other hand, the disguised anal and urinary imagery associated with these same rituals allowed for the disguised gratification of that same unconscious hostility.

This same argument, I think, deepens our understanding of why rounding rituals and the patrons associated with them fell from favor. I have already suggested that the class interests of the local clergy, who were recruited mainly from the tenant farmer class, was critical in causing this decline. But it is also the case, as any number of commentators have noted, that the values of the tenant farmer class came to predominate among Irish Catholics generally, especially in the decades following the Famine. One of those values was an emphasis upon strict submission to authority within the family, and indeed it was precisely this value that predisposed Irish Catholics—as Hynes suggested—toward the variant of Catholicism being proposed by Roman authorities in the nineteenth century. What this means is that the great resistance to hierarchal subordination in religious matters that had long been a part of Irish tradition, and which was (at least under the argument being offered here) responsible for the repressed hostility toward the Counter-Reformation Church's demand for subordination, evaporated. Deprived of the unconscious hostility that had always served—quite literally—as the wellspring of their popularity, rounding rituals and patterns also evaporated.

Epilogue

I began this book by telling the story of Margaret Fogarty Larkin, the ancestor of mine who came over from Ireland in the early years of the Great Famine. It is now time to finish that story.

I don't know how Margaret and her family supported themselves for their first decade or so in the United States. Eventually, however, they made their way to Covington, Kentucky. It was there, in 1861, that Margaret's daughter—also named Margaret, and the one who had fallen off her chair "dead drunk" on that very first day in Cincinnati—married John Corcoran. John too had been driven out of Ireland by the Famine. He was a blacksmith by trade and had a small farm in the Covington area, and this is where he brought his bride. The elder Margaret Larkin moved in with the newlyweds and never moved out.

From what I can tell, the Corcorans did moderately well for themselves. They had eight children, all of whom survived, and the farm, along with John's blacksmithing, provided the family with a steady income. However, things took a turn for the worse in the late 1800s when John lost his farm and his trade. Whether it was a cause or an effect (or both), he also increasingly turned to drink. In early 1890 he was even jailed briefly for some unknown offense. Late on the night of August 29, 1890, after a drunken binge, John took a shortcut across a railway trestle. He was hit by an oncoming train and his body was mangled and literally cut to pieces. He carried no identification but did have a tattoo on each arm (a pair of clasped hands on the left arm and a broken dagger on the right). The tattoos were duly described the next day in the *Kentucky Post*'s account of the accident. Neighbors who knew John read the account and informed his wife and she went to the morgue to identify what was left of his body.

Epilogue

Margaret Corcoran's greatest regret, it appears, was that her husband had died without the last rites.

In 1896, exactly fifty years after she had arrived in the United States from Ireland, the elder Margaret Larkin also died and her funeral was held at Covington Cathedral. The Corcorans and the Larkins, you see, had remained Catholic. What had changed since their arrival in the United States is that they had stopped being Irish.

Sometime between the late 1840s and the 1890s my Larkin and Corcoran ancestors underwent a cultural metamorphosis that made them "southerners" first and foremost. They never denied their roots in Ireland; this just never figured much in how they thought of themselves. Their experience was by no means unique. Long before the Famine, starting really in the early eighteenth century, a substantial number of Irish emigrants had settled in the U.S. South. Grady Mc-Whiney (1988), a southern historian, has gone so far as to suggest that those elements that most of all distinguished the culture of the antebellum South from the culture of the northern states—including the southern emphasis on hospitality, herding, leisure, feuding, and hostility toward the English and—by extension, New Englanders—have their roots in the traditions brought to the South by Celtic groups from Wales, Scotland, and, most of all, Catholic Ireland. Whether McWhiney is right or not, it seems obvious that Irish emigrants would have found in the culture of the South something that resonated easily with the Irish experience.

One small and very personal consequence of my ancestors' cultural metamorphosis was that when my paternal grandmother told me stories about the Corcorans and the Larkins (and she was a wonderful storyteller) they were never stories about Ireland. Instead they were about leaving money on a fencepost and coming back later to find a jar of moonshine (and about how the money would never move and the moonshine would never appear if you tried to keep an eye on your money) and about hoofbeats in the night that were (supposedly) the sounds of the Klan doing the things that the Klan did. Her favorite story though, or really *my* favorite, was about the time Yankee soldiers arrived at the Corcoran farm near Covington. Kentucky did not secede from the Union during the Civil War, but support for the South was strong and the Corcorans and the Larkins were a part of that support. Yankee soldiers, I was told, burst into the Corcoran house and thrust their bayonets up the chimney in order to flush out any Confederates who might be hiding there. In hearing my grandmother tell the story, it seemed obvious that thrusting a bayonet up someone's chimney epitomized Yankee bad manners. Those same soldiers also wanted milk from the family cow, and being the savage creatures that any good southerner knows them to be, they slit the cow's udders. They got their milk, but the cow was useless from then on. Even in her eighties my grandmother's face took on an ashen scowl whenever she talked of that poor cow. It was a good story, and like all the others she told me, I enjoyed it. But my link to pre-Famine Ireland had been cut.

I grew up Catholic in the years before Vatican II and went to Catholic schools dominated by Irish-American kids from working-class backgrounds. In this environment "being Catholic" meant attending Sunday Mass, going to confession and communion, and saying the rosary a lot; it also meant giving money for pagan babies and getting time off school to see Hollywood's account of the Fatima apparitions. I found Irish-American Catholicism to be intensively conservative, overly concerned with appearance, and eminently unappealing. I much preferred the Catholicism of my mother's Italian relatives.

Italian-Americans also went to Mass, received communion, and said the rosary, but here and there it was possible to catch sight of Catholic beliefs and devotions that had no analogue in the Catholicism I knew from school. From my grandfather, I learned stories about venal priests and the foolish things they did. Most modern commentators, I suspect, would see in such stories evidence of Italian anticlericalism. At the time they simply conveyed to me that priests were ordinary men very much like, well, me and my grandfather. My favorite places in San Francisco's North Beach, apart from my grandfather's Italian restaurant on Grant Avenue, were the chapels at the back of SS. Peter and Paul's, the Italian national church. These chapels contained a treasure trove of statues and pictures depicting a variety of madonnas and saints. Unlike the generic (and insipid) Mary-dressed-in-blue-and-white favored in my local parish church, the madonnas at SS. Peter and Paul's exhibited color and variety and were associated with particular communities in Italy.

Epilogue

Those back chapels also had statues of saintly women who bled from the stigmata in their hands and feet, of saintly men with strong Italian names like "Rocco" who had open sores on their bodies, and of ordinary (but naked!) men and women writhing in the flames of Purgatory. It was great. In retrospect, it hardly seems surprising that my first detailed investigation of popular Catholicism in a particular national context would involve Italian Catholicism.

As I came to know and explore Italy as an adult, I came to love the dizzying array of madonnas who were sisters to one another but who each had a strong and independent personality. I sought out their sanctuaries, which even now are often located on hilltops in the beautiful Italian countryside. While it would be too much to say that I truly believed in their existence, there is no denying that I often felt a sense of exhilaration and peace in their presence. I sought out, too, saintly bodies still preserved incorrupt (of which Italy has a greater number than any other Catholic country); the blood relics at Naples and Ravello that still liquefy; the sanctuary of the beheaded souls at Palermo; sanctuaries dedicated to the skeletal dead at Milan; and a range of other sanctuaries and cults once popular in Italy and now in decline. I wanted to write about these things but I also wanted to get as close to them physically as I could, and I enjoyed the experience. The Italian Catholicism that emerged from the documentary record and from the churches and shrines I visited was even more vibrant and diversified than the statues in the back chapels of SS. Peter and Paul had suggested.

What I now know, however, is that I was wrong about Irish Catholicism. Once we get past the rigidly Tridentine version of Catholicism that rose to prominence among Irish Catholics at home and abroad during the devotional revolution, and past the cultural amnesia that came to characterize many of the emigrants who left Ireland, we encounter a variant of popular Catholicism that was in its time as distinctive as the variant that developed in Italy. As we have seen, supernatural power was as fragmented in Ireland as it was in Italy, though in Ireland that power was far more likely to be associated with a male saint having an unpronounceable Irish name than with a localized madonna. Then too, the image and relic cults so central to Italian Catholicism were generally missing in Ireland; in their place we find holy wells and shapeless piles of stone around which people walk in endless circles. These differences, however, should not obscure the similarities.

In both cases, religion was physical. While the official Church may have regarded the Eucharistic host as the preeminent example of the fusion of sacred power with the material world, the people of Italy and Ireland knew differently. The fusion of sacredness with the material world was experienced during the ordinary course of their popular devotions. Statues and relics had to be touched (in Italy) and pilgrims to holy places had to feel the rocks beneath their feet or dip their hands into the spring's water (in Ireland). In both cases the local clergy allied themselves with the laity in pursuing devotions that both considered to be eminently "Catholic" even though these devotions would later be written off as "superstition" by scholarly commentators. But the similarity that most unites the variant of popular Catholicism that developed in Italy with the variant that developed in Ireland is that each was developed by local populations who sought to develop new and creative ways of "being Catholic" within the constraints imposed on them by the official Church and by the historical situations in which they found themselves.

Unfortunately, in the case of Irish popular Catholicism we cannot go to the back rooms of any church to look at artifacts that evoke a sense of what this variant of Catholicism was like. All we can do is piece together its story from the odd bits of evidence we have; that is what this book has been about.

Notes

Introduction

1.   For a more detailed discussion of De Rosa's work, see Carroll (1996, 6–12).

2.   For additional examples of studies of popular religion that emphasize popular creativity, see the various essays in Badone (1990).

Chapter 1 Popular Catholicism before the Famine

1.   The typical "Mass-house" was a simple and unadorned building, often no more than a hut or shed, which provided a sheltered place for saying Mass. On Mass-houses, see Brady and Corish (1971, 58–67).

2.   Although conceding that St. Sunday's Well was of "pretious estimation among the Irish (I meane) amongst the Popish sort of the Irish, that doe flocke thither so thicke upon Sunday mornings, in the summer season," Rich (1610, 53) could not resist ridiculing the idea of naming a well after someone called St. Sunday: "I cannot tell what countrey man Sa. Sunday was himselfe . . . [and] I am sure if Saint Sunday were there in person to read a Lecture about the New Testament, they had rather go altogether to an alehouse then they would travell so farre to see him." Rich's sarcasm notwithstanding, the well he is describing was almost certainly dedicated either to St. Dominic, who was sometimes called St. Sunday (Bradshaw 1974, 102), or to *Rí an Domhnaigh*, the King of Sunday, who is the "Jesus Christ" of the Tridentine Church.

3.   During the 1820s, the British ordnance department began a massive topographical survey of Ireland. In the 1830s, several Irish scholars were hired to gather information on the Irish names given to the various sites that would be marked on the Ordnance Survey maps. The term *site* was interpreted broadly, and included anything that might be of antiquarian, archeological, historical, or ecclesiastical interest. While some of the scholars associated with the Ordnance Survey concentrated on the place-name information found in old Irish manuscripts, others went into the field to collect information from the people living in an area, and their reports from the field are the Ordnance Survey Letters (OSL). Most of this fieldwork was con-

ducted by one man, John O'Donovan. As he visited each Irish county in turn, O'Donovan quickly found himself becoming a sort of "one-man local-history department" (Andrews 1975, 128). The Ordnance Survey investigators made a special point of asking about any holy wells in the areas, including both those still holy and those that were remembered as being holy in the recent past. For a more detailed discussion of the Ordnance Survey and O'Donovan, see Andrews (1975); Boyne (1987); Gailey (1988). Typed copies of the OSL were made under the supervision of the Rev. Michael O'Flanagan in 1930. I used the copy available at the Royal Irish Academy in Dublin.

4. For a discussion of ex-votos in Italy, see Carroll (1992, 82–87).

5. For a detailed discussion of the ways in which local priests participate at patterns, see Donnelly (1988, 25–28).

6. The incident involving Heneas MacNichaill is reported in the Register of Primate Dowdall. A summary of that register, which includes a summary of this incident, appears in Gwynn (1946, 268–69).

7. On the centrality of image cults to the Catholic experience in Italy, see Carroll (1996, 16–76).

8. For an account of the apparitions at Knock, see Carroll (1986, 202–11).

9. For an overview of apparitions in Italy and Spain, respectively, see Carroll (1992, 52–59); Christian (1981; 1996).

Chapter 2 The Rise of the "Celtic Origins" Hypothesis

1. Another version of this same story appears in *The Tripartite Life of St. Patrick* (see Stokes 1:1887, 123), a collection of Patrician legends likely compiled in the tenth or eleventh century.

2. For textual references to the various stories in which these miraculous methods are used to produce wells, see Plummer (1910, cxlviii).

3. For an overview of these early (and often impressionistic) linguistic investigations, see Morgan (1983). Mallory (1989, 95–107) provides a succinct account of the precise relationships that are now seen to exist among the various Celtic languages.

4. For an account of some of the other writers in the Romantic tradition who contributed to this romanticized vision of Celtic society, see Kenny (1966, 57–59); Snyder (1923); Chapman (1992).

5. There is now a fairly extensive literature dealing with the links between Irish historiography and Irish politics; for an introduction to that literature see Ellis (1991) and Foster (1983), as well as the works already cited.

6. Bieler (1963) presents the texts of all known Irish penitentials in English translation. Connolly (1995) provides an overview of these penitentials and the historical context in which they emerged. For a discussion of the use of these handbooks in Continental Europe, see Frantzen (1979).

7.   Medieval references to holy wells are more plentiful in England. Rattue's (1995) review of these references leads to a number of conclusions that seem worth repeating here. First, it seems unlikely on the basis of the available textual evidence that any substantial number of these wells were of pagan origin. Second, there seems to have been a dramatic increase in the number of such wells as we approach the modern period. (This, however, may only reflect an increasing concern with boundary demarcation—since many of these wells may have served as boundary markers—and/or an increase in the construction of ecclesiastical buildings.) Finally, Rattue brings forward no evidence from the medieval period suggesting that these English wells served as the focus of ritual activities that attracted large numbers of people.

8.   Camden (1610, 140) attributes the report to an English priest named "J. Good" who was in Ireland sometime around 1566; on the identification of "J. Good" with the Jesuit priest William Good, see Quinn (1966, 28).

9.   For an account of David Wolfe's mission to Ireland, see Jones (1967, 8–13). The Italian-language text of Wolfe's report, written in 1574, is reproduced in Begley (1927, 494–515).

Chapter 3 New Rituals for Old at Patrick's Purgatory

1.   For an overview of these accounts, see the various essays in Haren and de Pontfarcy (1988).

2.   By the twelfth century, Ireland was divided into four ecclesiastical sees (Armagh, Tuam, Cashel, and Dublin). The archbishop of Armagh, in addition to being head of the See of Armagh, was also considered to be the titular head of the Irish Church generally.

3.   For Mannini's account, see Picard (1988).

4.   For a listing of the pilgrimage sites mentioned in different annalistic sources, see Harbison (1991, 52).

5.   Michael O'Clery was born about 1580 in Donegal and entered the Franciscan Order in 1623. During the early 1630s, he headed a team of scholars, Franciscans like himself, who set about compiling a work entitled *Annals of the Kingdom of Ireland*. This they did mainly by copying passages from ancient manuscripts which described various historical events involving important personalities from the Year of the World 2242 (taken to be forty days before the biblical Deluge) to 1616 A.D. and arranging them in chronological order. Over time the work came to be called *The Annals of the Four Masters*, in deference to O'Clery and his three primary assistants. There are several surviving annalistic accounts in Ireland, but *The Annals of the Four Masters* is generally seen as being the most comprehensive. For more on O'Clery, see Boyne (1987, 81–84).

6.   Pollard and Redgrave (1976, 221) indicate that Jones's 1647 book is a reissue, with some new preliminary material, of a book on St. Pat-

rick's Purgatory published at Dublin c. 1632; unfortunately, no copies of that original book are known to exist.

7.   Peter Lombard (1555–1625), the archbishop of Armagh, included an account of the pilgrimage experience at Lough Derg in a book on Ireland that was written around 1600 but only published in 1632 (see Lombard 1868, 119–21). Although somewhat less detailed than the accounts considered here, Lombard does say that pilgrims several times "went around" the different stations on bare feet and then entered the water of the lake. The stations in Lombard's account included the church, a "cemetery" near the church (an enclosed area that seems to have contained what other accounts call St. Patrick's Altar), and the seven cells, or penitential beds, dedicated to different Irish saints.

8.   The Franciscans had been appointed custodians of this pilgrimage site in 1631; see Millett (1964, 303).

9.   For a detailed discussion of the events associated with the papal order to dismantle St. Patrick's Purgatory, see Haren (1988).

10.   The "cave" described by Chiericati is an oblong structure with a slight "bend" in its final four feet. The window apparently was nothing more than an open space at the outside angle of this bend.

11.   For more detailed versions of the story about the discovery of these relics, see Mant (1840, 65–67); O'Laverty (1878, 285–89).

12.   A detailed account of Chiericati's life and career can be found in Foa (1980).

13.   These changes to the pilgrimage experience at Lough Derg suggest that Ireland may well have been experiencing precisely the same sort of devotional surge that has been documented for other parts of Europe in the decades immediately preceding the Reformation. In German-speaking regions, for example, the late fifteenth century witnessed a dramatic increase in pilgrimage and other devotional forms associated with Mary and the saints (Moeller, 1971; Sargent 1986). Closer to home (or at least, more relevant to the Irish case), Eamon Duffy (1992) has demonstrated that lay piety—in the form of pilgrimages, the invocation of saints, and image and relic cults—was flourishing in England just before the Reformation. The hypothesis that Ireland experienced a devotional surge during this same period is also consistent with Bradshaw's (1988) finding that in the port cities of Cork, Limerick, and Galway the decades immediately preceding the Reformation were characterized by a spate of church building heavily financed by lay endowments and by the success of the reform movement associated with the observant arm of the various mendicant orders.

Chapter 4 Ireland's Catholic Heartland

1.   For a summary of the archival records for the Province of Armagh that deal with this case, see Gwynn (1946, 268–69).

2. A "faction fight" was a scheduled encounter between two local groups, usually involving free-for-all physical assaults, for the purpose of articulating a feud; faction fights will be discussed in more detail later in this chapter.

3. For Peacock's painting see illustration 8 in Harbison (1991).

4. On David Rothe's commitment to Trent and his efforts to implement the Tridentine reforms in his diocese, see Ó Fearghail (1990).

5. The relevant portion of the original text reads "diebus etiam dominicis et festivis, convenit maiestratus et cives illuc, stationesque ibi faciunt, et obationes seu eleemosinas pro animabus defunctorum." In Classical Latin *maiestratus* (a variant of *magistratus*) would usually be translated as "magistrate," or (when a collective noun) as "magistrates." By the modern era, however, the term was often used more generally to designate an individual or set of individuals who wielded civil authority in an area; see the entry for *magistratus* in Thomas 1972 [1587].

6. A vicar-general is a priest who administers a diocese on behalf of a bishop. During the seventeenth century, the use of vicar-generals in Ireland became a common way of evading the legal restrictions placed on Catholic bishops. Kirwan first acted as vicar-general for the Franciscan Florence Conry, who had been appointed Archbishop of Tuam in about 1619, and then as vicar-general for Malachy Queely, appointed in about 1629.

7. Ireland was by no means unique in witnessing an upsurge in the popularity of cults organized around saints during the Counter-Reformation; the same thing happened in Italy. The reason for this seems clear. Precisely because Protestantism rejected the cult of the saints, embracing the cult of the saints was a visible sign of having rejected Protestantism. It was thus very much in the political interest of Church authorities to promote devotion to the saints. For the full argument here, see Carroll (1996, 163–78).

Chapter 5 The Two Devotional Revolutions

1. For more examples of Irish prelates who straddled the boundary between Catholic and Protestant in the early decades of the Reformation, see Mooney (1967).

2. For a map showing the geographical distribution of the monasteries dissolved in 1534–37, see Bradshaw (1984).

3. For a discussion of the Irish Colleges on the Continent, see Giblin (1971, 3–26); Hammerstein (1971); Silke (1976).

4. I say "likely had" because the oaths are in Latin and in several cases surnames seem to have been Latinized phonetically—with the result that there is sometimes uncertainty as to what the original English or Gaelic surname was.

5. Miller (1986) would later reject his own theory on the grounds that it was simplistic.

6. The account of a station of confession in Hardy's (1840, 77–88) book on holy wells is an abridged version of Carleton's account.

Chapter 6 The Psychology of Pre-Famine Catholicism

1. Freud aside, the view that the essence of anality consists in the blurring of boundaries continues to be used by investigators to gain insight into behaviors that would otherwise seem quite puzzling; see, for instance, Rosegrant (1995).

2. In retrospect, it seems clear that this newer perspective on obsessional neurosis was to some extent implicit in some of Freud's own writings, especially if we pay less attention to his general theoretical pronouncements and more attention to his analysis of particular case studies. In his analysis of the obsessional ceremonies associated with the so-called Rat Man, for example, Freud argues that these ceremonies were shaped by the patient's unconscious rage toward his dead father and that this rage derived ultimately from demands the father had made—and to which the patient had acceded—when the patient was a child.

3. For a list of studies that discuss the distinctive organization of the early Irish Church, see Bradshaw (1989).

4. For a more detailed discussion of the institutions of coarbship and erenaughship, see Mooney (1969, 10–16).

Bibliography

Anderson, Alan, and Marjorie Anderson, eds. 1991. *Adomnán's Life of Columba.* Oxford: Clarendon Press.

Andrews, J. H. 1975. *A Paper Landscape: The Ordnance Survey in Nineteenth-Century Ireland.* Oxford: Clarendon Press.

Anonymous. 1766. "Extract of a letter from an English Gentleman who made a tour of Ireland last Summer." *Gentleman's Magazine* 35 (February): 60–61.

Anonymous. 1851. *Irish Topography—Wilde's "Boyne and Blackwater." Dublin University Magazine* 37: 327–33.

Arensberg, Conrad M. 1968 [1937]. *The Irish Countryman: An Anthropological Study.* Garden City, N.Y.: Natural History Press.

Arensberg, Conrad, and Solon T. Kimball. 1968 [1940]. *Family and Community in Ireland.* Second Edition. Cambridge: Harvard University Press.

Badone, Ellen, ed. 1990. *Religious Orthodoxy and Popular Faith in European Society.* Princeton: Princeton University Press.

Barrett, Michèle. 1992. "Psychoanalysis and Feminism: A British Sociologist's View." *Signs* 17 (2): 455–66.

Begley, John. 1906. *The Diocese of Limerick Ancient and Medieval.* Dublin: Browne and Nolan.

———. 1927. *The Diocese of Limerick in the Sixteenth and Seventeenth Centuries.* Dublin: Browne and Nolan.

Bieler, Ludwig. 1958. "Letter of Credence by Donatus Magrahe, Prior of Lough Derg, for Nylanus O Ledan, Priest and Pilgrim." *Clogher Record* 5: 257–59.

———, ed. 1963. *The Irish Penitentials.* Dublin: Dublin Institute for Advanced Studies.

———. 1979. *The Patrician Texts in the Book of Armagh.* Dublin: Dublin Institute for Advanced Studies.

Birdwell-Pheasant, Donna. 1992. "The Early Twentieth-Century Irish Stem Family: A Case Study from County Kerry." In *Approaching the Past: Historical Anthropology through Irish Case Studies,* ed. Marilyn Silverman and P. H. Gulliver, 205–35. New York: Columbia University Press.

Bibliography

Bliss, Alan. 1976. "The English Language in Early Modern Ireland." In *A New History of Ireland*, volume 3, ed. T. W. Moody, F. X. Martin, and F. J. Byrne, 546–60. Oxford: Clarendon Press.

Boate, Gerard. 1652. *Ireland's Natural History.* London: John Wright.

Bossy, John. 1970. "The Counter-Reformation and the People of Catholic Europe." *Past and Present* 47 (May): 51–70.

———. 1971. "The Counter-Reformation and the People of Catholic Ireland, 1596–1641." *Historical Studies* 8: 155–69.

Bottigheimer, K. 1985. "The Failure of the Reformation in Ireland: Une question bien posée." *Journal of Ecclesiastical History* 36 (2): 196–207.

Boullaye le Gouz, M. de la. 1837 [1657]. *The tour of the French traveller M. de la Boullaye le Gouz in Ireland, A. D. 1644*, ed. T. Crofton Croker. London: T. and W. Boone.

Boyle, Patrick. 1913. "Irish Colleges, on the Continent." In *The Catholic Encyclopedia*, 8: 158–63. New York: Encyclopedia Press.

Boyne, Patricia. 1987. *John O'Donovan (1806–1861)*. Kilkenny: Boethius.

Bradshaw, Brendan. 1974. *The Dissolution of the Religious Orders in Ireland under Henry VIII.* Cambridge: Cambridge University Press.

———. 1979. *The Irish Constitutional Revolution of the Sixteenth Century.* Cambridge: Cambridge University Press.

———. 1984. "Map: The Dissolution of the Religious Houses, 1534–1610." In *A New History of Ireland*, volume 9, ed. T. W. Moody, F. X. Martin, and F. J. Byrne, 33. Oxford: Clarendon Press.

———. 1988. "The Reformation in the Cities: Cork, Limerick, and Galway, 1534–1603." In *Settlement and Society in Medieval Ireland*, ed. John Bradley, 445–75. Kilkenny: Boethius Press.

———. 1989. "Nationalism and Historical Scholarship in Modern Ireland." *Irish Historical Studies* 26 (Nov.): 329–51.

———. 1993. "Geoffrey Keating: Apologist of Irish Ireland." In *Representing Ireland: Literature and the Origins of Conflict, 1534–1660*, ed. B. Bradshaw, A. Hadfield, and W. Maley, 166–90. Cambridge: Cambridge University Press.

Brady, Ciaran. 1994. *The Chief Governors: The Rise and Fall of Reform Government in Tudor Ireland, 1536–1588.* Cambridge: Cambridge University Press.

Brady, John. 1965. *Catholics and Catholicism in the Eighteenth-Century Press.* Maynooth: Catholic Record Society of Ireland.

Brady, John, and P. J. Corish. 1971. "The Church under the Penal Code." In *A History of Irish Catholicism*, volume 4, ed. P. J. Corish, 1–88. Dublin: Gill and Macmillan.

Brady, W. Maziere, ed. 1868. *State Papers Concerning the Irish Church.* London: Longmans, Green, Reader, and Dyer.

Brand, John. 1849. *Observations on the Popular Antiquities of Great Britain.* Three volumes. London: Henry G. Bohn.

Bibliography

Burke, Nuala. 1974. "A Hidden Church? The Structure of Catholic Dublin in the Mid-Eighteenth Century." *Archivium Hibernicum* 32: 81–92.

Burke, William P. 1969 [1914]. *The Irish Priests in the Penal Times (1660–1760).* Introduction by Patrick Corish. Shannon: Irish University Press.

Burrows, Michael A. J. 1989. "Fifteenth-Century Irish Provincial Legislation and Pastoral Care." In *The Churches, Ireland, and the Irish,* ed. W. J. Sheils and Diana Wood, 55–67. Oxford: Basil Blackwell.

Calendar of State Papers, Ireland, Elizabeth, 1596 July–1597 December. 1893. Edited by George Atkinson. London: Eyre and Spottiswoode.

Camden, William. 1610. *Britain, Or a Chorographicall Description of the Most Flourishing Kingdomes, England, Scotland, and Ireland, and the Ilands Adioyning, out of the depth of Antiquitie.* London: G. Bishop and J. Norton.

Cannadine, David. 1983. "The Context, Performance, and Meaning of Ritual: The British Monarchy and the 'Invention of Tradition,' c. 1820–1977." In *The Invention of Tradition,* ed. Eric Hobsbawm and Terence Ranger, 101–64. Cambridge: Cambridge University Press.

Canny, Nicholas. 1975. *The Formation of the Old English Elite in Ireland.* Dublin: National University of Ireland.

———. 1976. *The Elizabethan Conquest of Ireland: A Pattern Established, 1565–1576.* Hassocks, Sussex: Harvester Press.

———. 1979. "Why the Reformation Failed in Ireland: Une Question Mal Posée." *Journal of Ecclesiastical History* 30 (4): 423–50.

———. 1987. "The Formation of the Irish Mind: Religion, Politics, and Gaelic Irish Literature, 1580–1750." In *Nationalism and Popular Protest in Ireland,* ed. C. H. E. Philpin, 50–79. Cambridge: Cambridge University Press.

Carey, John. 1996. "Saint Patrick, the Druids, and the End of the World." *History of Religions* 36 (1): 42–53.

Carleton, William. 1867. *Traits and Stories of the Irish Peasantry.* Seventh edition. London: William Tegg.

Carrigan, Rev. William. 1905. *The History and Antiquities of the Diocese of Ossory.* Four volumes. Dublin: Sealy, Bryers, and Walker.

Carroll, Michael P. 1986. *The Cult of the Virgin Mary.* Princeton: Princeton University Press.

———. 1989. *Catholic Cults and Devotions.* Montreal: McGill-Queens University Press.

———. 1992. *Madonnas That Maim: Popular Catholicism in Italy since the Fifteenth Century.* Baltimore: Johns Hopkins University Press.

———. 1996. *Veiled Threats: The Logic of Popular Catholicism in Italy.* Baltimore: Johns Hopkins University Press.

Cartwright, Julia. 1903. *Isabella d'Este, Marchioness of Mantua, 1474–1539: A Study of the Renaissance.* Volume 2. London: John Murray.

Bibliography

Chapman, Malcolm. 1992. *The Celts: The Construction of a Myth.* New York: St. Martin's.

Chodorow, Nancy J. 1989. *Feminism and Psychoanalytic Theory.* New Haven: Yale University Press.

Christian, William A., Jr. 1981. *Apparitions in Late Medieval and Renaissance Spain.* Princeton: Princeton University Press.

———. 1992. *Moving Crucifixes in Modern Spain.* Princeton: Princeton University Press.

———. 1996. *Visionaries: The Spanish Republic and the Reign of Christ.* Berkeley: University of California Press.

Cipriani, Roberto, Giovanni Rinaldi, and Paolo Sobrero. 1979. *Il simbolo conteso.* Roma: Editrice Ianua.

Clark, Samuel. 1979. *Social Origins of the Irish Land War.* Princeton: Princeton University Press.

Clark, Samuel, and James S. Donnelly Jr. 1983. *Irish Peasants: Violence and Political Unrest, 1780–1914.* Madison: University of Wisconsin Press.

Cogan, A. 1862–70. *The Diocese of Meath, Ancient and Modern.* Three volumes. Dublin: Joseph Dollard.

Comella, Annamaria. 1981. "Tipologia e diffusione dei complessi votivi in Italia in epoca medio—e tardo repubblicana." *Mélanges de l'École Française de Rome* 93 (2): 717–804.

Connolly, Hugh. 1995. *The Irish Penitentials.* Dublin: Four Courts Press.

Connolly, S. J. 1982. *Priests and People in Pre-Famine Ireland.* Dublin: Gill and Macmillan.

Cooney, Gabriel. 1996. "Building the Future on the Past: Archaeology and the Construction of National Identity in Ireland." In *Nationalism and Archaeology in Europe*, ed. M. Díaz and T. Champion, 146–63. London: UCL Press.

Corish, Patrick J. 1968. "The Origins of Catholic Nationalism." In *A History of Irish Catholicism*, volume 3, part 8. Dublin: Gill and Son.

———. 1981. *The Catholic Community in the Seventeenth and Eighteenth Centuries.* Dublin: Helicon Limited.

———. 1985. *The Irish Catholic Experience: A Historical Survey.* Wilmington, Del.: Michael Glazier.

———. 1994. Review of *The Fall and Rise of the Irish Nation: The Catholic Question, 1690–1830. Catholic Historical Review* 80 (1): 166–67.

Cousin, Bernard. 1977. "Devotion et société en Provence: les ex-voto de Notre Dame de Lumières." *Richerche di storia sociale e religiosa—nuova serie* 2: 303–42.

Crawford, W. H. 1986. "The Patron, or Festival of St. Kevin at the Seven Churches, Glendalough, Country Wicklow 1813." *Ulster Folklife* 32: 37–47.

Cregan, Donal F. 1979. "The Social and Cultural Background of a Counter-

Bibliography

Reformation Episcopate, 1618–60." In *Studies in Irish History Presented to R. Dudley Edwards,* ed. A. Cosgrove and D. McCartney, 85–117. Dublin: University College.

Cunningham, Bernadette. 1991. "The Culture and Ideology of Irish Franciscan Historians at Louvain 1607–1650." In *Ideology and the Historians,* ed. Ciaran Brady, 11–30. Dublin: Lilliput Press.

Curtis, L. Perry. 1968. *Anglo-Saxons and Celts: A Study of Anti-Irish Prejudice in Victorian England.* Bridgeport, Conn.: Conference on British Studies at the University of Bridgeport.

D'Alviella, Goblet. 1922. "Circumambulation." In *Encyclopaedia of Religion and Ethics* 3:657–59. New York: Charles Scribner's Sons.

Danaher, Kevin. 1958. "The Holy Wells of Country Dublin." *Reportoriun Novum: Dublin Diocesan Historical Record* 2 (1): 68–87.

———. 1960. "The Holy Wells of Country Dublin: A Supplementary List." *Reportoriun Novum: Dublin Diocesan Historical Record* 2 (2): 233–35.

Davis, Natalie Zemon. 1974. "Some Tasks and Themes in the Study of Popular Religion." In *The Pursuit of Holiness in Late Medieval and Renaissance Religion,* ed. C. Trinkaus and H. A. Oberman, 307–36. Leiden: E. J. Brill.

deGategno, Paul. 1989. *James Macpherson.* Boston: Twayne Publishers.

Delooz, Pierre. 1969. *Sociologie et canonisations.* La Haye: Martinus Nijhoff.

Delumeau, Jean. 1977 [1971]. *Catholicism between Luther and Voltaire: A New View of the Counter-Reformation.* London: Burns and Oates.

de Paor, Liam. 1971. "The Aggrandisement of Armagh." *Historical Studies* 8: 95–110.

de Pontfarcy, Yolande. 1988. "Accounts and Tales of Lough Derg or of the Pilgrimage." In *The Medieval Pilgrimage to St. Patrick's Purgatory: Lough Derg and the European Tradition,* ed. Michael Haren and Yolande de Pontfarcy, 35–57. Enniskillen: Clogher Historical Society.

De Rosa, Gabriele. 1983. *Vescovi, popolo e magia nel Sud.* Second Edition. Napoli: Guida editori.

de Voragine, Jacobus. [Jacobo de Voragine]. 1993. *The Golden Legend.* Two volumes. Translated by William Ryan. Princeton: Princeton University Press.

Dietler, Michael. 1994. "'Our Ancestors the Gauls': Archeology, Ethnic Nationalism, and the Manipulation of Celtic Identity in Modern Europe." *American Anthropologist* 96 (3): 584–605.

Donnelly, James S., Jr. 1983. "Pastorini and Captain Rock: Millenarianism and Sectarianism in the Rockite Movement of 1821–4." In *Irish Peasants: Violence and Political Unrest, 1780–1914,* ed. Samuel Clark and James S. Donnelly Jr., 102–39. Madison: University of Wisconsin Press.

———. 1988. "Patterns, Magical Healing and the Decline of Traditional Popular Religion in Ireland." Unpublished lecture delivered at McGill University, Montreal, November 10, 1988.

Bibliography

Dubisch, Jill. 1995. *In a Different Place: Pilgrimage, Gender, and Politics at a Greek Island Shrine.* Princeton: Princeton University Press.

Duffy, Eamon. 1992. *The Stripping of the Altars.* New Haven: Yale University Press.

Dulaney, Siri, and Alan Fiske. 1994. "Cultural Rituals and Obsessive-compulsive Disorder: Is There a Common Psychological Mechanism?" *Ethos* 22 (3): 243–83.

Dundes, Alan. 1987. "Couvade in Genesis." In his *Parsing through Customs: Essays by a Freudian Folklorist,* 145–66. Madison: University of Wisconsin Press.

———. 1988. "The Flood as Male Myth of Creation." In *The Flood Myth,* ed. Alan Dundes, 167–82. Berkeley: University of California Press.

———. 1989. *Life Is Like a Chicken Coop Ladder.* Detroit: Wayne State University Press.

Durkheim, Emile. 1912. *Les formes élémentaires de la vie religieuse: le système totémique en Australie.* Paris: Alcan.

Dwelly, Edward. 1911. *The Illustrated Gaelic-English Dictionary.* Glasgow: Alex MacLaren and Sons.

Easting, Robert. 1988. "The English Tradition." In *The Medieval Pilgrimage to St. Patrick's Purgatory: Lough Derg and the European Tradition,* ed. Michael Haren and Yolande de Pontfarcy. Enniskillen: Clogher Historical Society.

Egan, Martha. 1991. *Milagros: Votive Offerings from the Americas.* Santa Fe: Museum of New Mexico Press.

Ellis, Steven. 1985. *Tudor Ireland.* London: Longman.

———. 1991. "Historiographical Debate: Representations of the Past in Ireland: Whose Past and Whose Present." *Irish Historical Studies* 28 (Nov.): 289–308.

Erasmus, Desiderius. 1975. *The Correspondence of Erasmus,* volume 5. Translated by R. A. B. Mynors and D. F. S. Thomson. Annotated by Peter G. Bietenholz. Toronto: University of Toronto Press.

Evans, E. Estyn. 1957. *Irish Folk Ways.* London: Routledge.

Fahey, J. 1891. "The Lough Derg Pilgrimage." *Irish Ecclesiastical Record* 12 (Nov.): 973–84.

Ferenczi, Sandor. 1914. "The Ontogenesis of the Interest in Money." In his *Sex in Psychoanalysis,* 269–79. New York: Dover, 1956.

Finegan, F. 1967. "Irish Colleges on the Continent." In *The New Catholic Encyclopedia,* 7:638–39. New York: McGraw-Hill.

Fitzgerald, Walter. 1900. "Inscriptions at St. John's Well, Killone Abbey, County Clare." *Journal of the Royal Society of Antiquaries of Ireland* 10 (3): 245–46.

Fitzpatrick, William John. 1861. *The Right Rev. Dr. Doyle, Bishop of Kildare and Leighlin.* Two volumes. Dublin: James Duffy.

Bibliography

Flood, W. H. Grattan. 1913. "The Diocesan Manuscripts of Ferns during the Rule of Bishop Sweetman (1745–1786)." *Archivium Hibernicum* 2: 100–105.

———. 1914. "The Diocesan Manuscripts of Ferns during the Rule of Bishop Sweetman (1745–1786)." *Archivium Hibernicum* 3: 113–23.

Foa, A. 1980. "Chiericati, Francesco." In *Dizionario biografico degli Italiani,* 24:674–81. Rome: Istituto Enciclopedia Italiana.

Ford, Alan. 1986. "The Protestant Reformation in Ireland." In *Natives and Newcomers: Essays on the Making of Irish Colonial Society, 1534–1641,* ed. Ciaran Brady and Raymond Gillespie, 50–74. Dublin: Irish Academic Press.

Foster, R. F. 1983. "History and the Irish Question." *Transactions of the Royal Historical Society* (fifth series) 33: 169–92.

Frantzen, Allen J. 1979. "The Significance of the Frankish Penitentials." *Journal of Ecclesiastical History* 30 (4): 409–21.

Frazer, James G. 1987 [1892]. *The Golden Bough: A Study in Magic and Religion.* Abridged edition. London: Macmillan.

French, Dorothea. 1994. "Ritual, Gender and Power Strategies: Male Pilgrimage to Saint Patrick's Purgatory." *Religion* 24 (2): 103–15.

Freud, Sigmund. 1900. *The Interpretation of Dreams.* In *The Standard Edition of the Complete Psychological Works of Sigmund Freud* (hereafter *Standard Edition*), volumes 4 and 5. London: Hogarth, 1953.

———. 1905. "Three Essays on the Theory of Sexuality." In *Standard Edition,* volume 7, 123–245. London: Hogarth, 1953.

———. 1907. "Obsessive Actions and Religious Practices." In *Standard Edition,* volume 9, 115–27. London: Hogarth, 1959.

———. 1908. "Character and Anal Eroticism." In *Standard Edition,* volume 9, 167–75. London: Hogarth, 1959.

———. 1909. "Notes upon a Case of Obsessional Neurosis." In *Standard Edition,* volume 10, 151–249. London: Hogarth, 1955.

———. 1913a. *Totem and Taboo.* In *Standard Edition,* volume 13, 1–161. London: Hogarth, 1953.

———. 1913b. "The Disposition to Obsessional Neurosis: A Contribution to the Problem of Choice of Neurosis." In *Standard Edition,* volume 12, 311–26. London: Hogarth, 1958.

———. 1916–17. *Introductory Lectures on Psychoanalysis.* In *Standard Edition,* volumes 15 and 16. London: Hogarth, 1963.

———. 1917. "On Transformations of Instinct as Exemplified in Anal Eroticism." In *Standard Edition,* volume 17, 125–33. London: Hogarth, 1955.

———. 1924. "A Short Account of Psychoanalysis." In *Standard Edition,* volume 19, 189–200. London: Hogarth, 1961.

———. 1925. "An Autobiographical Study." In *Standard Edition,* volume 20, 1–74. London: Hogarth, 1959.

————. 1927. *The Future of an Illusion.* In *Standard Edition,* volume 21, 1–56. London: Hogarth, 1953.

————. 1933. *New Introductory Lectures on Psychoanalysis.* In *Standard Edition,* volume 22, 1–182. London: Hogarth, 1964.

Gailey, Alan. 1988. "Folk-life Study and the Ordnance Survey Memoirs." In *Gold under the Furze: Studies in Folk Tradition,* ed. Alan Gailey and Dáithí Ó hÓgáin, 150–64. Dublin: Glendale Press.

Gandelman, Claude. 1996. ""Patri-arse": Revolution as Anality in the Scatological Caricatures of the Reformation and the French Revolution." *American Imago* 53 (1): 7–24.

Gentilcore, David. 1992. *From Bishop to Witch: The System of the Sacred in Early Modern Terra d'Oltranto.* Manchester: Manchester University Press.

Giblin, Cathaldus. 1971. "Irish Exiles in Catholic Europe." In *A History of Irish Catholicism,* volume 4, 1–65. Dublin: Gill and Macmillan.

Giovacchini, Peter L. 1987. *A Narrative Textbook of Psychoanalysis.* Northvale, N.J.: Jason Aronson.

Giraldus Cambrensis. 1951. *The First Version of The Topography of Ireland.* Translated by John J. O'Meara. Dundalk: Dundalgan Press.

Glasberg, Ronald. 1990. "Eulenspiegel's Rebellion against the Civilizing Process: A Psychohistorical Perspective." *Psychoanalytic Review* 77 (3): 423–45.

Graham, B. J., and L. J. Proudfoot. 1993. "A Perspective on the Nature of Irish Historical Geography." In *An Historical Geography of Ireland,* ed. B. J. Graham and L. J. Proudfoot, 1–18. London: Academic Press.

Gramsci, Antonio. 1966. *Il materialismo storico e la filosofia di Benedetto Croce.* Turin: Giulio Einaudi editore.

Greeley, Andrew. 1995. *Religion as Poetry.* New Jersey: Transaction Publishers.

Green, Miranda, 1986. *The Gods of the Celts.* Gloucester: Alan Sutton.

————. 1995a. "Celtic Religion." In *Cultural Identity and Cultural Integration: Ireland and Europe in the Early Middle Ages,* ed. Doris Edel, 129–43. Portland, Oreg.: Four Courts Press.

————. 1995b. "The Gods and the Supernatural." In *The Celtic World,* ed. Miranda J. Green, 465–488. London: Routledge.

Guinnane, Timothy W. 1997. *The Vanishing Irish: Households, Migrations, and the Rural Economy in Ireland, 1850–1914.* Princeton: Princeton University Press.

Gwynn, Aubrey. 1946. *The Medieval Province of Armagh, 1470–1545.* Dundalk: Dundalgan Press.

Hackett, William. 1861–62. "The Irish Bacach, or Professional Beggar, Viewed Archaeologically." *Ulster Journal of Archaeology* 9: 256–71.

Haderlein, Konrad. 1992. "Celtic Roots: Vernacular Terminology and Pagan Ritual in Carloman's *Draft Capitulary* of A. D. 743, Codex Vat. Pal. Lat. 577." *Canadian Journal of Irish Studies* 18 (1): 1–30.

Bibliography

Hagan, J. 1914. "Miscellanea Vaticano-Hibernia, 1580–1631." *Archivium Hiberni-cum* 3: 227–365.

Hall, Mr. and Mrs. S. C. 1841–43 *Ireland: Its Scenery, Character, &c.* Three volumes. London: Virtue and Co.

Hammerstein, Helga. 1971. "Aspects of the Continental Education of Irish Students in the Reign of Queen Elizabeth I." *Historical Studies* 8:137–53.

Handler, Richard, and Jocelyn Linnekin. 1984. "Tradition, Genuine or Spurious." *Journal of American Folklore* 97 (385): 273–90.

Hanson, Allan. 1989. "The Making of the Maori: Culture Invention and Its Logic." *American Anthropologist* 91: 890–902.

Harbison, Peter. 1991. *Pilgrimage in Ireland: The Monuments and the People.* London: Barrie and Jenkins.

Hardy, Philip Dixon. 1840. *The Holy Wells of Ireland.* Dublin: Hardy and Walker.

Haren, Michael. 1988. "The Close of the Medieval Pilgrimage: The Papal Suppression and Its Aftermath." In *The Medieval Pilgrimage to St. Patrick's Purgatory: Lough Derg and the European Tradition,* ed. Michael Haren and Yolande de Pontfarcy, 190–201. Enniskillen: Clogher Historical Society.

Haren, Michael, and Yolande de Pontfarcy, eds. 1988. *The Medieval Pilgrimage to St. Patrick's Purgatory: Lough Derg and the European Tradition.* Enniskillen: Clogher Historical Society.

Hartnett, P. J. 1947. "Holy Wells of East Muskerry, Co. Cork." *Journal of the Cork Historical and Archaeological Society* 52: 5–17.

Hennessy, William, ed. 1871. *The Annals of Loch Cé.* London: Her Majesty's Stationery Office.

Hewson, Rev. 1727 [1701]. "A Description of St. Patrick's Purgatory in Lough-Derg and an Account of the Pilgrim's Business There." Reprinted in *The Great Folly, Superstition, and Idolatry of Pilgrimage in Ireland, Especially of That to St. Patrick's Purgatory,* John Richardson, 127–36. Dublin.

Hobsbawm, Eric. 1983. "Mass-producing Traditions: Europe, 1870–1914." In *The Invention of Tradition,* ed. Eric Hobsbawm and Terence Ranger, 263–307. Cambridge: Cambridge University Press.

Hogan, John. 1874. "Patron Days and Holy Wells in Ossory." *The Journal of the Royal Archaeological Society* (fourth series) 2: 261–81.

Hughes, Harry. 1991. *Croagh Patrick.* Westport, Ireland: Harry Hughes.

Hughes, Kathleen. 1960. "The Changing Theory and Practice of Irish Pilgrimage." *The Journal of Ecclesiastical History* 11 (1): 143–51.

Hutchinson, John. 1987. *The Dynamics of Cultural Nationalism: The Gaelic Revival and the Creation of the Irish Nation State.* London: Allen and Unwin.

Hynes, Eugene. 1978. "The Great Hunger and Irish Catholicism." *Societas* 8 (2): 137–55.

———. 1988. "Family and Religious Change in a Peripheral Capitalist Soci-

Bibliography

ety: Mid-Nineteenth-Century Ireland." In *The Religion and Family Connection: Social Science Perspectives*, ed. Darwin L. Thomas, 161–74. Provo, Utah: Religious Studies Center, Brigham Young University.

———. 1990. "Nineteenth Century Irish Catholicism, Farmer's Ideology, and National Religion: Explorations in Cultural Explanation." In *Sociological Studies in Roman Catholicism: Historical and Contemporary Perspectives*, ed. Roger O'Toole, 45–69. Lewiston: Edwin Mellen Press.

Inglis, Tom. 1987. *Moral Monopoly: The Catholic Church in Modern Irish Society.* Dublin: Gill and Macmillan.

J. E. 1984. "St. Patrick's Purgatory." *The Canadian Journal of Irish Studies* 10 (1): 7–40.

Jackson, Patricia. 1977/86. "The Holy Wells of Co. Kildare." *Journal of the Kerry Archaeological Society* 16: 133–61.

Jennings, Brendan. 1934. "Brussels ms. 3947: Donatus Moneyus, de Provincia Hiberniae S. Francisci." *Analecta Hibernica* 6 (Nov.): 12–138.

Johnston, E. M. 1983. "Problems Common to Both Protestant and Catholic Churches in Eighteenth-Century Ireland." In *Irish Culture and Nationalism, 1750–1950*, ed. Oliver MacDonagh, W. F. Mandle, and Pauric Travers, 14–39. London: Macmillan.

Jones, Ernest. 1951. "The Madonna's Conception through the Ear." In his *Essays in Applied Psycho-analysis*, 2:266–357. London: Hogarth Press.

———. 1955. *The Life and Work of Sigmund Freud.* Volume 2. New York: Basic.

Jones, Frederick M. 1967. "The Counter-Reformation." In *A History of Irish Catholicism*, volume 3, part 3. Dublin: Gill and Son.

Jones, Henry. 1647. *Saint Patrick's Purgatory, Containing the Description, Originall, Progress, and Demolition of That Superstitious Place.* London: Richard Royston.

Joyce, P. W. 1875. *The Origin and History of Irish Names of Places.* Fourth Edition. Dublin: McGlashan and Gill.

Keenan, Desmond J. 1983. *The Catholic Church in Nineteenth-Century Ireland: A Sociological Study.* Dublin: Gill and Macmillan.

Kenny, James F. 1966 [1929]. *The Sources for the Early History of Ireland: Ecclesiastical.* New York: Octagon Books.

Keogh, Dáire. 1993. *The French Disease: The Catholic Church and Irish Radicalism, 1790–1800.* Blackrock, Co. Dublin: Four Courts Press.

Knowlson, T. Sharper. 1910. *The Origin of Popular Superstitions and Customs.* London: T. Werner Laurie.

Kurzweil, Edith. 1995. *Freudians and Feminists.* Boulder, Colo.: Westview Press.

Laing, Lloyd, and Jennifer Laing. 1979. *Anglo-Saxon England.* London: Routledge and Kegan Paul.

Larkin, Emmet. 1972. "The Devotional Revolution in Ireland, 1850–75." *American Historical Review* 77 (3): 625–52.

Bibliography

———. 1980. *The Making of the Roman Catholic Church in Ireland, 1850–1860.* Chapel Hill: University of North Carolina Press.

———. 1984. *The Historical Dimensions of Irish Catholicism.* Washington, D.C.: Catholic University of America Press.

———. 1996. *The Roman Catholic Church and the Emergence of the Modern Irish Political System, 1874–1878.* Dublin: Four Courts Press.

Lecky, William. 1913. *A History of Ireland in the Eighteenth Century: Volume I.* London: Longmans, Green, and Co.

Leclercq, H. 1912. "Station Days." *The Catholic Encylopedia*, 14:268–69. New York: Encyclopaedia Press.

Ledwich, Edward. 1790. *Antiquities of Ireland.* Dublin: A. Grueber.

Le Goff, Jacques. 1984. *The Birth of Purgatory.* Chicago: University of Chicago Press.

Lehrhaupt, Linda. 1985. "Processional Aspects of Irish Pilgrimage." *Drama Review* 29 (3): 48–64.

Lennon, Colm. 1986. "The Counter-Reformation in Ireland, 1542–1641." In *Natives and Newcomers: Essays on the Making of Irish Colonial Society, 1534–1641*, ed. Ciaran Brady and Raymond Gillespie, 75–92. Dublin: Irish Academic Press.

———. 1989. "The Rise of Recusancy among Dublin Patricians, 1580–1613." In *The Churches, Ireland, and the Irish*, ed. W. J. Sheils and Diana Wood, 123–32. Oxford: Basil Blackwell.

———. 1991. "The Sixteenth Century." In *Irish Church History Today*, ed. Réamonn ó Muirí. Armagh: Cumann Seanchais Ard Mhacha.

———. 1995. *Sixteenth-Century Ireland: The Incomplete Conquest.* New York: St. Martin's Press.

Leslie, Shane. 1961. *St. Patrick's Purgatory.* Dublin: Colm O Lochlainn at the Sign of the Three Candles.

Logan, Patrick. 1980. *The Holy Wells of Ireland.* Gerrard's Cross: Colin Smythe Limited.

Lombard, Peter. 1868 [1632]. *De Regno Hiberniae, Sanctorum Insula.* Edited by Patrick Moran. Dublin: James Duffy.

Lynch, John. 1848–52 [1662]. *Cambrensis Eversus: The History of Ancient Ireland Vindicated.* Translated by Matthew Kelly. Three volumes. Dublin: Printed for the Celtic Society.

———. 1848 [1662]. *The Portrait of a Pious Bishop, or, The Life and Death of the Most Reverand Francis Kirwan.* Translated by C. P. Meehan. Dublin: James Duffy.

Mac Cana, Proinsias. 1987. "Celtic Religion." In *The Encyclopaedia of Religion*, ed. Mircea Eliade, 148–66. New York: Macmillan.

———. 1988. "Placenames and Mythology in Irish Tradition: Places, Pilgrimages, and Things." In *Proceedings of the First North American Congress*

Bibliography

of Celtic Studies, ed. Gordon W. MacLennan, 319–41. Ottawa: Chair of Celtic Studies, University of Ottawa.

———. 1991. "Celtic Religion and Mythology." In *The Celts*, ed. Sabatino Moscati et al., 596–604. New York: Rizzoli.

MacCulloch, J. A. 1911. *The Religion of the Ancient Celts*. Edinburgh: T. & T. Clark.

———. 1922. "Festivals and Fasts (Celtic)." In *Encyclopaedia of Religion and Ethics* 5:838–43. New York: Charles Scribner's Sons.

MacDonagh, Oliver. 1983. *States of Mind: A Study of Anglo-Irish Conflict 1780–1980*. London: George Allen and Unwin.

Macpherson, James. 1771. *An Introduction to the History of Great Britain and Ireland*. London: T. Becket and P. A. De Hondt.

Mallory, J. 1989. *In Search of the Indo-Europeans: Language, Archeology, Myth*. London: Thames and Hudson.

Mant, Richard. 1840. *History of the Church of Ireland*. London: John W. Parker.

Martin, F. X. 1979. "Confusion Abounding: Bernard O'Higgin, O.S.A., Bishop of Elphin." In *Studies in Irish History Presented to R. Dudley Edwards*, ed. A. Cosgrove and D. McCartney, 38–84. Dublin: University College.

Martin, Martin. 1716. *A Description of the Western Islands of Scotland*. Second Edition. Photographic reproduction by Mercat Press, Edinburgh, 1970.

Mason, William Shaw. 1814–1819. *A Statistical Account, or Parochial Survey of Ireland, Drawn up from Communications of the Clergy*. Three volumes. Dublin: Graisberry and Campbell.

McCone, Kim. 1991. *Pagan Past and Christian Present in Early Irish Literature*. Maynooth: An Sagart.

McCourt, Desmond. 1971. "The Dynamic Quality of Irish Rural Settlement." In *Man and His Habitat: Essays Presented to Emyr Estyn Evans*, ed. R. H. Buchanan, Emyrs Jones, and Desmond McCourt, 126–64. London: Routledge and Kegan Paul.

McCullough, Mavis. 1992. "The Changing Relationship between Bishops, Priests, and Parishioners in Pre-Famine Ireland." Master's thesis, University of Western Ontario (Department of Sociology), London, Ontario.

McGrath, Thomas G. 1991. "The Tridentine Evolution of Modern Irish Catholicism, 1563–1962: A Re-examination of the 'Devotional Revolution' Thesis." *Recusant History* 20 (4): 512–23.

McNeil, John T. 1923. "The Celtic Penitentials, Chapter IV: Special Features of the Celtic Penitentials, as Affected by Pre-Christian Customs." *Revue Celtique* 40: 320–41.

McWhiney, Grady. 1988. *Cracker Culture: Celtic Ways in the Old South*. Tuscaloosa: University of Alabama Press.

Melis, Francesca, and Stefania Quilici Gigli. 1982. "Luoghi di culto nel Territorio di Ardea." *Archeologia classica* 34: 1–37.

Bibliography

———. 1983. "Votivi e luoghi di culto nella campagna di Velletri." *Archeologia classica* 35: 1–44.

Miller, David W. 1975. "Irish Catholicism and the Great Famine." *Journal of Social History* 9: 81–98.

———. 1986. "Irish Catholicism and the Historian." *Irish Economic and Social History* 13: 113–16.

Millett, Benignus. 1964. *The Irish Franciscans, 1651–1665.* Rome: Gregorian University Press.

———. 1965. "Calendar of Volume I (1625–68) of the Collection *Scritture riferite nei congressi, Irlanda* in Propaganda Archives." *Collectanea Hibernica* 6/7: 18–211.

———. 1991. "The Seventeenth Century." In *Irish Church History Today*, ed. Réamonn Ó Muirí, 42–62. Armagh: Armagh Diocesan Historical Society.

Mitchell, Timothy. 1990. *Passional Culture: Emotion, Religion, and Society in Southern Spain.* Philadelphia: University of Pennsylvania Press.

Moeller, Bernd. 1971. "Piety in Germany around 1500." In *The Reformation in Medieval Perspective*, ed. Steven Ozment. Chicago: Quadrangle Books.

Mooney, Canice. 1967. "The First Impact of the Reformation." In *A History of Irish Catholicism*, volume 3, part 3. Dublin: Gill and Son.

———. 1969. "The Church in Gaelic Ireland: Thirteenth to Fifteenth Centuries." In *A History of Irish Catholicism*, volume 2, part 5. Dublin: Gill and Macmillan.

Mooney, Desmond. 1990. "Popular Religion and Clerical Influence in Prefamine Meath." In *Religion, Conflict, and Coexistence in Ireland: Essays Presented to Monsignor Patrick J. Corish.* Dublin: Gill and Macmillan.

Moran, Dr. [Patrick F.]. 1864. *History of the Catholic Archbishops of Dublin, since the Reformation.* Volume 1. Dublin: James Duffy.

———. 1874. *Spicilegium Ossoriense: Being a Collection of Original Letters and Papers Illustrative of the History of the Irish Church from the Reformation to the Year 1800.* Dublin: W. B. Kelly.

———. 1884. *The Analecta of David Rothe, Bishop of Ossory.* Dublin: M. H. Gill and Son.

Morgan, Prys. 1983. "From a Death to a View: The Hunt for the Welsh Past in the Romantic Period." In *The Invention of Tradition*, ed. Eric Hobsbawm and Terence Ranger, 43–100. Cambridge: Cambridge University Press.

Murphy, J. A. 1965. "The Support of the Catholic Clergy in Ireland, 1750–1850." In *Historical Studies* V, ed. J. L. McCracken, 103–21. London: Bowes and Bowes.

Murphy, Michael A. 1912. "Royal Visitation of Cashel and Emly, 1615." *Archivium Hibernicum* 1: 277–311.

Bibliography

———. 1914. "The Royal Visitation, 1615: Diocese of Killaloe." *Archivium Hibernicum* 3: 210–26.

Nadel-Klein, Jane. 1995. "Occidentalism as a Cottage Industry: Representing the Autochthonous "Other" in British and Irish Rural Studies." In *Occidentalism: Images of the West*, ed. James Carrier, 109–34. Oxford: Clarendon Press.

Newenham, Thomas. 1809. *A View of the Natural, Political, and Commercial Circumstances of Ireland.* London: T. Cadell and W. Davies.

Ní Chatháin, Próinseas. 1988. "The Later Pilgrimage—Irish Poetry on Loch Derg." In *The Medieval Pilgrimage to St. Patrick's Purgatory: Lough Derg and the European Tradition*, ed. Michael Haren and Yolande de Pontfarcy. Enniskillen: Clogher Historical Society.

Nolan, Mary Lee. 1983. "Irish Pilgrimage: The Different Tradition." *Annals of the Association of American Geographers* 73 (3): 421–38.

Nolan, Mary Lee, and Sidney Nolan. 1989. *Christian Pilgrimage in Modern Western Europe.* Chapel Hill: University of North Carolina Press.

O'Carroll, Joseph. 1994. *Historic Kilkenny.* Kilkenny: Kilkenny People Ltd.

Ó Coindealbhain. 1946. "Holy Wells." *Journal of the Cork Historical and Archaeological Society* 51: 158–63.

Ó Danachair, Caoimhín [Kevin Danaher]. 1955. "The Holy Wells of Co. Limerick." *Journal of the Royal Society of Antiquities of Ireland* 85: 195–217.

———. 1958a. "The Holy Wells of North County Kerry." *Journal of the Royal Society of Antiquities of Ireland* 88: 153–63.

———. 1958b. "The Holy Wells of County Dublin." *Reportorium Novum: Dublin Diocesan Historical Record* 2 (1): 68–87.

———. 1960a. "The Holy Wells of Corkaguiney, Co. Kerry." *Journal of the Royal Society of Antiquities of Ireland* 90: 67–78.

———. 1960b. "The Holy Wells of County Dublin: A Supplementary List." *Reportorium Novum: Dublin Diocesan Historical Record* 2 (2): 233–35.

O'Doherty, D. J. 1913. "Students of the Irish College Salamanca (1595–1619)." *Archivium Hibernicum* 2: 1–36.

O'Donovan, John. 1854. *Annals of the Kingdom of Ireland by the Four Masters.* 7 vols. Dublin: Hodges, Smith and Co.

Ó Fearghail, Feargus. 1990. "The Catholic Church in County Kilkenny." In *Kilkenny: History and Society*, ed. William Nolan and Kevin Whelan, 197–249. Dublin: Geography Publications.

O'Halloran, Clare. 1989. "Irish Re-creations of the Gaelic Past: The Challenge of Macpherson's Ossian." *Past and Present* 124 (Aug.): 69–95.

O'Laverty, James. 1878. *An Historical Account of the Diocese of Down and Connor, Ancient and Modern.* Volume 1. Dublin: James Duffy and Sons.

Ó Muirgheasa, Énrí. 1936. "The Holy Wells of Donegal." *Bealoideas* 6 (2): 141–62.

Bibliography

Orsi, Robert. 1996. *Thank You, St. Jude: Women's Devotion to the Patron Saint of Hopeless Causes.* New Haven: Yale University Press.

O'Shea, James. 1983. *Priests, Politics, and Society in Post-Famine Ireland: A Study of County Tipperary 1850–1891.* Dublin: Wolfhound Press.

Ostow, Mortimer. 1972. "Religion and Morality: A Psychoanalytic View." In *Moral Values and the Superego Concept in Psychoanalysis,* ed. Seymour C. Post, 321–39. New York: International Universities Press.

O'Toole, Edward. 1933. "The Holy Wells of County Carlow." *Bealoideas: Journal of the Folklore of Ireland* 4 (1): 3–23.

Parliamentary Gazetteer of Ireland: Volume I (A–C), 1844. Dublin: A. Fullarton.

Paul, Robert A. 1985. "David and Saul at En Gedi." *Raritan* 4: 110–32.

———. 1996. *Moses and Civilization: The Meaning behind Freud's Myth.* New Haven: Yale University Press.

Petrie, George. 1841. "St. Senan's Well, County of Clare." *Irish Penny Journal* 1 (51): 401–2.

Picard, Jean-Michel. 1988. "The Italian Pilgrims." In *The Medieval Pilgrimage to St. Patrick's Purgatory: Lough Derg and the European Tradition,* ed. Michael Haren and Yolande de Pontfarcy, 169–89. Enniskillen: Clogher Historical Society.

Piers, Henry. 1981 [1682]. *A Chorographical Description of the County of West-Meath.* Tara, County Meath: Meath Archaeological and Historical Association.

Plummer, Charles. 1910. *Vitae Sanctorum Hiberniae.* Volume 1. Oxford: Clarendon Press.

———. 1968 [1922]. *Bethada Náem nÉrenn: Lives of Irish Saints.* Two volumes. Oxford: Clarendon Press.

Pollard, A. W., and G. R. Redgrave. 1976. *A Short-title Catalogue of Books Printed in England, Scotland, and Ireland.* Volume 2. Second Edition, Revised and Enlarged. London: Bibliographical Society.

Power, P. 1914. *Life of St. Declan of Ardmore and Life of St. Mochuda of Lismore.* London: Irish Texts Society.

Power, Thomas. 1993. *Land, Politics, and Society in Eighteenth-Century Tipperary.* Oxford: Clarendon.

Purcell, Mary. 1987. "St. Patrick's Purgatory: Francesco Chiericati's Letter to Isabella d'Este." *Seanchas Ardmhacha* 12 (2): 1–10.

Quinn, David Beers. 1966. *The Elizabethans and the Irish.* Ithaca: Cornell University Press.

Quinn, D. B., and K. W. Nicholls. 1976. "Ireland in 1534." In *A New History of Ireland,* volume 3, ed. T. W. Moody, F. X. Martin, and F. J. Byrne, 1–38. Oxford: Clarendon Press.

Rambo, Elizabeth L. 1994. *Colonial Ireland in Medieval English Literature.* Selingrove, Penn.: Susquehanna University Press.

Bibliography

Rank, Otto. 1959. *The Myth of the Birth of the Hero.* New York: Vintage.

Rattue, James. 1995. *The Living Stream: Holy Wells in Historical Context.* Wood-bridge, Suffolk: Boydell Press.

Reeves, William. 1847. *Ecclesiastical Antiquities of Down, Connor, and Dromore.* Dublin: Hodges and Smith.

———. 1854. "Irish Itinerary of Father Edmund MacCana." *Ulster Journal of Archaeology* 2: 44–59.

Renehan, Laurence F. 1861. *Collections on Irish Church History.* Dublin: C. M. Warren.

Rich, Barnaby. 1610. *A New Description of Ireland.* London: Thomas Adams.

———. 1624. *A New Irish Prognostication, or Popish Callender.* London: Francis Constable.

Roberts, Paul E. W. 1983. "Caravats and Shanavests: Whiteboyism and Fac-tion Fighting in East Munster 1802–11." In *Irish Peasants: Violence and Political Unrest, 1780–1914,* ed. Samuel Clark and James S. Donnelly Jr., 64–101. Madison: University of Wisconsin Press.

Ronan, M. V. 1941a. "Royal Visitation of Dublin, 1615." *Archivium Hibernicum* 8: 1–55.

———. 1941b. "Archbishop Bulkeley's Visitation of Dublin, 1630." *Archivium Hibernicum* 8: 56–98.

Rosegrant, John. 1995. "The Anal World of a Six-year-old Boy." *International Journal of Psycho-analysis* 76 (6): 1233–44.

Rossi, Annabella. 1969. *Le feste dei poveri.* Bari: Editori Laterza.

Rutty, John. 1767. *An Essay towards a Natural, Experimental, and Medical History of the Mineral Waters of Ireland.* Dublin: Printed for the author.

Ryan, William Granger. 1993. "Introduction." In *The Golden Legend: Readings on the Saints,* volume 1, ed. Jacobus de Voragine, xiii–xviii. Princeton, N.J.: Princeton University Press.

Sargent, Steven. 1986. "Miracle Books and Pilgrimage Shrines in Late Medi-eval Bavaria." *Historical Reflections* 13 (2/3): 455–71.

Schneiderman, Stuart. 1986. *Rat Man.* New York: New York University Press.

Schroeder, H. J. 1950. *Canons and Decrees of the Council of Trent.* St. Louis, Mo.: B. Herder Book Co.

Silke, John J. 1976. "The Irish Abroad, 1534–1691." In *A New History of Ireland,* Volume 3, ed. T. M. Moody, F. X. Martin, and F. J. Byrne, 587–633. Oxford: Clarendon Press.

Silverman, Marilyn, and P. H. Gulliver. 1992. "Historical Anthropology and the Ethnographic Tradition: A Personal, Historical, and Intellectual Account." In *Approaching the Past: Historical Anthropology through Irish Case Studies,* ed. M. Silverman and P. H. Gulliver, 1–72. New York: Columbia University Press.

Silverman, Martin A. 1996. "The Neuroses." In *Textbook of Psychoanalysis,* ed.

Bibliography

Edward Nersessian, 189–230. Washington, D.C.: American Psychiatric Press.

Smith, W. Robertson. 1972 [1889]. *The Religion of the Semites.* New York: Schocken Books.

Smyth, Alfred P. 1992. *Faith, Famine, and Fatherland in the Irish Midlands.* Dublin: Four Courts Press.

Smyth, William J. 1988. "Society and Settlement in Seventeenth-Century Ireland: The Evidence of the '1659 Census.'" In *Common Ground: Essays on the Historical Geography of Ireland,* ed. William J. Smyth and Kevin Whelan, 55–83. Cork: Cork University Press.

———. 1992. "Making the Documents of Conquest Speak: The Transformation of Property, Society, and Settlement in Seventeenth-Century Counties Tipperary and Kilkenny." In *Approaching the Past: Historical Anthropology through Irish Case Studies,* ed. Marilyn Silverman and P. H. Gulliver, 236–90. New York: Columbia University Press.

Snyder, Edward D. 1923. *The Celtic Revival in English Literature, 1760–1800.* Cambridge: Harvard University Press.

Stafford, Fiona J. 1988. *The Sublime Savage: A Study of James Macpherson and the Poems of Ossian.* Edinburgh: Edinburgh University Press.

Stark, Rodney. 1991. "Normal Revelations: A Rational Model of Mystical Experiences." In *Religion and the Social Order: New Developments in Theory and Research,* ed. David G. Bromley, 239–51. Greenwich, Conn.: JAI Press.

———. 1992. "Do Catholic Societies Really Exist?" *Rationality and Society* 4 (3): 261–71.

Stark, Rodney, and Laurence R. Iannaccone. 1991. "Sociology of Religion." In *Encyclopedia of Sociology,* volume 4, ed. Edgar F. Borgatta and Marie L. Borgatta, 2029–37. New York: Macmillan.

Stokes, Whitley, ed. 1887. *The Tripartite Life of St. Patrick, with Other Documents Relating to That Saint.* Two volumes. London: Her Majesty's Stationery Office.

———, ed. 1890. *Lives of Saints from The Book of Lismore.* Oxford: Clarendon Press.

———. 1896. "The Annals of Tigernach: Third Fragment." *Revue Celtique* 17 (2): 47–263.

Stokes, William. 1868. *The Life and Labours in Art and Archaeology of George Petrie, LL.D, M.R.I.A.* London: Longman's, Green, and Co.

Stubbs, Major-General. 1908–11. "Holy Wells in County Louth." *Journal of the County Louth Archaeological Society* 2: 40.

Suggett, Richard. 1996. "Festivals and Social Structure in Early Modern Wales." *Past and Present* 152 (Aug.): 79–112.

Taylor, Lawrence J. 1989. "Bás inEirinn: Cultural Constructions of Death in Ireland." *Anthropological Quarterly* (Oct.): 149–87.

————. 1990. "Stories of Power, Powerful Stories: The Drunken Priest in Donegal." In *Religious Orthodoxy and Popular Faith in European Society*, ed. Ellen Badone, 163–84. Princeton: Princeton University Press.

————. 1992. "The Languages of Belief." In *Approaching the Past*, ed. M. Silverman and P. H. Gulliver, 142–75. New York: Columbia University Press.

————. 1995. *Occasions of Faith: An Anthropology of Irish Catholics*. Philadelphia: University of Pennsylvania Press.

Thackeray, William M. 1985 [1843]. *The Irish Sketch Book*. Belfast: Blackstaff Press.

Thomas, Thomas. 1972 [1587]. *Dictionarium Linguae Latinae et Anglicanae*. Menston, Eng.: Scolar Press.

Thurston, Herbert. 1905. "Croagh Patrick." *The Month* 105 (November): 449–61.

Trevor-Roper, Hugh. 1983. "The Invention of Tradition: The Highland Tradition of Scotland." In *The Invention of Tradition*, ed. Eric Hobsbawm and Terence Ranger, 15–41. Cambridge: Cambridge University Press.

Tubach, Frederic C. 1969. *Index Exemplorum*. Helsinki: Finnish Academy of Science and Letters.

Tylor, Edward B. 1871. *Primitive Culture: Researches into the Development of Mythology, Philosophy, Religion, Art, and Custom*. London: Murray.

Vane, Charles, ed. 1849. *Memoirs and Correspondence of Viscount Castlereagh*. Twelve volumes. London: Henry Colburn, Publisher.

Wakefield, Edward. 1812. *An Account of Ireland, Statistical and Political*. Two volumes. London: Longman, Hurst, Rees, Orme, and Brown.

Walshe, Helen Coburn. 1989. "Enforcing the Elizabethan Settlement: The Vicissitudes of Hugh Brady, Bishop of Meath, 1563–84." *Irish Historical Studies* 26 (Nov.): 352–76.

Ware, James. 1654. *De Hibernia & Antiquitatibus ejus, Disquisitiones*. London: J. Grismond.

Webster, Jane. 1995. "Sanctuaries and Sacred Places." In *The Celtic World*, ed. Miranda J. Green, 445–64. London: Routledge.

Weinstein, Donald, and Rudolph M. Bell. 1982. *Saints and Society*. Chicago: University of Chicago Press.

Westropp, Thomas J. 1911. "A Folklore Survey of County Clare." *Folk-Lore* 22: 203–13, 332–41.

————. 1912. "The Promontory Forts and Early Remains of the Coasts of County Mayo: Part I—The North Coast (Tirawley and Erris)." *Journal of the Royal Society of Antiquaries of Ireland* 92: 101–15.

Whelan, Kevin. 1985. "The Catholic Church in County Tipperary 1700–1900." In *Tipperary: History and Society*, ed. William Nolan and Thomas G. McGrath, 215–55. Dublin: Geography Publications.

————. 1988. "The Regional Impact of Irish Catholicism, 1700–1850." In *Com-*

mon Ground: Essays on the Historical Geography of Ireland, ed. W. J. Smyth and K. Whelan. Cork: Cork University Press.

———. 1990a. "Catholic Mobilisation 1750–1850." In *Culture et pratiques en France et en Irlande XVIe–XVIIe siècle.* Paris: Centre de Recherches Historiques.

———. 1990b. "The Catholic Community in Eighteenth-Century County Wexford." In *Endurance and Emergence: Catholics in Ireland in the Eighteenth Century,* ed. T. P. Power and K. Whelan. Dublin: Irish Academic Press.

———. 1991. "Settlement and Society in Eighteenth-Century Ireland." In *The Poet's Place,* ed. Gerald Dawe and John Wilson Foster. Belfast: Institute of Irish Studies.

Wilde, William. 1850. *The Beauties of the Boyne, and Its Tributary, the Blackwater.* Second Edition. Dublin: James McGlashan.

———. 1873. "Memoir of Gabriel Beranger and his Labors in the Cause of Irish Art, Literature from 1760 to 1780." *Journal of the Royal Historical and Archaeological Association of Ireland* 2: 445–85.

Wood-Martin, W. G. 1902. *Traces of the Elder Faiths of Ireland.* Volume 2. London: Longmans, Green.

Zimdars-Swartz, Sandra L. 1991. *Encountering Mary: From La Salette to Medjugorje.* Princeton: Princeton University Press.

Index

Index

Index

druids, 8, 54, 56, 64, 66
Drury, William, 139
Dubisch, Jill, 13
Dublin (city), 22, 36, 46, 108, 122, 123, 139
Dublin, County, 21, 26, 50, 107, 123
Duffy, Eamon, 136, 196
Dulaney, Siri, 171
Dundes, Alan, 169, 183
Durkheim, Emile, 175–76
Dwelly, Edward, 60

Easting, Robert, 94
Edgar (king), 57–58
Edward VI, 51, 136, 138
Egan, Martha, 34
Egyptians, 59
Elizabeth I, 136, 139, 140
Ellis, Steven, 179, 180, 194
England, 27, 32, 33, 57–58, 75
Enlightenment, 61–62
Erasmus, 99–100
erenaughs, 179
Eulenspiegel, 183, 184–85
evangelization, 149
Evans, E. Estyn, 7, 20
ex-votos. See votive offerings
exempla, medieval, 83

faction fight, 115, 127–30, 197
fairies, 79
"Fairy Doctor," priest as, 48
family solidarity, 155
Famine, the, 1–2, 105, 107, 150, 156, 188
fasting, as penance, 37–38, 75, 78
Fatima, apparitions at, 190
Ferenczi, Sandor, 184
Ferns, Diocese of, 48
fertility magic, 45
feuding, 125–26, 127–30, 188. See also faction fight
figurative emphasis, absent from Irish Catholicism, 49–52
flagellation, 167
Fleming, Thomas, 88
Flood, W.H.G., 47, 48
folklore, vs. religion, 7
Ford, Alan, 136, 140
Fore, 112
Forty Hours, 105

Foster, R. F., 194
France, 27–28, 33, 124
Franciscans, 28, 46, 51, 84, 90, 103, 120, 180, 194, 196
Frantzen, Allen, 194
Frazer, James, 69
French, Dorothea, 83
French Revolution, 183
Freud, Sigmund: on anal-eroticism, 171–75, 183, 184; on obsessional neurosis, 169–75; on religious belief and ritual, 168–70; scholarly reactions to, 167
funerals, Irish, 46, 78–79
Future of an Illusion, The (Freud), 168

Gaelic: Catholicism, 110, 146–47, 179–80; culture, 109–10, 126; language, 67, 150
Gailey, Alan, 194
Galway (city), 23, 196
Galway, County, 26, 116
Gandelman, Claude, 183
Gentilcore, David, 13, 33
Germany, 27
Giblin, Cathaldus, 197
Giraldus Cambrensis, 76–78, 81, 82
Glasberg, Ronald, 183, 184–85
Glendalough, 19–20, 84, 91, 112–13; pattern at, 115–16, 128
godparenthood, 125
Golden Legend (de Voragine), 83
Good, William, 78, 180, 195
Graham, B. J., 66
Gramsci, Antonio, 12, 40
Greek Orthodox shrine, at Tinos, 13–14
Greeley, Andrew, 14
Green, Miranda, 70, 71, 72
Guinnane, Timothy, 7, 10
Gwynn, Aubrey, 138, 194, 196

Hackett, William, 34, 52, 102, 103
hagiography, Irish, 27–29
Hall, Mr. and Mrs. S. C., 55, 130
Hammerstein, Helga, 142, 197
Handler, Richard, 8
Hanson, Allan, 8
Harbison, Peter, 20, 85–87, 111, 132–33, 195, 197
Hardy, Philip D., 55, 103, 116–17, 118, 119, 131, 158, 198

Index

Index

Mac Cana, Proinsias, 73
MacCulloch, J. A., 56, 58
MacDonagh, Oliver, 66
MacNichaill, Heneas, 43, 111, 138, 194
Macpherson, James, 62–65, 69
magic, 45, 77, 78, 79
Malachi (bishop), 98
Malinowski, Bronislaw, 38
Mallory, J., 194
Mant, Richard, 196
marriage, 125
Martin, Martin, 32
Martyrology of Donegal (O'Clery), 28, 29, 84
Mary (queen), 136, 139
Mary, devotion to, 16, 25, 50, 52, 196
Mason, William S., 35, 117, 119
Mass, attendance at, 19, 105–6, 148
Mass-houses, 19, 193
Maynooth, 154
Mayo, County, 30, 31, 37–40
McCourt, Desmond, 9
McGrath, Thomas, 105–6
McWhiney, Grady, 189
Meath, County, 21, 35, 36, 50, 54, 107
medieval legislation, and holy wells, 57–58
Mediterranean Catholicism, 28–29
Medjugorje, 15
mercantile class, 5, 108–9, 122
Miller, David, 106–7, 150, 197
Millett, Benignus, 46, 90–91, 196
Mitchell, Timothy, 13
M'Mahon, Hugh, 122–23
Modreeny, 112
Monaincha, 91, 112, 113, 119
monasteries, dissolution of, 141
monasticism, Irish, 65, 66, 77
Mooney, Canice, 197, 198
Mooney, Desmond, 150
Mooney, Donatus, 120
Moran, Patrick, 51, 88, 89, 90, 113, 119, 122, 137, 139, 140
Morgan, Prys, 8, 194
Munster, 17

Nadel-Klein, Jane, 69
Nangle, Richard, 138
Navaho, 59

New English, 143
New Introductory Lectures on Psychoanalysis (Freud), 168
Ní Chatháin, Próinseas, 84–87
Nolan, Mary Lee and Sidney, 26, 52

oaths, at Irish colleges, 146
obedience, to father, 155
Observant reforms, 180
obsessional neurosis, 169–75, 198
O'Carroll, Joseph, 23
O'Clery, Michael, 28, 84–89
Ó Danachair, Caoimhím. *See* Danaher, Kevin
O'Devany, Cornelius, 119
O'Donovan, John, 24, 31, 39, 68, 69, 84, 152, 193. *See also* Ordnance Survey
Ó Fearghail, Fergus, 197
Office of the Dead, 82
O'Flanagan, Michael, 194
O'Halloran, Clare, 64
Old English, 109, 110, 126. *See also* Anglo-Irish
orderliness, as defense mechanism, 171–73, 178
Ordnance Survey, 9, 67, 193
Ordnance Survey Letters, 24, 26, 30, 39, 151, 153, 193
Orsi, Robert, 14
O'Shea, James, 154
OSL. *See* Ordnance Survey Letters
Ossian. *See* Macpherson, James
Ossory, Diocese of, 21, 26, 47, 113, 119
Ostow, Mortimer, 174

pagan survivals hypothesis, 6–7. *See also* "Celtic origins" hypothesis
Pale, 107, 108
Paris, 142
parish registers, 108, 147
Parnell, Charles, 154
patrons. *See* patterns
patterns, 35–37, 45; at Ardmore, 130–33; at Glendalough, 114–15, 129; Irish bishops and, 44–45, 48–49; social composition of crowds at, 114–24
Paul, Robert, 169, 171, 183
Paul V, 112, 120
Peacock, Joseph, 116, 128, 197

Index

Penal Laws, 19, 41, 91, 106, 107, 122, 155, 159

penitential activity, 30–35; standing in cold water as, 98–99. *See also* penitentials, Irish

penitentials, Irish, 75–76

Petigo, 118

Petrie, George, 56, 57, 67

Phoenicians, 64

Picard, Jean-Michel, 198

Picts, 55–56

Piers, Henry, 129–30

pilgrimage: to Croagh Patrick, 37–40; in early Irish Church, 42–43; in Europe, 26; rituals at holy wells as, 43–44; to Saint Patrick's Purgatory, 81–104

pilgrimage sites, Irish: assessing popularity of, 111–14; associated with male saints, 25–26. *See also names of specific pilgrimage sites*

Plummer, Charles, 29, 91, 94, 113

popular Catholicism, framework for studying, 15–16, 152

popular religion, approaches to the study of, 11–15

Power, Thomas, 155

priests, Irish (local clergy): class background, 41–42, 153–54, 157–58; and holy well cults, 41–42; ratio of, to people, 151–53

Protestantism, in Ireland, 127, 136–38. *See also* Church of Ireland; Reformation

psychoanalysis, and religion, 167–75. *See also* anal-eroticism; Freud, Sigmund

Purcell, Mary, 95, 99

Queely, Malachy, 197

Rambo, Elizabeth, 76

Rank, Otto, 169

Rattue, James, 195

recusancy, 139–40

Reformation, 5, 32, 113, 114, 123; in Ireland, 136–38, 149; in Wales, 8–9

relic cults, 6, 91, 97–98

Renehan, Laurence, 44

repetition, as defense mechanism, 171–73, 176

Rí an Domhnaigh, 25, 193

Rich, Barnaby, 22, 36, 45, 46, 193

Rinuccini, Giovanni, 90, 126

Roberts, Paul, 155

Roman religion, influence on Celtic religion, 70–72

Romantic movement, 61–65

Rome, 59, 112

Rosegrant, John, 198

Rothe, David, 113, 119–20, 121, 197

Rouen, 142

rounding rituals: at Ardmore, 131–32; and Celtic religion, 58–60; at Croagh Patrick, 38–39; and Irish holy wells, 30–35; as penance, 41, 75; psychoanalytic perspective on, 177; at Saint Patrick's Purgatory, 91–92, 99–100; and Tridentine Catholicism, 110, 119–22

Rousseau, Jean Jacques, 62

Royal Irish Academy, 2, 64

Ryan, William, 83

Sacred Heart of Jesus, 105

Saint Augustine, 23, 26

Saint Brigid, 26, 30, 35, 78

Saint Ciarán, 26, 74

Saint Columba, 42–43, 55–56, 74, 95, 97–98

Saint Dolock (Dolough), 22

Saint John, 47, 117, 122

Saint Kevin, 19, 91, 112–13

Saint Patrick, 26, 27, 37–38, 56, 78, 95, 97–99

Saint Patrick's Purgatory, 17, 36, 41, 43; developmental phases of, 100–101; earliest stories about, 81–84; in 15th and 16th centuries, 93–100; from 17th century onward, 84–93, 118–19, 121–23, 196

Saint Sunday, 22, 193

saint's bed, 31, 90, 92

saints, Irish: and holy well dedications, 25–27; legends about, 55–57; number of, *vs.* other national traditions, 27–30. *See also specific saints*

Saint's Island, 82. *See also* Saint Patrick's Purgatory

Salamanca, 142, 146

Samuel, Book of, 183

Index

Index